Contemporary Issues in the Early Years

Contemporary Issues
in the
Early Years

Fourth Edition

Edited by

Gillian Pugh and Bernadette Duffy

SAGE Publications
London • Thousand Oaks • New Delhi

First edition published 1992
Second edition published 1996
Third edition published 2001
This edition published 2006

Reprinted 2006

© Gillian Pugh and Bernadette Duffy 2006
Chapter 1 © Gillian Pugh 2006
Chapter 2 © David Hawker 2006
Chapter 3 © Tricia David 2006
Chapter 4 © Jenny Andreae and Peter Matthews 2006
Chapter 5 © Y. Penny Lancaster 2006
Chapter 6 © Bernadette Duffy 2006
Chapter 7 © Cathy Nutbrown 2006
Chapter 8 © Iram Siraj-Blatchford 2006
Chapter 9 © Sheila Wolfendale and Mary Robinson 2006
Chapter 10 © Trevor Chandler 2006
Chapter 11 © Lucy Draper and Bernadette Duffy 2006
Chapter 12 © Kathy Sylva and Helen Taylor 2006
Chapter 13 © Sue Owen 2006

 SAGE Publications
1 Oliver's Yard
London EC1Y 1SP

SAGE Publications Inc
2455 Teller Road
Thousand Oaks, California 91320

SAGE Publications India Pvt Ltd
B-42, Panchsheel Enclave
Post Box 4109
New Delhi 110 017

Library of Congress Control Number: 2005938891

A catalogue record for this book is available from the British
Library

ISBN 10: 1-4129-2106-6   ISBN 13: 978-1-4129-2106-0
ISBN 10: 1-4129-2107-4 (pbk)   ISBN 13: 978-1-4129-2107-7 (pbk)

Typeset by Dorwyn Ltd, Wells, Somerset
Printed in Great Britain by Cromwell Press, Trowbridge, Wiltshire
Printed on paper from sustainable resources

Contents

v

LO3

Biographical details of contributors

Jenny Andreae was an Her Majesty's Inspector (HMI) for 14 years and was responsible for early years and the foundation stage for the maintained and non-maintained sectors. She was involved in the development of inspection frameworks for care, learning and education, guidance for inspectors, schools and settings, the training of inspectors and for the quality assurance of inspections. She is now an educational consultant. Prior to being an HMI she was a head-teacher, adviser/inspector for two local education authorities (LEAs) and an educational researcher at Lancaster University.

Trevor Chandler qualified as a social worker in 1977. He came to Pen Green Centre as Deputy Head of Centre in 1986. In 1995 he became Head of Centre and was awarded an OBE in 2003 for his services to early years education in Northamptonshire. He is married with two children, Rachel and David.

Professor Tricia David worked at Canterbury Christ Church University for seven years and prior to that at Warwick University for ten years, having been a head-teacher of both nursery and primary schools earlier in her career. Tricia's research and writing mainly concerned with the earliest years (birth to age 6). Her publications include 15 books (single authored or edited by her) and over 70 journal articles and chapters in books. Tricia is known internationally for her work with l'Organisation Mondiale pour l'Education Préscolaire (OMEP), the OECD (Organisation for Economic Co-operation and Development) and the British Council. Her most recent book (with Kathy Gooch, Sacha Powell and Lesley Abbott) was a *Review of Research for the Birth to Three Matters Framework*, published by the Department for Education and Skills (DfES). In 2005 Tricia was awarded the title Honorary Emeritus Professor of Early Childhood Education by the University of Sheffield.

Lucy Draper is co-ordinator of Coram Parents Centre, which offers a wide range of parenting support and education to families from the Kings Cross area of the London Borough of Camden. She is also involved in the training of practitioners to work with parents. Lucy originally trained as a teacher, and has since worked in a variety of early years settings, as an early years training officer and as a counsellor and group worker with parents.

Bernadette Duffy is Head of Centre at Thomas Coram Centre for Children and Families in Camden which has been designated as a Sure Start Children's Centre. The centre offers fully integrated care and education for young children in partnership with their parents and local community. Bernadette was part of the Qualification and Curriculum Authority (QCA) Foundation Stage Working Party which devised the Curriculum Guidance for the Foundation Stage and had a particular input into the section on creativity. She was also part of the Working Group for the Birth to Three Matters project. Bernadette has contributed to a number of publications and is author of *Supporting Creativity and Imagination in the Early Years* published by Open University Press. Bernadette has acted as Sure Start and Early Years Adviser for the Office of the Deputy Prime Minister's Beacon Authority Scheme and Foundation Stage Adviser for the QCA. She is Vice Chair of the British Association for Early Childhood Education, a fellow of the Royal Society of Arts, a member of the DfES Early Education Advisory Group and was awarded the OBE in 2005.

David Hawker is Director of Children, Families and Schools for Brighton and Hove City Council, where he has worked since 1999. He was previously head of Curriculum and Assessment at the Qualifications and Curriculum Authority, where he had responsibility, among other things, for supervising the development of the Early Learning Goals. He trained originally as a teacher and his career has spanned schools, examination boards, local government and central government. He is chair of the Association of Directors of Education and Children's Services.

Y. Penny Lancaster is the project director of the Coram Family's Listening to Young Children project and co-author of the *Listening to Young Children* resource pack (Open University Press, 2003). After five years experience of primary school teaching in New Zealand Penny moved to the Netherlands to work for an international voluntary organisation. She was responsible for preparing practitioners to work within 'cross-cultural' situations and delivering social inclusion projects, first, to drug addicts in Amsterdam and, then, within Europe, the Middle East and Africa, to people who were experiencing armed conflict and forced migration. Penny is currently delivering *Listening to Young Children* training and consultancy across the UK.

Dr Peter Matthews is a Visiting Professorial Fellow at the Institute of Education, University of London, a Schools Adjudicator and consultant evaluator. As an HMI, he was Head of Inspection Quality in Ofsted, responsible for the inspection frameworks and the conduct of school inspections, the training of inspectors and the quality assurance of inspections of schools and nurseries. He was previously a local authority chief adviser and has taught in schools and higher education. He has published research in both science and education, and recently completed, with Professor Pam Sammons, the first comprehensive evaluation of Ofsted's work, *Improvement through Inspection*. His interests lie in education leadership and evaluation, and school effectiveness and improvement. He is currently working in partnership with the University of Nottingham to evaluate aspects of the London Leadership Strategy for the National College for School Leadership. He was awarded an OBE in 2003 for services to education.

Dr Cathy Nutbrown began her career as a teacher of young children and has since worked in a range of settings and roles with children, parents, teachers and other early childhood educators. At the University of Sheffield, her research interests include children's early learning and development, their literacy, assessment, children's rights and work with parents. Over 30 publications in the field of early childhood education include *Early Literacy Work with Families: Research, Policy and Practice* (Sage, 2005), *Threads of Thinking* (Sage, 2006) and *Inclusion in the Early Years* (Sage, 2006).

Sue Owen is Director of the Early Childhood Unit at the National Children's Bureau and was, before that, Deputy Director of the Early Years National Training Organisation. She takes part in frequent consultations and advisory groups on training, qualifications and workforce issues as part of the government's children's workforce strategy.

Dr Gillian Pugh has recently retired as Chief Executive of Coram Family, a leading children's charity which aims to develop and promote best practice in the care and support of very vulnerable children and their families. She worked previously at the National Children's Bureau in a number of posts, including establishing and directing the Early Childhood Unit. Over the past 30 years Gillian has advised governments in the UK and overseas on the development of policy for children and families and has published widely. She was a founder member and is chair of the Parenting Education and Support Forum and a trustee of the National Family and Parenting Institute. She has been an adviser to the Children, Young People and Families Directorate at the Department of Education and Skills, is a board member of the new Children's Workforce Development Council and the Training and Development Agency, and is visiting Professor at the Institute of Education. She was awarded the DBE in 2005 for services to children and families.

Mary Robinson is a senior educational psychologist in the London Borough of Redbridge and is also a tutor on the MSc in Educational Psychology at the University of East London. Prior to her current post, she led the early years team within the Educational Psychology Service in the London Borough of Newham, where she gained experience of the key issues involved in including young children within mainstream education. With Sheila Wolfendale, she had co-ordinated the National Early Years Interest Group for educational psychologists, which meets twice yearly at the University of East London. Mary has written chapters and articles on early years, of which two recent ones had been co-authored with Sheila.

Professor Iram Siraj-Blatchford is Professor of Early Childhood Education at the Institute of Education, where she has been working for over a decade. She is co-director of the major, ten-year, DfES Effective Preschool and Primary Education Project and she directed the DfES Researching Effective Pedagogy in the Early Years (REPEY) Project. She is currently evaluating the Welsh Foundation Phase for the Welsh Assembly. Iram is committed to research and practice which combats disadvantage for children and families.

Professor Kathy Sylva is Professor of Educational Psychology at the University of Oxford, Department of Educational Studies. After earning a PhD at Harvard University she moved to Oxford, where her book *Childwatching at Playgroup and Nursery School* broke new ground by questioning an unbridled 'free play' ideology. She has also carried out research on early literacy in reception and year 1. A dominant theme throughout her work is the impact of education not only on 'subject knowledge' but on children's problem-solving, social skills and dispositions. A related theme in her work is the impact of early intervention in combating social disadvantage and exclusion. She is one of the leaders of the DfES research on Effective Provision of Pre-school Education (EPPE). In 2000–01 she served as specialist adviser to the House of Commons Select Committee on Education and Skills in its Early Years enquiry. In 2004–05 she advised the Select Committee on enquiries into Every Child Matters and also Teaching of Reading.

Helen Taylor graduated from Oxford University in 2004, with a BA in Experimental Psychology. Since then, she has worked as a Research Officer in the Families, Early Learning and Literacy research group in the Department of Educational Studies, Oxford University. She carried out fieldwork as part of a team working on the 'Millennium Cohort Study' and she has analysed observational data from a variety of studies of quality in Early Childhood settings.

Professor Sheila Wolfendale was a primary school, special needs teacher and educational psychologist in several LEAs. Most recently she directed a postgraduate doctoral programme for practising educational psychologists at the University of East London. Sheila wrote many books, chapters, articles, manuals on areas of educational psychology, special needs, early years, parental involvement, parenting support, family literacy and baseline assessment. During 2003–04 Sheila was consultant to a European Union funded family literacy programme led by Malta that took place in six countries. Very sadly, Sheila died just before this book was published.

Introduction

Bernadette Duffy

When Gillian Pugh asked me to act as assistant editor to this, the fourth edition, of *Contemporary Issues in the Early Years* I was honoured and delighted. I was also somewhat daunted! *Contemporary Issues* is a classic. Since it was first published in 1992 each edition has reflected the changing nature of the early years in England and it has become a key text for many early years practitioners.

In this edition we are attempting to reflect the early years at a time of great change. Children and their families are now a priority within national debate and impressive plans exist to have high-quality joined-up services at national, local authority and community levels. This is a great step forward, but with this step comes dangers, for what works well as innovative one-off projects may be much harder to roll out across the whole country. Innovative projects are frequently developed by people with vision, inspiring leadership and un-bounded energy – finding enough of them to run children's services throughout the country may be a challenge!

The Every Child Matters agenda is changing our view of services for all children. In many ways early years is ahead of the game with its history of com-bined centres, early excellence centres and Sure Start local programmes. We have a long history of joined-up services and it is important that we use this history to influence the development of integrated services right across the early years and the rest of the children's services system more generally.

The 2004 Children Act builds on the Green Paper *Every Child Matters* (DfES, 2003b). The aim of *Every Child Matters* is to ensure that every child and young person has the opportunity to fulfil their potential and that no child slips through the net. *Every Child Matters* sets out five outcomes for children which services should support them to achieve:

- Being healthy: enjoying good physical and metal health and living a healthy lifestyle.
- Staying safe: being protected from harm and neglect and growing up to look after themselves.
- Enjoying and achieving: getting the most out of life and developing broad skills for adulthood.

- Making a positive contribution: to the community and to society and not engaging in antisocial or offending behaviour.
- Economic well-being.

If children are to achieve these outcomes, they will require better access to high-quality universal services and there will need to be more targeted, specialist, support for vulnerable groups, such as looked after children, children on the child protection register, young carers, children of asylum seekers or prisoners, and disabled children.

The ten-year childcare strategy *Choice for Parents, the Best Start for Children* was published in December 2004 (HMT, 2004) and the Childcare Bill to implement this policy is currently going through Parliament. It builds on the 2004 Children Act and *Every Child Matters* and aims to help deliver the outcomes by giving a clear direction of travel and long-term goals. Its vision is to ensure that every child gets the best start in life and that parents are given more choice about how to balance work and family life.

This is an ambitious agenda and in response major changes are under way to make it a reality. Local authorities are reforming their education and social services to create integrated children's services, the Office for Standards in Education (Ofsted) has developed a new inspection framework, workforce reforms are being consulted on, and children's centres and extended schools are being introduced into every community. As I write, there is still so much to be decided and much to play for.

But while this is a time of great change, the major themes in this book remain the same. How can we work together to better meet the needs of young children and their families? How do we ensure that all children have equality of opportunity? How do we use what we know from research and practice to create children's services that truly put the child at the centre?

At a time when everything matters it can be hard to decide where to start, but our contributors have risen to the challenge. The book is in two main parts – policy and practice, both informed by research, and two additional chapters, one looking at research and the other at training.

The first four chapters focus on policy. In Chapter 1 Gillian Pugh reviews the main developments in national policy in recent years. She provides us with a clear understanding of how we have got to where we are, the success we have achieved and the challenges that lie ahead. In Chapter 2 David Hawker gives the background to the drive towards integrated services and describes one local authority's approach to children's services. Chapter 3 looks at the world picture and Tricia David provides an insight into some of the ways early years services are viewed around the world, looking at the role of early childhood services, the continuing education/care divide, and models of early childhood education. Jenny Andreae and Peter Matthews in Chapter 4 look at the changing nature of inspection. The chapter reviews the evolution of inspection and quality assurance of childcare and nursery education, and discusses recent developments.

In the second part of the book are seven chapters focusing on practice. Penny Lancaster writes the first chapter in this section and draws on Coram Family's Listening to Young Children project to focus on some of the issues to be addressed in implementing the government's social inclusion policy for children and their families. She shows how practitioners can enable young children to articulate their feelings, experiences and ideas. Chapter 6 is written by Bernadette Duffy and looks at what we mean by the term 'curriculum', current curriculum frameworks, the issues surrounding them, and where the curriculum needs to go next. In Chapter 7 Cathy Nutbrown explores the question of assessment. She discusses how early childhood educators can understand young children's capabilities and learning needs, and asks 'What is assessment'? 'Why assess'? and 'How best to assess'? with due respect to children. Diversity is the theme for Iram Siraj-Blatchford's chapter and in it Iram challenges the hidden assumptions which disadvantage children on the grounds of ethnic background, gender or socio-economic class. Sheila Wolfendale and Mary Robinson pick up these themes in Chapter 9 in relation to children with special needs, examining recent developments and emerging practice in meeting special needs within inclusive settings. In Chapter 10 Trevor Chandler describes the process of leading and developing multi-agency teams drawing on his experiences at the Pen Green Centre in Corby. He describes the complex nature of the task and the benefits of success. Lucy Draper, assisted by Bernadette Duffy, in Chapter 11 draw on their experiences at the Thomas Coram Centre to explore the ways that parents and practitioners can work together for the benefit of children, parents and practitioners.

Part 3 focuses at research and Kathy Sylva and Helen Taylor look at the messages from research projects such as the Effective Provision of Pre-School Education (EPPE) project and their impact on policy.

In Part 4 Sue Owen explores the training challenge and discusses the workforce reforms that are currently under way. She describes the radical changes needed in the field of training and qualifications and stresses the importance of ensuring that early years work becomes a career which is valued and recognized by society.

The contributors to this book are all nationally or internationally known for their contribution to the early years debate. Many have been actively involved in the research and development of policies and practice that this book discusses. All share a commitment to the well-being of young children and their families. It is a crucial time for the early years. If we get it wrong we will have lost a golden opportunity to ensure that the young children that are the focus of this book are encouraged to grow and develop in a way that meets their needs now and in the future. But if we get things right now, we will have established a legacy to be proud of.

PART 1
POLICY

1

The Policy Agenda for Early Childhood Services

Gillian Pugh

Chapter contents

- A brief history
- Every Child Matters: a national policy for children and young people
- An integrated strategy for young children and their parents?
- Availability, affordability and sustainability of early years services
- Joined-up services: Sure Start local programmes and children's centres
- Quality in service provision
- Support for parents – or parents as supporters?
- Staff training and qualifications
- Some challenges

While the nineteenth century was distinguished by the introduction of primary education for all and the twentieth century by the introduction of secondary education for all, so the early part of the twenty first century should be marked by the introduction of pre-school provision for the under fives and childcare available to all. (Rt. Hon. Gordon Brown MP, Chancellor of the Exchequer, 2004 Comprehensive Spending Review)

The past few years have seen considerable developments in the availability and organization of early childhood services. This chapter considers these changes within the context of the broader Every Child Matters agenda for children's services and raises a number of issues that are considered further in the chapters that follow.

A brief history

Since the establishment of the first nursery school by Robert Owen, in Scotland in 1816, the development of early education in the UK has been remarkably slow by comparison to much of mainland Europe. In 1870, publicly funded education became compulsory at the age of 5 years, but from the earliest days children as young as 2 years were admitted to primary schools. During the course of the twentieth century successive governments supported the principle of free nursery education but seldom found the resources to fund it. Even with the gradual establishment of nursery schools and, during the 1914–18 war, some public daycare centres, the predominant form of early education in the UK has always been state primary schools. The lack of appropriate provision within the education system led to two parallel developments: on the one hand, the emergence during the 1960s through the voluntary sector of the playgroup movement and, on the other, the growth since the 1990s through the private sector of day-care centres to meet the needs of working parents who needed full day care for their children.

This legacy is important in understanding the state of early childhood services at the beginning of the twenty-first century. A review in 1988 found a patchwork of fragmented and uncoordinated services, showing wide variations between one part of the country and another, within the context of a 'low national commitment to developing and resourcing preschool services, and the absence of a national policy on what services should be provided, for whom and by whom' (Pugh, 1988: 80). This review concluded that the challenge for government was to provide an overall framework within which services could be developed flexibly at local level. The second edition of this book, published in 1996, described services in the UK as discretionary, with low levels of public funding compared with mainland Europe, with a heavy reliance on the private and voluntary sectors, with diversity of provision but little choice for parents, lacking in co-ordination between providers from different agencies, and with different services having different aims and purposes, and being used by different client groups – working parents, children 'in need' and parents able to use part-time nurseries (Pugh, 1996).

The levels of concern expressed here were reflected in a number of prestigious national reports published during the 1990s, notably the Rumbold Report *Starting with Quality* (DES, 1990), largely ignored by the government at the time, but very widely used subsequently as the basis for best practice in early years settings (and see also National Commission on Education, 1993; Ball, 1994; Audit Commission, 1996).

During the 1980s and early 1990s there was a lack of political conviction that young children mattered and a view that children were the private responsibility of their parents. But there were also unclear and conflicting messages about what was required – should an early years policy be most concerned about preparing children for school, or with day care for working parents? Should it provide stimulation for a developing brain, or equal opportunities for women? Was it about cost savings for employers, able to retain staff when they became parents, or about reducing the benefit bill for single parents, enabling them to return to the workforce? Or was prevention the main driver – whether of developmental delay in children or juvenile crime?

The establishment in 1993 of the Early Childhood Education Forum (now known as the Early Childhood Forum) bringing together all the national agencies in the field, was one response to the lack of clarity over what a policy for early childhood services should look like. As the Forum gathered strength, with a membership of 45 national organizations by 1998, and as report after report called for an expansion in services and for better co-ordination, the government took action. In 1995 additional funding for the education of 4-year-olds was announced but, controversially, the funding was to be made available to parents through vouchers which could be redeemed in private, voluntary or local authority nurseries. A pilot scheme was rolled out amid mounting criticism, but full implementation was stopped by the election of a Labour government in 1997. Eight years later the expansion of services for our youngest children has been considerable, and this chapter assesses the extent to which the vision of what was called for during the 1990s has been realized.

Every Child Matters: a national policy for children and young people

The publication in 2003 of the Green Paper *Every Child Matters* (DfES, 2003b) was described by the Prime Minister at its launch as the most significant develop-ment for children in over 30 years. Although much of the expansion of early childhood services was already under way by 2003, I will briefly describe the bigger picture at this point so that we can see where services for younger chil-dren fit into the whole. The Green Paper was initially planned as a response to the report by Lord Laming on the circumstances surrounding the death of Vic-toria Climbié in 2002 at the hands of two people who were supposed to be caring for her. Her case was known to social services, the health service and the police in two boroughs, but on ten separate occasions they failed to protect her. The government remit was to focus on children at risk but, after discussion with many working in the field, the report took prevention as its starting point and accepted the view that to support all children better through well co-ordinated mainstream services was more likely to benefit those in need and at risk than a separate child protection service. Based on a review of relevant research and widespread consultation with professionals and young people, the five key themes of *Every Child Matters* are

- strong foundations in the early years
- a stronger focus on parenting and families
- earlier interventions and effective protection
- better accountability and integration locally, regionally and nationally
- reform of the workforce.

The overall aim of the Green Paper and the subsequent 2004 Children Act is to improve outcomes for all children and narrow the gap between those who do well and those who do not, through reconfiguring services around children and families. The focus is on entitlements for children through five main (and many subsidiary) outcomes:

- Being healthy – enjoying good physical and mental health and living a healthy lifestyle.
- Staying safe – being protected from harm and neglect.
- Enjoying and achieving – getting the most out of life and developing the skills for adulthood.
- Making a positive contribution – being involved with the community and society and not engaging in antisocial or offending behaviour.
- Economic well-being – not being prevented by economic disadvantage from achieving their full potential in life.

The long-term vision that emerges through the Children Act and the implementation paper *Every Child Matters: Change for Children* (DfES, 2004b) is

- the development of integrated education, health and social care, through children's centres, extended schools and improved services for young people
- better support for parents
- provided by better qualified staff
- targeted services planned and delivered within a universal context.

At central government level, responsibility for most services for children, young people and families has been brought within a single directorate at the Department for Education and Skills under the direction of a Minister for Children. The exception is children's health which remains with the Department of Health, although a parallel National Service Framework for children's health has been developed (DH and DfES, 2004), and youth justice which remains with the Home Office. In local areas, the existing directors for social services and education are being replaced by a director for children's services, and an integrated mechanism for planning and delivering services – a Children's Trust. Chapter 2 explores the implications of these changes in one local authority and examines integration in the delivery of services. There is also a common assessment framework, an integrated workforce strategy and a common core of training (see Chapter 13), and an integrated inspection framework (see Chapter 4). It is a huge and ambitious agenda – for all children.

An integrated strategy for young children and their parents?

It is in the early years that there has been the most substantial commitment to expanding services, as is evident from the Chancellor of the Exchequer's statement which opened this chapter. The Labour government had 17 years in opposition to consider its priorities, and both the Prime Minister and the Chancellor have stated their commitment to eliminating child poverty by 2020 as a high priority. It is this commitment that has driven the increase of childcare as a means of enabling women to return to work and thus increase family income, together with the substantial body of research which has underpinned the importance of high-quality early learning. Research studies include new thinking looking at the contribution of early learning to the development of the brain, revisiting long-established studies on early attachments between children and their parents and carers (see, for example, Gerhardt, 2004) , and the longitudinal EPPE study (Sylva et al., 2004, and Chapter 12), as well as research into parenting and parental involvement. The government's own summary of the research evidence in its 2004 ten-year childcare strategy (HMT, 2004) concludes that:

- During the first year of a child's life, in the majority of cases it is good for the child to receive consistent one-to-one care. For health reasons (eg breast feeding) mothers should have a genuine choice as to the main carer in the early months of a child's life. There are also child development benefits that derive from close parental contact in the early years.
- Early education before a child starts school has a very positive effect on child development.
- The quality of early years and childcare provision is directly related to child outcomes. High quality care after the age of two can produce a range of benefits to the social, emotional and cognitive development of the child.
- Disadvantaged children benefit particularly from high quality services.
- Children will benefit in the short and long run from at least one parent working and from not growing up in poverty. Parents need to strike a balance between the demands of work and home life. Growing up in a workless, low income family can significantly damage children's long term outcomes.
- The quality of the home learning environment makes a strong difference to children's pre-school intellectual and social development. (HMT, 2004: 71)

It is this combination of factors – the anti-poverty agenda driving the 'day care' agenda, and the research into child development and children's learning driving the 'education' agenda – that has led to an increase in provision but also to tensions between increasing the quantity of provision while ensuring that high quality is maintained.

The policy agenda since 1997 has been considerable:

- the National Childcare Strategy (DFEE, 1998), which included an expansion of nursery education and child care from birth to 14, together with the establishment of Sure Start local programmes and early excellence centres, and a programme of neighbourhood nurseries
- additional financial support for families on low incomes, including what is now called working tax credit
- more family friendly policies in the workplace, including improved parental leave and encouragement on employers to offer more flexible working arrangements
- the establishment of the Foundation Stage of early education for children aged from 3 to end of reception year

- national qualifications and training framework for the early years
- an integrated inspection service for all early years services within OFSTED
- a recognition that services must meet the needs of parents as well as children
- and most recently – drawing many of these developments together and taking them forward – the ten-year childcare strategy, *Choice for Parents, the Best Start for Children* (HMT, 2004), and the 2005 Childcare Bill.

The following sections look at some of these developments in more detail.

Availability, affordability and sustainability of early years services

Expenditure of services for young children has increased substantially, with a 75 per cent increase (from £2billion to £3.5billion) between 1997 and 2003, as can be seen from Figure 1.1. Nursery education – currently available for 12.5 hours a week in term time, but increasing to 15 hours by 2010 and 20 hours in due course – is free and is now more or less universally available for all 3- and 4-year-olds, with the numbers of children using a place having risen by over 40 per cent since 1998 (NAO, 2004). The public funding for these places is available to nursery and primary schools in the statutory sector, as well as to private and voluntary sector nurseries so long as they meet nationally approved standards. Figure 1.1 summarizes government expenditure on early years between 1997 and 2003. Expenditure between 1996–97 and 2007–08 will quadruple – from £1.1billion to £4.4billion (HMT, 2004).

However, as is evident from Figure 1.2, parents still make the major financial contribution to the cost of services, particularly before and after the free nursery education, in holidays, and all provision for children under 3. This accounts for around 45 per cent of the national childcare bill in 2002–03. Working tax credit, introduced in 1998 as childcare tax credit, was intended to assist low-income families with up to 70 per cent of their childcare costs. However the take-up has been low. Only 15 per cent of eligible couples and 24 per cent of lone families receive the childcare element, and some 20 per cent of low-income parents still pay all the costs themselves (NAO, 2004). Even for those who do claim, the amount received is far from the actual cost of a place. In one London borough, for example, in 2004 it cost on average £250 per week for a place, and in order for parents to be able to afford this the borough had to subsidize all places by £80 per week to help parents bridge the gap (London Borough of Camden, 2004). The precarious nature of the funding and of parents' ability to pay creates challenges for nurseries in the private and voluntary sectors, and each year there are nearly half as many closures of nurseries as there are new places (NAO, 2004). The overall increase in places, however, is still considerable. Although numbers of places with childminders dropped from 365,000 to 322,000 between 1997 and 2004, the number of full day-care places has more than doubled – from 194,000 to 484,000.

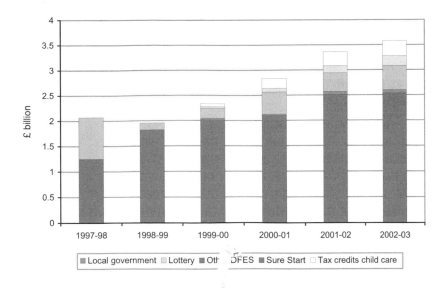

Figure 1.1 *Government expenditure   early years since 1997 (NAO, 2004)*

Some of these challenges are recognized in the ten-year childcare strategy (HMT, 2004) and subsequent Childcare Bill 2005. There is greater recognition of the need for parents to be able to balance work and family life, with 12 months paid maternity leave promised by the end of the next Parliament and nine months from April 2007. Eligible childcare costs that the working tax credit can cover have now increased from £135 to £175 a week; and there is a new duty on local authorities to 'secure sufficient provision to meet local childcare needs'. Apart from a £125 million Transformation Fund, there is as yet no additional funding to support this duty and it remains to be seen how far this money will go.

Joined-up services: Sure Start local programmes and children's centres

Although these statistics paint a picture of a divided care and education system, there are continuing attempts to create provision that integrates care and education – a task that would be eased if a satisfactory term could be found to describe this 'educare' provision. An early example was the targeted community based Sure Start programme, originally established in 1998 with £540 million to fund 250 local programmes covering 150,000 children. The government official responsible for the programme described Sure Start as

> a radical cross-departmental strategy to raise the physical, social, emotional and intellectual status of young children through improved services. It is targeted at children under four and their families in areas of high need. It is part of the

Government's policy to prevent social exclusion and aims to improve the life chances of younger children through better access to early education and play, health services for children and parents, family support and advice on nurturing. It will be locally led and locally delivered, but will be based on evidence from the UK and elsewhere on 'what works' in terms of improving life chances for children and their parents. (Glass, 1999: 257)

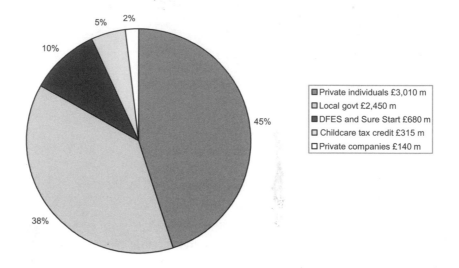

Figure 1.2 *How early years provision is paid for, 2002–03 (NAO, 2004)*

In a statement that foreshadows the even more ambitious Every Child Matters agenda, Glass continues: 'The Sure Start programme represents a new way of doing things both in the development of the policy and in its delivery. It is an attempt to put into practice "joined-up thinking" but it is also an outstanding example of evidence based policy and open, consultative government' (Glass, 1999: 264).

A substantial evaluation programme was commissioned, and even before the ink was dry on the contract the scheme was expanded to 520 communities. Sure Start has been enormously popular with local parents, although the first major evaluation report shows – not surprisingly – modest outcomes as yet (DfES, 2005a). However, the goal posts have been moved yet again, with further expansion of the Sure Start concept but through the establishment of children's centres rather than through separate Sure Start schemes (HMT, 2004). While there is a welcome for the expansion of the concept, there is fear that the same level of funding will be spread over a wider area much more thinly; and the House of Commons Education Select Committee (2005) has criticized the government for making significant changes before the evidence is available.

The concept of children's centres, as referred to above, is not a new one, and indeed goes back to the vision of Robert Owen in the early 1880s and the work of the McMillan sisters in the early 1900s. The first combined nursery centre in more recent times opened in 1971 and since then there have been many calls for these integrated centres to become the model for early years provision (see Pugh, 1994; Makins, 1997). The government's 'early excellence centre' programme was launched in 1997 to encourage the development of centres that would provide integrated care and education for children, a range of support services for parents, and access to adult education and training. Most of the centres that were awarded early excellence status were not new centres, but were able to add to their existing provision and take on a training and dissemination role. Preliminary evaluation of the first 60 such centres, which included Pen Green (see Chapter 10) and Thomas Coram (see Chapter 11) suggested substantial benefits for children, families and the wider community through the bringing together of a range of services that met families' needs without the stigma attached to specialist provision (Bertram et al., 2002).

In 2003 the government changed direction, perhaps concerned at the cost of early excellence centres, and announced a children's centres programme, building on early excellence centres and neighbourhood nurseries, through a promise of a centre in the 20 per cent most disadvantaged communities. Children's centres are less generously funded than early excellence centres, but they do have an additional emphasis on health, being required to provide a base for midwives, health visitors, and speech and language therapists, as well as information and support for parents, and training and support for childcare workers (see Pugh, 2003). The ten-year childcare strategy goes further and promises 2,500 children's centres by 2008 and 3,500 by 2010 (HMT, 2004), though there is concern as to how these will be funded.

Quality in service provision

Despite the arguments in the Rumbold Report (DES, 1990) of the importance of the context of learning and the process of learning – the way in which children acquire the disposition to learn – there were widespread concerns at the end of the 1990s that the National Curriculum and the national literacy and numeracy strategies were leading to pressure to formalize education at the earliest opportunity. It was therefore with some enthusiasm that a working party of early years experts developed the *Curriculum Guidance for the Foundation Stage* (QCA, 2000), which provides a clear and unambiguous statement of the principles which should underpin both learning and teaching. The guidance argues that effective early education requires a relevant curriculum, one that builds on what children can already do and which includes opportunities for children to engage in activities planned by adults as well as those they plan or initiate themselves. Children are innately curious and eager to learn. They learn best through play, through talk and through direct experience; and they learn when they feel confident and secure. The guidance argues that early learning experiences should encourage in children a positive attitude and disposition towards learning, and the confidence to work on their own and with others to solve problems and make choices. The guidance also reinforces the need for early education practitioners who understand how young children learn and develop; who can observe children and respond appropriately, planning for children's learning, both as individuals and in groups; who can create a stimulating and well-organized learning environment; and who can work in partnership with parents.

The Foundation Stage curriculum has been well received, as has *Birth to Three Matters* (DfES, 2003a), a framework for all practitioners working with children under 3. Work is currently ongoing to develop a single Early Years Foundation Stage Framework bringing together these two documents. This is described further in Chapter 6.

The EPPE research noted above, commissioned by government to inform its policy-making, has played a key role in ensuring that, despite the requirement to expand provision as quickly as possible, the needs of children are not lost. Key findings have been that the best quality has been found in settings integrating care and education, and there is high correlation between well-qualified staff and better outcomes for children, with quality indicators including warm interactive relationships and a good proportion of trained teachers on the staff (Sylva et al., 2004; see also Chapter 12).

There are, however, a number of concerns about the quality of provision, across all sectors. With regard to children in reception classes in primary schools, a recent report concluded that

> if the purpose of the Foundation Stage [FS] was to extend to four and five year olds in the primary/infant schools the best practice in the education of three and four year olds, then it has not succeeded. There is a demonstrable gap between the quality of children's experiences in the reception classes (the second year of the FS) and the quality of their experiences in the first year in our best nurseries and family centres. (Adams et al., 2004)

The downwards pressure from Key Stages 1 and 2 has not gone away. (See also Chapter 6)

Evidence from 19,000 inspections of private and voluntary sector providers, cited in Chapter 4, shows over half of the childcare provision was considered good and the majority of the rest was satisfactory (Ofsted, 2005a).

Support for parents – or parents as supporters?

A recognition of the need for greater support for parents has featured strongly in government policy over the past eight years, first in the Green Paper *Supporting Families* (Home Office, 1998), then in the establishment of Sure Start programmes, and most recently in *Every Child Matters*. Acknowledgement of the importance of the relationships between parents and their children, and a recognition that bringing up children is a challenging and sometimes difficult task for which help should be universally available before things start to go wrong (see Pugh et al., 1994) is finally leading to the establishment of a wider range of services, from informal through to the more structured (see Chapter 11). However, the current emphasis on improving outcomes for children has also reinforced the concept of parents as their children's first educators. Pulling together a wide body of research, Desforges and Abouchaar (2003) confirm the view that parental involvement in schools and early years settings, and above all the educational environment of the home, have a positive effect on children's achievement and adjustment. At its best this is building on partnerships between parents and professionals that have been central to good early years provision for many years. But there is a danger that an instrumentalist view of parents as the key to better behaved and more highly achieving children can also lead to undue pressure on parents at a time when they are also under pressure to return to paid employment.

Staff training and qualifications

As the EPPE research notes, the qualifications of the staff are a critical ingredient in securing good outcomes for children, and yet the early years sector has always suffered from low levels of qualified staff and of pay. The government workforce strategy (DfES, 2005f) and the newly established Children's Workforce Development Council quite rightly see the early years as a high priority. Many of those within the sector are not well qualified, particularly those working in the voluntary and private sectors, and non-teaching staff are poorly paid. Staff across the sector are seen as having low status, and even within the teaching profession early years teachers are seen as of lower status than secondary school teachers.

There is an urgent need for a graduate workforce, with a range of qualifications and experience, and with teachers playing a key role in curriculum leadership. However, the current training of early childhood teachers is no longer well suited to the multi-agency role of children's centres, nor does it encompass the development and learning needs of children under 3. The majority of early years staff are not qualified to graduate level, and while some have both skills and experience, the workforce strategy recognizes that many have a low level of qualifications. There are thus considerable challenges in equipping the early years workforce with the skills required to deliver the services that are needed, and the new qualifications and career structure that the workforce strategy envisages will require considerable additional expenditure if it is to deliver a high-quality workforce (for further discussion see Chapter 13) .

Some challenges

The achievements of the past eight years are remarkable, and there is much to applaud in the expansion that we have seen and the promise of the ten-year strategy (HMT, 2004) and 2005 Childcare Bill. But a number of challenges remain.

The first is one of sustainability and affordability, and of whether sufficient public funding can be secured to realize the very ambitious programme outlined in the ten-year childcare strategy. It is already evident that, with the exception of the 15 hours a week of 'nursery education' for 3- and 4-year-olds, the move towards a universal entitlement for integrated care and education for all children is heavily dependent on parental purchasing power and on their subsidizing a service that is provided largely through the voluntary and private sectors. The Childcare Bill requires additional services but provides no additional funding, and the promise of a children's centre in every community could mean a 'virtual' centre in many areas, with little provision beyond what is currently available. As the ring fence is removed from around local Sure Start programmes and requirements on local authorities to provide children's centres take shape, it remains to be seen whether the funding is sufficient to provide all that is envisaged in the government's strategy (see also Chapter 2).

The challenges of recruiting and training a workforce fit for the early years services of the future are also considerable, both in terms of front-line staff but, equally importantly for the leaders, the heads of services and centres who will have to drive the agenda forward.

The second challenge is to ask where early years services fit within the overall pattern of provision for children, and particularly how they relate to schools – what could be described as the 'L-shaped dilemma'. As the horizontal at the foot of the L (all services for children under 5) becomes greater in number and better integrated, and the extent of the funding and staffing challenge becomes more apparent, the question arises as to whether early years services are the first part of the education system (the upright of the L, going from 0 to 19) or part of a completely different system. Although most 3- and 4-year-olds are actually in nursery or reception classes of primary schools, the government describes the early years as 'child care' as in the ten-year strategy for childcare, or as 'early years provision' as in the Childcare Bill. The new Children's Workforce Development Council is responsible for the overall strategy for recruitment, retention and training of early years workers who are not teachers, while the Training and Development Agency is responsible for teachers, including early years teachers. If the Foundation Stage is to be really effective, I would argue that it should be revised to cover the years from birth (or whenever a child starts in out of home care) to 6 years, including both reception and year 1 in primary school, that this should be seen as the first stage of the education system.

This proposal does not, however, assume that the current emphasis on preparing children for school is appropriate. A far more important question, in my view, is to ask whether schools are ready for children. We need to pay more attention to how children learn, and the role of schools overall in promoting learning, if early education is to be effective. We also need to recognize how much of what is best in the early years is also the foundation stone for the Every

Child Matters agenda – a curriculum which places emphasis on personal, social and emotional as well as cognitive development, and children's centres in which well-trained staff from different professional backgrounds work well together and in which parents are closely involved.

Finally, is it possible to devise a policy that meet the needs of both parents and children? Many parents currently feel torn by the dual messages coming out of government – return to work in order to earn your way out of poverty, on the one hand, but parenting is the most important role that you will play and your child's future depends on the quality of your relationship, on the other. Balancing work and family life is a challenge for parents of children of all ages, but is particularly acute for parents of young children.

As the ten-year childcare strategy rolls out, it will be important to ensure that quality of service provision is maintained as the quantity increases, that children's needs remain paramount, and that parents really do feel that they have choice.

Points for discussion

- ❖ How do you think local authorities are going to be able to increase the availability of day care without additional public funding?
- ❖ What further measures would improve the integration of care and education in early years settings?
- ❖ Has government stuck the right balance between parents being encouraged to return to work and caring for their young children?

2

Joined up Working – the Development of Children's Services

David Hawker

A key driving principle behind *Every Child Matters* (DfES, 2003b), and the Children Act 2004, which enshrines it in legislation, is to create a single integrated service for children and young people covering education, social care and health. The rationale for this is the strongly held belief – supported in part by experience on the ground – that integrated services will result in improved outcomes for children. Children's Trusts are to be the standard-bearers for the new integrated services.

This chapter gives some of the background to this development, charts one local authority's efforts in making it happen for early years services, and highlights some of the knotty issues which are being addressed as we do so.

Children's Trusts

In many respects the template for integrating services in the way envisaged by the creation of Children's Trusts was developed and pioneered in local Sure Start programmes. Children's Trusts are not mentioned as such in the 2004 Act, but are being promoted through the *Guidance on the Duty to Co-operate* under the Act (DfES, 2005d). The term 'Children's Trust' originated in the early work on the *Every Child Matters* Green Paper, in 2002, and deliberately used language familiar to the National Health Service (NHS). It would be to children's services what a 'Care Trust' was to adult services – a vehicle for integrating council-run social care services with NHS-run community health services via the freedoms allowed under Section 31 of the NHS Act 1999. The difference was that, whereas Care Trusts were envisaged as NHS organizations, Children's Trusts were conceived more as an extension of local government.

With one or two exceptions, the early 'pathfinder' Children's Trusts did not plan to become separate legal entities. They were essentially partnerships between local government and local NHS bodies, principally Primary Care Trusts. There was a lively debate during 2004 about how 'hard edged' a Children's Trust should be. Should it be merely a renamed Children and Young People's Strategic Partnership, or should it be an organization in its own right, effectively replacing existing organizational structures? Most local partnerships preferred the former, and this was reflected in the successive terms used by the Department for Education and Skills to describe the new idea – 'children's trust approach', 'children's trust arrangements', or even 'children's trust way of working'. None of these terms gave a very clear idea of what was intended. But local government was generally reluctant to embark on a programme of structural change without being convinced of its benefits in terms of improved services.

During 2004, however, an increasing number of local authorities decided to bring together their education and children's social care functions and create children's services departments ahead of the statutory schedule (of 2008) envisaged by the government. The process accelerated following the passing of the Children Act so that, by late 2005, over 80 per cent of the 150 top-tier local authorities in England had appointed a Director of Children's Services. Thus, ironically, the same local government constituency that had declared itself sceptical about the wisdom of engaging in large-scale structural change had, by 2005, not only reconciled itself to one of the main changes, but was already moving ahead of the government's timetable.

Inevitably this had a bearing on the way in which Children's Trusts started to be conceived. If new children's services departments were becoming a reality, there was more sense in viewing Children's Trusts as their organizational extension into the health-care and wider partnership field. The government was then able to set out a realistic expectation for all local authority areas to have one by 2008, and to build on this expectation by writing them firmly into its plans for the future management of these services. This found notable expression in the *Youth Matters* Green Paper (DfES, 2005g). So far as government thinking is concerned, therefore, children's trusts seem to have emerged as the basic organizational building blocks for the integrated service of the future.

In late 2004, the debates about the nature of Children's Trusts crystallized around what has come to be known as the 'onion diagram' (see Figure 2.1). The diagram sets out a specification for a reformed system of integrated services which is just firm enough to ensure that Children's Trusts have a recognizable existence, but flexible enough to allow local partnerships to develop in the way, and at the pace, which suits local circumstances.

Figure 2.1 *The Children's Trust in action (DfES, 2004b: 13)*

The onion diagram places outcomes for children and their families at the centre, signalling an intention to try to design the services around children rather than to expect them to fit into the pigeon-holes provided by traditional services. It also signals an intention to consult with them over the design of those services, and listen to what they say. There is of course a strong emphasis in *Every Child Matters* on children's rights and children's participation. In terms of early years, putting the child at the centre, and involving families in the design of local services, are already key aspects of the Sure Start programme, at least in theory.

Out from the centre, the four concentric rings in the onion diagram describe, in turn, the 'integrated front-line delivery', the 'integrated processes', the 'integrated strategy', and finally the 'inter-agency governance' arrangements, which are to be the foundational design features of children's services in the future.

Integrated front-line delivery

The intention is that teams of professionals will work together in a multidisciplinary context, meeting children's needs in the round, without using cumbersome referral procedures. Services for a particular age group will be co-located in children's centres, schools and youth centres as appropriate, rather than being spread across a number of different service-specific locations. Managers of integrated teams will be able to deploy resources to best meet the needs, shift them from one service area to another, and resolve conflicting demands. Good quality consultative processes with children and families will ensure that the services provided are what people want and need.

Integrated processes

The service will use the Common Assessment Framework, will have information sharing protocols in place, and the lead professional role will operate within the front line teams.

Integrated strategy

The local partnership will have an agreed commissioning strategy, a shared vision for children, young people and families, a shared set of goals and objectives (expressed as a set of local priorities 'owned' by all the partner organizations), and a single set of organizational arrangements.

Inter-agency governance arrangements

A board or other high-level policy and decision-making body will operate, representative of the various stakeholders and linked effectively to the partner organizations' existing decision making bodies through formal constitutional agreements.

Bringing a local Children's Trust into being

Fig 2.2 shows the governance structure of the Brighton and Hove Children's Trust as at December 2005.

Other local Children's Trusts have different structures. As one of the original pathfinders, our structure originated in mid-2003, with an agreement between the city council and the local Primary Care Trust to establish joint commissioning and strategic planning arrangements for children's services. Our first step was to make a joint staff appointment of a children's services commissioner, supported by a small team of change managers. This small team then devised and led a strategy for systematically reviewing and re-commissioning the whole range of services across health, education and social care. The vision was, and remains, for a seamless service for all children, young people and families in the city. The core of the service will be a single organizational entity bringing together the management of education, social care, youth work (including Connexions) and children's community healthcare. It will have commissioning and partnership arrangements with a range of other bodies in the statutory, voluntary and private sectors, including schools, general practitioners (GPs) and child-care providers. The plan is underpinned by a realization that, in order to improve outcomes for children significantly over the longer term, the local agencies need to move beyond partnership working and bite the bullet of structural integration. At the time of writing (December 2005), most of this management integration is in place, and plans are in place to complete the process by mid-2006.

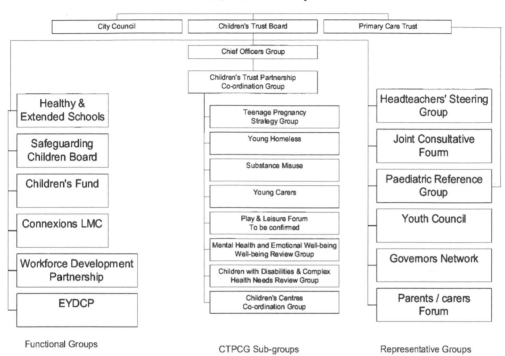

Figure 2.2 *Brighton and Hove's Children's Trust Partnership*

Needless to say, converting plans for management integration into a fully integrated service on the ground is a complex and lengthy business. Our target date for completing the reshaping of our service and seeing it make a real difference to children's lives is 2009.

So we can say that our Children's Trust is simultaneously up and running (that is, planning and implementing change) and under development (that is, gradually moving the services into their final shape). The overall agenda is daunting by any standards: implementing the Common Assessment Framework; introducing the Lead Professional role, better information-sharing arrangements, and multidisciplinary teams working as part of the new children's centres; developing extended schools; reforming youth provision and the Connexions Service; establishing local Safeguarding Boards; reforming Child and Adolescent Mental

Health Services; the list goes on and on. All demand attention. What it means is that local partnerships are faced with the need to make wholesale changes to a range of key services all at once, and to manage it all as one large-scale and multifaceted change programme. Needless to say, local authorities, as the lead partners in this process, are feeling the strain in terms of their capacity to manage and support it. And, of course, the amount of extra money available for the whole change programme is nowhere near enough to fully resource it.

The remarkable fact is that, by and large, there continues to be widespread support for the whole change programme. This is partly due to the power of the vision originally set out in *Every Child Matters*, and partly to the way that vision has been built on through a process of consultation and dialogue between central government and its local and national partners, which has been refreshingly inclusive.

The outcome of all this is that the ideas underpinning the establishment of Children's Trusts are steadily gaining support as more and more local areas start to move in the same direction. It is not too fanciful to envisage a time when the local Children's Trust becomes such a clear organizational entity and that it will take over from the local authority as the public face of all children's services locally, in the way its original proponents intended.

Implications of Children's Trusts for early years services

In Brighton and Hove, we decided to review all services for 0–5-year-olds across the city as part of the establishment of our Children's Trust. We were driven partly by the fact that we wanted to give them priority, and partly by the government's timetable for establishing children's centres (DfES, 2004d, 2005h; HMT, 2004). In our case, we had to establish five by April 2006, and a further nine by 2008 – 14 in all, serving a population of 260,000 and an under-5s cohort of around 10,000.

It was clear to us that the funding would not pay for 14 all-singing-all-dancing centres. Government guidance required us to provide a full service children's centre in the most deprived 30 per cent of areas, but we were free to vary the offer in other areas according to local need. But like so many local authorities, our demography is rather lumpy. So, although many of our deprived areas are concentrated in certain parts of the city, others are sprinkled around, and pockets of deprivation exist in close proximity to areas of relative affluence.

As a result of previous funded programmes we had been able to invest in the main areas of deprivation, but were concerned about the many other smaller pockets which did not have equal access to the services that these previous programmes had funded. So we decided to develop a strategy which would be able to respond to this complex geographical pattern of need by building on and expanding existing provision, and at the same time setting up a city-wide infrastructure which would ensure equitable access to services for all who needed them. In mid-2004 we embarked on a year-long redesign and consultation process, involving parents, professionals and local communities. Over 1,200 people took part in meetings and surveys across the city, and we were thus able to gauge very clearly what people's priorities were for the provision of early years services in the future. Some key results of the survey are set out in Table 2.1.

Table 2.1 *Summary of consultation on early years services, Brighton and Hove*

A better future for your family – headlines of consultation findings	
Parents perceived benefits in the development of children's centres and community teams	• More accessible services at Children's Centres • More integrated services via community teams • More efficient service provision • Potential for extending the support to whole families
8/10 staff supported the idea of bringing professionals together in Children's Centres and Multi-Disciplinary Community Teams	• Help them learn new skills • Improve communication and information sharing • Improve services and outcomes for families • Reduce duplication and repetition for parents

Both parents and staff perceived similar benefits, but staff were more likely to suggest that integrated working would have professional benefits.

The consultation process resulted in a specification for a city-wide service based initially on the first five centres, but growing over the first two years into a full 'hub and satellite' model (with apologies for the mixed metaphor). The consultation also introduced the concept of a 'family health plan', where every family would be entitled to a specified range of core services, such as health visiting, integrated childcare/early education, and basic advice services, and would have automatic access to enhanced services based on assessed need. The core services would be provided in all the centres, but the enhanced services would be managed from, and mostly located in, the 'hub' centres.

Of our five or six hubs, two are already in being as part of the local Sure Start programmes, a further two are being established in a large regeneration area in east Brighton, the fifth is being built on the site of an expanded nursery in the west of the city, and a possible sixth will be built at a venue yet to be identified in Hove. These full-offer centres based in the most disadvantaged areas of the city will use most of the capital funding available. The other eight or nine will be satellite centres, with one or two attached to each hub in order to offer the full service entitlement. Almost all the satellite centres will be carved out of existing facilities or co-located with them, and will link with our extended schools strategy. Schools, GPs, youth centres and community groups will form local clusters with their local children's centre and integrated service teams, to provide what we hope will become a seamless offering for children aged 0–19 and their families.

The managers of the hub children's centres will be designated 'early years service managers', each responsible to an overall area children's services director. Each manager will:

- manage the hub and satellite centres and the integrated early years teams in their area
- link with the schools, GPs, community groups and other service providers in their area
- ensure that the list of children in need is kept up to date
- determine, in conjunction with their local steering committee/Sure Start Board, how the services should be designed and the money spent, based on a single agreed specification for the city as a whole.

Each local steering committee, involving local parents and service providers, will report to the city wide Children's Trust Board, and thus be part of the overall governance arrangements for the Trust. In the case of the two existing local Sure Start Partnerships, these steering groups will develop out of the current Sure Start Boards.

Five key challenges

Through the consultative process we also identified five major sets of challenges, which again are common to local services across the country:

1 How to build a wider partnership.
2 How to develop new, more integrated ways of working.
3 What the new service model should look like.
4 Striking the right balance between central specification and local autonomy.
5 Sustainability.

Building a wider partnership

The first of our key challenges is how to develop effective partnership working between the children's centre based services, GPs and schools.

So far as GPs are concerned, it is not yet clear how the future practice-based commissioning arrangements will work. For us, commissioning is essentially a partnership activity, which starts from the joint identification of needs in the city. This will inevitably involve the GP practices working in partnership with their local clusters. The sharpest discussions locally have been around the management and deployment of health visitors, who will in future be based in the children's centres rather than in GP practices. Each cluster will need to build a new commissioning relationship with the GP practices in its area .

A similar situation applies with schools. As essentially autonomous institutions, with their own budgets and governing bodies, they are not under a legal duty to co-operate. But by agreeing cluster arrangements where they can work together with their local children's centre to plan joint support to families, they inevitably become part of the commissioning arrangements. In essence the relationship between schools and their local cluster partners is a voluntary one. We find that most schools want to join in, because they know that most of the families receiving children's centre services will also have older children at school. And many schools will also play host to some of the children's centre services themselves.

Inevitably there will always be difficult choices to make, even in the most harmonious of partnerships. One of our children's centres is located on a campus with an adjacent primary school. There is a private neighbourhood nursery that was originally set up to provide wrap-around childcare for the 100-place nursery class in the school next door. Should the integrated early education and childcare be located in the neighbourhood nursery that already offers day care, or in the school that has the qualified teachers? There is not enough funding, and there would not be enough children, to justify creating two separate facilities as part of the same children's centre. In the end we decided on the private provider, for a range of complex reasons, but the decision could quite legitimately have gone the other way.

In another children's centre the childcare provision is part of a neighbourhood nursery which in turn is part of the local state nursery school. As a school, it has a delegated budget and is governed autonomously, but also needs to be part of the local governance arrangements of the children's centre. We are still debating how the relationship can be made to work out to everyone's benefit.

Another challenge, which is very particular to the early years sector, is ensuring that the large number of other local childcare and early education providers, within the voluntary and private sectors, including childminding networks, are fully integrated into the partnership arrangements. Generally speaking, most early years partnerships have been quite successful in supporting the private and voluntary sector providers, and thus have built a good foundation for the local collaborative arrangements envisaged for children's centres. Our aim locally will be to ensure that all providers are linked to one of the hubs for training, advice, quality monitoring and support, as part of a city-wide specification, building on what the Early Years Development and Childcare Partnership (EYDCP) already does.

Developing new, more integrated ways of working

Integrated, multi-professional teams are a basic design principle of the 'onion diagram' (Figure 2.1), but as yet there is no single agreed model for one. Integration means different things to different people, and the various aspects where agreement will be needed, such as 'supervision' or 'performance management', certainly mean different things to people from different services.

There is a relatively strong tradition of interdisciplinary working in specialist early years settings. In Brighton we have a very successful pre-school special needs service, which works in a close partnership with specialist professionals in the speech and language service, the children's hospital and our home support service. In many people's eyes this would be seen as integrated working. However, the separate services are still separate – they work well in co-operation, but are not under a single management structure.

So we have explored, in our specification for the children's centres, what it would mean to set up a fully integrated team in each centre. What would be the implications of a team of health visitors, speech therapists or childcare workers being managed by someone from a different professional background? Would it bring about more effective management of the needs of the families, or introduce unnecessary risk to the specialist work involved? Would the professionals in the team benefit from sharing the caseload with other professionals? How would their professional practice be supervised and their standards monitored? Where would they turn to for professional development? And, most crucially of all, what evidence is there that integrated working leads to better outcomes for children?

In our debates, we came to the conclusion that, from the point of view of management coherence and meeting the needs of families, we should ideally have integrated teams under a single line management. However, we were sharply conscious of the need to provide effective professional supervision for all members of the team, and that this would often mean that each professional had both a line manager (within the team) and a professional supervisor (offline). Moreover, in a relatively small service like ours, it is likely that a senior practitioner working in one team would also exercise professional supervision for more junior practitioners working in other teams.

Developing a new service model

With the roll-out of the government's programme, Sure Start will move from being a series of area-specific programmes to becoming a universal programme based around a network of children's centres.

One advantage of the old model was that it was perceived as providing universal non-stigmatized services to everyone in a defined geographical area. If you lived 10 metres beyond the border you did not get access to the services, but if you lived inside it you were entitled to everything, and there was no stigma attached if you took advantage of the enhanced services available.

The new model breaks down the geographical barriers in favour of universal accessibility, but provides the enhanced services on the basis of an assessment of need, thus targeting them in a way which some feel could stigmatize those families. So there is a fear that the change will lead to a 'social services' feel about the way the enhanced services will be offered to people. This fear is reinforced by an expectation that, because funding for the children's centres will in future come via local authorities, there will be a shift in emphasis from local people taking pride in their own development to becoming once again the recipients of local authority services.

One thing which is both good and bad in recent government practice is the use of earmarked funding to deliver specific programmes in order to achieve specified outcomes. On the one hand, it has ensured that money which would otherwise be in danger of being squeezed by statutory or regulatory work is spent on preventive programmes. On the other hand, it has resulted in fragmentation, and sometimes duplication, of programmes, leading to the extra investment not necessarily achieving the best all-round outcomes.

The 2004 Children Act emphasizes that all children are entitled to have their needs met on a statutory basis. In theory this should ensure that money is spent in a more balanced way across the universal, targeted and specialist services. The most efficient way of planning and delivering this will be by treating it as a single budget. This principle is strengthened by Local Area Agreements which are now being introduced across the country, to allow local authorities and their partners greater flexibility over how they spend their money, on the understanding that they will deliver certain key outcomes.

So, in terms of the new service model, the distinction between 'core services' and 'additionality' disappears, to be replaced by the concept of a single shared budget across a local authority area. In principle, all the services for children aged 0–5 and their families, including those provided by GPs and schools, should therefore be regarded as part of a single budget. This budget should be managed jointly by the local cluster partnership, and the resources shifted around as agreed within the partnership to meet the needs identified. In a funding environment where local authorities are entering into Local Area Agreements, and both schools and GPs have their own budgets and devolved commissioning responsibilities, it will no longer be possible to ring-fence budgets as a way of guaranteeing the delivery of specified programmes. Instead, there will be a commissioning process whereby local partners agree a clear service specification matched to the overall resource available, and then agree to use their total budget flexibly to meet the needs on that basis.

But this approach requires the partnership to have reached a considerable level of maturity, and the partners to have developed a clear shared understanding of the needs, so that they can make these important decisions together.

It also requires a common performance framework, translating the five Every Child Matters outcomes into a common set of detailed objectives for the local cluster. There are challenges in bringing together the various disparate inspection and performance monitoring regimes to achieve this.

Balancing local autonomy with central specification

Since local authorities will become the overall budget holder, the existing local Sure Start Boards will have less autonomy than before. One of the key tasks at both national and local level is to clarify their relationship with the interagency governance arrangements of the Children's Trust. In our case, we have decided to build on the current Sure Start Boards, by asking them to expand their geographical reach and become cluster steering committees, joining with us in reviewing the needs of their whole cluster so that we can come to some joint decisions about how the money should be spent. The principle is that our city-wide service specification should leave enough flexibility to allow local clusters to develop their services in ways which best respond to the needs and aspirations of their local families. There is an important community dimension in this – one of our aims is to build capacity within local communities, so that local people continue to volunteer to run events, help out in the centre, manage fund-raising, social activities and all the other things which give life to a community-based resource. The key concept is of a service based on contributing rather than consuming.

Another issue to be clarified under the new arrangements is the relationship of the EYDCP to the Children's Trust. We have been fortunate in Brighton and Hove in having had an effective and well-led EYDCP. Nationally the picture is somewhat patchy. However, as things have become increasingly complex in the early years field, it has been apparent that many partnerships have found it difficult to respond effectively. This is hardly their fault – they were set up as voluntary partnerships and were never really fit for the purpose of leading the kind of complicated and multifaceted programme that early years and childcare has now become.

Nevertheless, we do not want to lose the particular overview which the EYDCP at its best can give. The government's consultation on the Childcare Bill (DfES, 2005a) proposes that every local authority/Children's Trust should have an early years service. We welcome this, because the idea of a coherent, integrated city-wide service fits well with our overall approach within the Children's Trust. But we want to make this service a reality both in operational and in partnership terms. We therefore intend to fully incorporate the EYDCP (perhaps renamed as the Sure Start Partnership) into the Children's Trust governance structure. The area-based cluster steering groups will have a direct relationship with the Children's Trust Board, who will approve their local delivery plan and agree their budgets. But each local cluster will also send representatives to the city-wide Sure Start Partnership, whose role will be to bring together the views of parents and providers across the city, in order to advise the Children's Trust Board on early years and childcare issues at a strategic level.

Sustainability

Last but not least, some of the long-standing issues relating to funding, sustainability, pay, status, training and quality management will become even more acutely felt as early years services become fully part of the Children's Trusts.

We know from research evidence that children from age 2 onwards have much to gain from good quality childcare, and that disadvantaged children benefit most. However, the government's policy for subsidizing childcare for children under 3 only helps those parents who return to work. Locally we are concerned that the most disadvantaged children will not access childcare if their parents do not return to work, even though they have the most to gain from it. This is also a sustainability issue as we struggle to persuade parents that returning to work is the best option for them, because it means they can get the childcare element of the working tax credit, and thus benefit from the childcare provided. Current take-up is too low in some areas for the provision to be sustainable.

The extension of free early education to 38 weeks and to 15 hours per week is good news to parents but, perversely, may exacerbate our existing sustainability problems. Our experience is that the current level of early education funding does not reflect the true cost of provision in a good quality day nursery which employs well-qualified staff, particularly where a qualified teacher is employed. In Brighton and Hove the government grant (now absorbed into the overall local government settlement) has allowed us to pay just under £8 for a two and a half hours early education session. However the true cost of a session is often over £10. The consultation on the new Code of Practice for funding early education (DfES, 2005i) states that parents cannot be charged for any part of the minimum free entitlement either directly or indirectly. This means that childcare providers may actually lose money by offering free early education places, unless they can subsidize them by charging parents for additional sessions or additional hours at a more economic rate. And, of course, the more hours they have to offer free of charge, the more money they will lose, and the fewer additional hours they will be able to charge for in order to help make ends meet. So the bottom line is that, unless the grant is raised significantly to reflect the actual cost of meeting the quality standards, including the employment of qualified teachers, providers of early education, particularly in disadvantaged areas, will struggle to survive.

Conclusion

There is little doubt that the move towards joined-up children's services, and the introduction of Children's Trusts in particular, will have a profound impact on early years provision. It will validate the best existing practice in early years pro-vision, and will challenge the whole sector to move in harmony. It will not of itself solve some of the more intractable issues about funding, sustainability and quality, but it will put them into a wider focus. But given the government's declared commitment to continue to invest in the early years, and the fact that so many of the changes in children's services are in line with what early years practitioners want, I think the sector can afford to be cautiously optimistic.

Points for discussion

❖ To what extent is the 'hub and satellite' model of children's centre provision helpful in planning to meet the needs of the communities in which you work, and does it help or hinder the establishment of integrated children's services across the whole age range?

❖ What strategies do you have, or can you put in place, to address the five key challenges set out in this chapter?

3

The World Picture

Tricia David

Clearly it takes more than a whole book to present a detailed account of Early Childhood Education and Care (ECEC) throughout the world! So in this chapter I try to provide a way of thinking about different types of societies and different understandings about early childhood, and how these influence the treatment of young children and their roles in those societies. I provide illustrations from a number of countries and raise issues about the consequences of different societies' priorities. The main aspects of ECEC focused on in different countries are:

- the role of early childhood services
- the continuing education–care divide
- models of early childhood education.

Young children: how different societies 'see' them

Writing this chapter in the days after the suicide bombings on 7 July 2005 in London, the classification of civilizations by Alvin and Heidi Tofler (1993) sprang to mind. They write about three waves – flashpoints when changes in the way of life for some groups in world population mean they come into conflict with an existing civilization. The Toflers argue that the First Wave occurred when some hunter-gatherer societies changed to an agricultural way of life. The Second Wave occurred with the advent of industrialization; and the Third Wave, as brain-based economies have meant that mass production is outmoded, customized products are 'cutting edge', and uneducated or unskilled workers are generally unemployed. Tofler and Tofler (1993: 22–3) add that in the postmodern, post-industrial, information society, the family too becomes 'de-massified' taking a variety of forms, and 'existing values are challenged or ignored ... The homogeneity of the Second Wave society is replaced by the heterogeneity of Third Wave civilisation'. They argue that since every society in the world is basically interdependent, de-coupling is not possible. Their typology does not imply a hierarchy. Rich nations cannot survive without the rest of the world and they should beware of exploiting, manipulating and damaging the environments in which different types of societies live. In addition they suggest that all the types of civilization will continue to arise, along with new forms we cannot yet envisage.

The aim of the Toflers' study was to provide an analysis of the future of war and how the mode of war in a civilization is associated to methods of production. They wanted to stimulate thinking, to continue the struggle for peace. Written over a decade ago, their conclusions are stunningly perceptive in relation to recent events, but how can such a study help our understandings about provision for young children? It is possible to see how their descriptions of different world civilizations can lead us to make sense of the different ways in which young children are brought up and cared for, as well as what is regarded as important for their learning, in terms of both content and process.

Recently, neuroscience has provided the field of ECEC with supportive evidence about early brain development, indicating that babies arrive ready programmed to socialize and to want to understand the society, or cultural group, in which they find themselves (Shore, 1997). Perhaps this push from neuroscientists and the politicians who have heeded them was responsible in part for the fact that the World Bank published a collection of papers entitled *From Early Child Development to Human Development: Investing in Children's Future* (Mustard, 2002). The papers show a shift in the discourse of social economics away from one about the development of planning models to one of developing people. Additionally, ministers of education of Organisation for Economic Co-operation and Development (OECD) member countries came to realize that the concept of lifelong learning no longer means adult education but learning 'from the cradle to the grave'. As a result they commissioned a study of provision for children from birth to primary-school admission age, initially in 12 member states (OECD, 2001).

The need for organized childcare

Konnor (1991) points out that multiple caring is not new, many cultures have adopted multiple caring for generations. He cites the example of the Efe people of Northern Zaire, who are hunter-gatherers. During the first few months of life the babies are cared for by their mothers for 40 per cent of the time but other women and girls spend time interacting with and sometimes breastfeeding them. Among the Fulani people of West Africa, fathers give their 5- or 6-year-old sons a calf that will form the basis of each boy's first herd (Johnson, 2000).[1] Children in this First Wave will thus be integrated early into the lives and work of their communities and they will be cared for by different members of the group, sometimes by older siblings or relatives. We know, too, that in the past in farming communities in Britain young children would have been taken to the fields and suckled by their mothers during breaks (see, for example, Hardy, 1891; Thompson, 1939).

The need for organized childcare arises principally when a Second Wave change occurs. It was in the industrial areas that the first group ECEC provision was set up in the UK. Robert Owen's New Lanarkshire infant school, dame schools, and the attendance of children as young as 2 in elementary schools in areas of high female employment, such as Yorkshire and Lancashire, are testament to this development. Similar patterns can be seen in the state nurseries in Eastern European countries during the communist era. Both women and men worked outside the home, so nurseries were needed to care for the children, and the nurseries were also considered necessary for the education of future citizens.

Different communities – different purposes for ECEC?

Rosenthal (2003) suggests that what and how a young child is educated appears to depend upon the role assigned to early childhood by the particular society. Societies whose way of life requires that the needs of the community takes precedence are likely to inculcate rules and knowledge, passed on by adults as superiors to children. Meanwhile, in individualistic societies, children are regarded as the equals of adults, encouraged to have and to express their own thoughts and ideas. Lubeck (1986) showed how two ECEC groups in the same North American city educated their children in ways that made sense according to the communities' contexts. The group in a poor black neighbourhood fostered the children's co-operative spirit, group solidarity, supportiveness and empathy; the group in the white affluent area encouraged independence, competitiveness and individuality. Lubeck bemoaned the fact that each group could have fruitfully learnt from each other and that the best of all possible worlds would be for all the children to have all the attributes, to be interdependent rather than either only independent or dependent. In another study Hartley (1993) found nurseries in Scotland to be providing differing educations according to assumptions staff made about the children's families and potential futures.

With the Second and, particularly, Third Wave civilizations (based as they are on 'brain work'), the range and complexity of what children are required to know or be able to do by the time they begin work has increased and this in turn influences what dominant members of that society believe important in the earliest years. However, at the same time, there is an increased likelihood that the adults predominantly responsible for their care (usually their mothers) will be employed outside the home in a setting alien to the young.

The role of early childhood services

Throughout the history of the development of ECEC services in the UK, as in many other countries, there has been confusion about the main role of such services. Should they be social care for children of 'feckless' or ill parents, care for children whose parents go out to work, or the first stage of the education system? Are they to aim to provide the best possible start for every child, or simply to ensure children are safe and healthy, offering cover for parents' hours of work, or to provide parental support, education and development, including community development? Or should ECEC services act as places where people of all ages, staff included, are seen as learners, democratically involved in community life?

It is notable that few countries originally set out to provide integrated care and education services. Sweden's *förskola* (pre-schools) were largely developed almost 50 years ago when the country had a labour shortage and needed to encourage mothers of young and school-age children to return to the workforce (Bergman, 1993). While the quality of the care provided was universally acclaimed and there was awareness about young children's learning, more recent developments have ensured that the 'education' aspect is attended to more consciously. The view of this education is broad, rather than narrowly conceived as subjects to be covered and targets to be reached. Despite being reported as highly successful in the recent OECD survey (OECD, 2001), Sweden's ECEC policy has been criticized (Dahlberg et al., 1999). Although early childhood institutions have been integrated into the national education system and are still financed by the state, these researchers argue that there is a growing trend towards regarding children, but more particularly parents, as *consumers*. Further, they contend that ECEC services are being transformed into production lines, 'a human resource for the market place' (Dahlberg et al., 1999: 69) where knowledge has become a commodity and children are shaped into future workers. In other words, the purposes and curricula of early childhood education are not value-free.

France's system of *écoles maternelles*, which is over 100 years old, was set up as an entitlement of its young children with the main aim of educating them to be and to become French citizens. The more recent developments in France have been a 'rebranding' of the *écoles maternelles* into pre-primary schools, which can result in narrower aims and schoolification according to Goutard (1993). However, France has also seen the provision of out-of-hours care services 'wrapped around' *école maternelle* and school hours to allow for parents' commitments. So can this be seen as a move in a similar direction to that observed in Sweden, but from a different starting point?

Both these systems of ECEC services have adapted to new thinking, responsive to issues related to parental employment but at the same time consciously emphasizing the children's educational entitlement. The discourses around curricula and pedagogy need to be viewed in the context of not only the relevant national histories and childhoods in the countries in question, but also in the light of contemporary economic policies.

Continuity and change in ECEC

Change is currently under way in China. During the Maoist communist era there was full care provision for babies and children up to age 6 because of parental employment, with some provision including weekly boarding. Now municipal authorities are advocating shorter hours, places for 2- to 5-year-olds and more attention to a play-based curriculum (David and Powell, 2005). There is a great interest in Western-style nursery education and brain studies, because at governmental levels China is eager to foster an entrepreneurial spirit among its population in order to compete in the global economy (Vong, 2005). So the new emphasis in China is upon how children learn and is less concerned with provision covering parents' working hours. In addition, much provision in China is now privately run and parents pay fees, with the result that children from low-income families cannot always access such provision. Exploring international differences using an ecological standpoint (Bronfenbrenner, 1979), one recognizes how practice grows out of political and economic conditions and traditions rather than from research about children's development (see also Penn, 2005).

Studying other countries' forms of provision creates challenges concerning services in one's own country. Such challenges to thinking and practice are beneficial. But one cannot simply transplant systems, curricula, pedagogical practices or understandings about young children from one society to another, and one certainly cannot impose them. In times of change it is important to pay attention to a need for continuity. The historical, economic, geographical and ideological context of each situation will determine how the ideas presented will be perceived and processed (David and Powell, 2005; Vong, 2005).

Where the role, or aims, of ECEC services are determined by government, the extent to which they will be thought appropriate by parents and providers – or indeed by children – at a local level is likely to depend on politicians' knowledge and understanding of young children's lives and learning. They will also depend on the extent to which governmental prescriptions (regulations about registration, inspections, curricula, and so on) are viewed as a minimal baseline upon which local communities can construct the kinds of services they deem high quality (Kagan, 2004).

The 'education'–'care' divide

Although the present UK government purports to be encouraging the development of high-quality educationally oriented services, many of its policies indicate the more urgent intention of increased levels of care services to enable mothers to work, especially single mothers living on benefits (Cohen et al., 2004; Campell-Barr, 2005). The argument about provision outside the home for young children continues to re-surface and at its centre are questions concerning children's and women's rights (see, for example, David, 1990). If the emphasis is on 'care' then it is sometimes argued that children's rights are being neglected; if on 'education' offered only part time or for school hours, then women's rights and opportunities are deemed to be jeopardized.

So what exactly is meant by the two terms? 'Care' in this context has traditionally meant the provision of facilities for children whose parents need them to be looked after while the parents themselves either work or study. There has also been a long tradition of care facilities for children of parents who are either too ill to care for them or who are deemed inadequate. The hours of provision would generally be day-long; staffing would be by health or care professionals in group settings. Meanwhile, care for children of working parents would often be provided by private nurseries or by relatively untrained 'family day-carers' (childminders) in the carers' homes.

'Education' would usually entail provision for a maximum equivalent to school hours, staff would usually include qualified teachers and the main aim would be to foster children's learning. The two forms of service would be administered by different government ministries and, as well as divisions along the lines of the service the family sought, there would be divisions within the birth to 5 or 6 age group, children under 2 generally being deemed to need 'care' and not 'education'.

Smith et al. (2000: 7), reviewing the literature for the New Zealand Ministry of Education, state:

> 'Care' suggests custodial physical caregiving, supervision and affectionate nurturing, whereas 'education' suggests planned activities designed to enhance children's learning. Care has sometimes been viewed as inferior to education, but no meaningful distinction can be made between care and education for

young children, regardless of the early childhood setting. The literature shows that if the social interactions, relationships and activities which comprise the early childhood education environment provide sensitive nurturance and care, they are likely to at the same time promote learning and development ... Nevertheless early childhood education involves planning and designing a learning environment for children and their families ... New Zealand was the first country in the world to integrate responsibility for all early childhood services within the education system.

They add that New Zealand's reforms supported the development of a holistic educare system,[2] by which they mean provision offers both education and care to the children and involves their families as a community resource.

The two researchers most involved in the recent OECD study (OECD, 2001) have subsequently published articles based on their analyses of the findings, arguing that the care–education divide continues to pose a problem in many of the countries surveyed but that the road to true integration is not simple (Bennett, 2003; Neuman, 2005).

The implications of the continuing care–education divide

Bennett states that negative consequences of a care–education divide include:

- an imbalance in the supply of services
- relative neglect of care
- an undermining of women's employment opportunities.

He adds that there are considerable economic advantages to governments in return for investment in ECEC services. Bennett (2003: 36–7) cites the NICHD (1997) study to support his argument that children are harmed 'at the time of purchase' as well as throughout life by policies which leave ECEC services to market forces. He adds the need for a strong infrastructure (such as ongoing training for staff and adequate funding), which governments are best placed to provide, and describes the increased tax revenues, reduced health and welfare spending accrued from various governments' initiatives.

Using international comparisons, Neuman (2005) analyses the governance of ECEC services through the themes of administrative integration, decentralization and privatization. She questions how these aspects at policy level impact at the level of provision for the children themselves. Most countries continue to administer 'care' and 'education' through two separate ministries (Australia, Belgium, France and Portugal for example). As has been the case in the UK for decades, this has led to differences in regulations; staff qualifications, training and conditions; funding; and even curricular variations which depend on differing understandings about young children and the role of the services.

Gradually, more countries are attempting to integrate provision under one government ministry.

The advantages of true integration of ECEC – and some of the challenges

Almost 20 years ago in Denmark an Inter-Ministerial Committee on Children was inaugurated, bringing together representatives from 15 ministries to foster cross-ministry working. A growing group of countries, including Sweden and England, have placed responsibility for ECEC services nationally in education ministries. The advantages include:

• all children, not just those defined as 'in need', are included, so avoiding stigmatization of children from vulnerable socio-economic groups and difficulties for families just above the threshold of the 'in need' definition
• policies should be more consistent
• curricula would be expected to have similar emphases
• children's experiences should be more coherent
• inequality should be less in evidence.

As long as staff retain, or gain, status equivalent to that of teachers in schools, being administered by a department of education can mean ECEC services are viewed as more significant than previously, with the corollary that early childhood itself is recognized as an important stage of learning. However, it is this recognition that early childhood is not simply a preparation for primary school and later (adult) life that causes some to worry that moving ECEC services to education might result in 'schoolification'. Nursery traditions and practices which value young children's curiosity and drive to explore may be eroded in favour of more formal top-down, academic practices, as has been witnessed in England (David et al., 2000; BERA, EYSIG, 2003).

There are clearly challenges, too, in integrating services without time being allowed for staff and communities to reflect and debate the purposes and practices of a setting. Anning (2005) details the complexity of enacting 'joined-up' policies requiring the integration of services. She also points to sophisticated and competing demands of traditional professional values and beliefs held by staff from different backgrounds, further complicated by a need for sensitivity to the values and beliefs of the local community. This conclusion is supported by that of Bertram et al. (2002), and by Cohen et al. (2004: 206) who argue that 'increased integration needs to go hand in hand with increased opportunities and capabilities for critical thinking among practitioners, parents, policy makers and politicians'. Cohen et al's study (2004: 208) demonstrated that Sweden's reforms have emanated from steady developments which 'have an evolutionary

feel' and in which 'Swedish society has reflected upon itself and
They add that, in contrast, top-down reforms in England and S
been technical, rather than sensitive to the historical contexts.

Models of early childhood education

Recent policies in England (QCA, 2000) have led to provision for children in the Foundation Stage (3- to 5-year-olds), being viewed as 'educational' provision. Bennett (2004) suggests that this type of prescription indicates that England is among those countries whose ECEC system is being required to adopt a pre-primary model (children are prepared for the primary school). Other countries in this group include Belgium, France, Ireland and the Netherlands, while the Nordic and central European countries Bennett regards as having a strongly social pedagogic tradition.

Social pedagogy is said to be fundamental to ECEC in Germany, where the concept originated (OECD, 2004: 19). Workers, called pedagogues, set out to:

> address the whole child, the child with body, mind, emotions, creativity, history and social identity. This is not the child only of emotions – the psycho-thera-peutic approach; nor only of the body – the medical or health approach; nor only of the mind – the traditional teaching approach. For the pedagogue, working with the whole child, learning, care and more generally upbringing … are closely related – indeed inseparable activities at the level of daily work. These are not separate fields needing to be joined up, but inter-connected parts of the child's life.

Oberhuemer (2004: 18) defines the identity of ECEC centres in Germany, with their strong community and social purpose as having a dominant educational philosophy: 'that has never been one of preparing children for school, or of focusing on academic skills. It has always been a wider under-standing … one which has in recent years seen kindergartens developing more and more into community resource centres, into neighbourhood centres for children and families'.

Despite the enormous challenges which faced Germany's ECEC services follow-ing reunification in 1990, their system is now regarded as second only to that of Nordic countries in its coverage (OECD, 2004). The high levels of public provision which existed in former East Germany (GDR) have been maintained, as far as pos-sible. Meanwhile former West Germany, where provision was generally run by voluntary groups, has increased levels of ECEC services. These are now part of the children and youth welfare system. Material resources and premises are relatively good and there is a committed workforce. Attention is being paid to out-of-school care and there is a strong push to develop services for children under three in the West, to match those in the East, with longer opening hours.

Perhaps one of the most important features of the German system is that it is non-profit-making, intended to reach all children. The system is decentralized, with responsibility being devolved to local governments within Germany's Federal government organization,[3] and to institutions. Each *Land* has its own funding arrangements, shared with the municipalities and parents, who pay between 10 and 20 per cent of the total costs.

Each *Land* sets its own standards for ECEC. The OECD team (2004) found these to be variable and undemanding, unlikely to contribute to efforts to improve quality. Family day-carers (*Tagesmütter* – childminders) are a key part of Germany's system and there has been debate about the lack of real regulation, leading to several *Länder* developing support systems and 'care licences'. *Land* Youth and Welfare Offices and voluntary providers also employ consultants to supervise standards and to offer practical professional development.

A broad framework has been produced upon which *Länder* will develop education plans. Nevertheless, Germany's ECEC programmes have been criticized as limited in 'stimulating and curiosity-triggering experiences' (Elschenbroich, quoted in Oberhuemer, 2004: 14). Clearly there are tensions in promoting a diversity of decentralized services while at the same time proposing 'quality criteria' set by a government agency. The high commitment to local autonomy can mean that there are barriers to the sharing of knowledge and ideas among practitioners, especially when there are insufficient pedagogical advisers.

Levels of policy-making and their impact on available models of services

In another federal country – Australia – ECEC comes under two departments at Commonwealth (national) level – Family and Community Services and the Department of Education, Training and Youth Affairs (DETYA). However, in some of Australia's states, childcare and education may be administered by one department. Australia has committed itself to expansion of ECEC services. Currently there is mixed and private provision – day care for children under 4, early education for 4- to 6-year-olds. Some services for disadvantaged children are subsidized, as are fees to parents from low-income groups using approved services. While a teaching qualification achieved through a three- or four-year university degree is required for pre-school employment, the levels of qualifications and training required to work in ECEC in Australia varies among the states, with staff in non-school services having relatively poor conditions of employment and being relatively untrained. Unsurprisingly, staff turnover is high and few males work in ECEC.

The OECD (2001) report notes the range of beliefs and understandings about childhood and early education in Australia, which appear to complicate the development of a coherent, forward-looking policy. Raban (forthcoming) points out that Australia is at the bottom of a list of 25 OECD countries in relation to expenditure on ECEC in 1999 as a percentage of gross domestic product (GDP), comparing Australia's 0.1 per cent with Norway's 0.8 per cent. She adds that the differences between states creates a hotchpotch of services across the country, with problems of access, and the lack of a coherent policy with respect to policy development and implementation (such as outcomes, staffing, evaluation and monitoring). In particular, Raban takes issue with targeted expansion programmes, citing Leseman's (2003) research indicating the need to embed early childhood services within a comprehensive family and community support policy, with a high degree of integration under a single, co-ordinating administration. In other words, all children should be targeted, all services (health, education, employment, training, housing, welfare, care, and so on) need coherent links and collaborative working practices, and shared responsibility among all the stakeholders – families, community groups, providers, employers, local and central governments.

Finally, Raban's analysis of Australian ECEC and future possibilities includes her description of a model for early childhood education. It is based on research and the new learning paradigm, where early childhood education does not mean 'preschool is a preparation for schooling with defined skills and abilities identified that children should have mastered before they enter primary school'. It is closer to the Scandinavian model, where services work 'in partnership with families and communities, contributing to each child's well-being and development at the time ... more emphasis is placed on fostering independence and autonomy in children. Their social and emotional development takes precedence over planning for cognitive gains in later schooling' (Raban, forthcoming: 5). She stresses the much stronger belief in these countries that early childhood involves experiences that can only occur at this time, they will not return and therefore need to be cherished in the present.

New understandings and resulting developments

Once a country has decided its system of ECEC should indeed involve both education and care for all its children, questions of appropriate education and training, pay and conditions of service for staff are also raised. This chapter has but touched on that discussion. Other issues such as the relationship between ECEC and the school system; universal entitlement; funding, privatization and profit; definitions of quality; challenging cultural assumptions; and the inclusion of children with special educational needs could also be discussed at greater length.

New understandings about young children's capacity for learning in the years between birth and 6 call into question the idea that they need only 'care', although undoubtedly as more and more mothers are involved in the workforce the care aspect and quality criteria are essential areas for debate and development. Further, the new understandings require an evaluation of policies which place the responsibility for children in their earliest years solely on parents and their ability to pay fees for ECEC services. Should young children's learning be viewed as a national investment or continue to be seen as a drain on the economy?

In some countries, ECEC provision is seen as a 'public good' and as an investment, not as a drain on the economy. Like Bennett (2003), Ball and Vincent's (2005: 567) research in the UK has convinced them that as an instrument of childcare policy 'the market is at present deeply flawed'. Like many before them, they call for a public debate about the purposes of ECEC.

In the global economy, with its cult of individualism, liberal theory neglects reciprocity and civic morality, while the market produces moral strangers (O'Neill, 1994). I began this chapter by delineating different forms of civilization. Keating and Mustard (1993: 102) point out, in their discussion of human development and economics, that

> In our 'continuing experiment with civilisation', the next century will see a contest between societies that practise capitalism in a narrow laissez-faire context and societies that evolve capitalism in a broader social context. At present, the latter have a much better record of creating societies that have a broad base for individual and societal health and well-being.

Points for discussion

❖ Why is it important to know about ECEC provision in other countries? Why is it not advisable to simply import or impose a system from one country to another?

❖ What are the advantages and disadvantages of encouraging private providers of ECEC to develop services?

❖ Brainstorm the range of roles that are required for a truly integrated, community-oriented system of ECEC. What aspects of training for workers might need to be universal and what aspects specialized?

❖ What different priorities might practitioners hold with respect to their work, depending on whether they viewed themselves as carers, educators, welfare or community workers?

Notes

1 I must add that in England, too, this can be a tradition in farming families. One of my former 5-year-old pupils asked for a pair of Golden Pheasants for Christmas, from which he intended to breed. His 15-year-old brother had by then a huge herd of pigs, started with the pair he had received ten years earlier.

2 Caldwell (1989) in the USA was the first to use this term to indicate the integration of education and care. The problem of terminology in English and the limited meaning of 'education and care' has been discussed by several writers (Dahlberg et al., 1999; Bennett, 2003). However, I believe that for many of us, the kind of provision we sought to promote has not been limited by our language. Narrow definitions of 'education' and 'care' do not do justice to the work of these services, nor to the histories of the two strands. For example, nursery provision and female employment has a long history in the Potteries (Stoke-on-Trent), an area in which the strong legacy of Tawney (1966) and the Workers' Educational Association (WEA) in the early twentieth century was inspirational, promoting a 'fellowship of learners' with educational opportunities available to all, and education depicted partly as the process by which we transcend barriers of isolation and become partners in a universe of interests with others, both living and dead.

3 There are three main levels in Germany's Federal system – federal, Länder and municipalities (local authorities).

4

Evaluating the Quality and Standards of Early Years Education and Care

Jenny Andreae and Peter Matthews

The introduction in 2000 of the Foundation Stage curriculum guidance and national standards for childcare signalled a major rationalization of policies for the education, early learning and care of young children in England. There has been additional government investment in nursery education since 1997, when public funding for nursery places in providers other than maintained schools became available. Subsequently, Sure Start was established to promote universal access to high-quality childcare. The development of early excellence centres heralded children's centres and extended schools. A vision for the care and education of children was expressed in the Green Paper, *Every Child Matters* (DfES, 2003b) which led to the 2004 Children Act. The government's commitment to greater provision for the early years was consolidated through the ten-year strategy for childcare (HM Treasury, 2004) which includes a commitment to an integrated framework for early development and learning by 2008.

The theme of 'quality' is a crucial aspiration of policy development for early childhood. The Foundation Stage curriculum, and the national childcare standards, set out expectations for providers in terms of the quality of their provision. The ten-year childcare strategy draws on the research of Sylva et al. (2003b) in support of its conclusions, for example, that: 'good quality early years provision can help redress the impact of growing up in poverty and disadvantage. Children from disadvantaged backgrounds should be able readily to access good quality childcare, and other forms of support' (HM Treasury, 2004: 17).

Since 1998, the levers for assuring and improving the quality of provision have been, first, funding – particularly for commercial providers – and, secondly, regulation and inspection, which together ensure that minimum standards are met and that quality is assessed independently and reported openly. The ten-year strategy also identifies the need for a high-quality workforce and presumes an influence on quality exerted by parents through their market power and the systematic incorporation of their views into the planning and 'delivery' of services (HM Treasury, 2004).

This chapter reviews the evolution of the inspection and quality assurance of childcare and nursery education and discusses recent developments. The latter are characterized by a number of tensions, for example, between: quality and compliance; inspection and audit; and different inspection arrangements for similar provision in maintained and non-maintained settings. We examine some of these issues and comment on the factors that affected them. We consider the strengths and weaknesses of recent approaches to inspection and regulation, and discuss whether the new inspection regimes established in autumn 2005 will bring cohesion to the quality assurance and inspection of early years provision under the umbrella of the philosophy of *Every Child Matters*.

The rise of accountability

Two milestones in raising the profile of accountability in provision for the early years were undoubtedly the Children Act 1989 and the 1992 Education Act. The former served to protect the interests of children by ensuring that their care, safety and protection were paramount. Children's interests were safeguarded through registration of their carers, and annual inspection to ensure their well-being. The inspections, undertaken by local authorities, amounted to audits of compliance with national and local regulations. Compliance, not quality, was the name of the game.

Maintained nursery classes and schools that catered for children aged 3 and 4 years, together with the reception classes for 4-year-olds in maintained schools were – and remain – exempt from Children Act inspections. It took the establishment of Ofsted through the 1992 Act to cause all maintained schools, including nursery schools, to be inspected on a regular cycle, which began in September 1994.

Thus there were two separate and independent regimes, covering the different sectors. Local authorities inspected childminding and day care. Maintained schools were inspected through Ofsted. Children Act inspections were necessary for the registration of providers; school (section 9) inspections reported to governors and parents about the quality and standards, management efficiency and ethos of their schools.

This distinction between two accountability regimes was challenged by the desire of successive governments to increase access to nursery education places. This was achieved initially through the nursery voucher scheme which led to the provision of funded nursery education places in non-maintained settings (such as day care providers). Public funding necessitates external accountability. This was established through section 5 of the 1997 Nursery Education and Grant Maintained Schools Act,[1] which provided for registered nursery inspectors (RgNIs) and specified that inspections should report in similar terms to those of schools.

Differences in the inspection frameworks for maintained schools and funded nursery education arose for legislative, practical and professional reasons. Practical considerations, for example, related to the fact that an inspection of a nursery education provider has to be completed by one RgNI in one day, unlike the inspection of even the smallest maintained school, which until September 2005 required a team of at least two inspectors for two or three days.

Some RgNIs were not teachers but had other qualifications appropriate to their work in nurseries. Funding dictated that they had to be trained in three days. There was sensitivity about whether these inspectors should inspect the work of any teachers they encountered, with the result that 'provision' rather than 'teaching' was evaluated. If there is equivocation about 'teaching', the dilemma is repeated in terms of judging standards. First, the notion of standards by the age of 5 was anathema to many nursery education practitioners, only partially dispelled by their diplomatic description as 'desirable learning outcomes' (DLOs) related to six 'areas of learning'. Secondly, any benchmark is purely notional, for few children remain in nursery settings until the age of 5, having already transferred to school reception classes. One solution, central to judging achievement in school inspections, is for inspectors to judge whether what they observe that children, initially aged 4 but later 3 and 4, know, understand and can do in each of the six areas of learning was appropriate in terms of their ages and capabilities. The task was simplified by asking the new cadre of RgNIs to judge whether the provision enabled children to achieve the DLOs by the age of 5 years! Other challenges were:

- the inspection of provision for a small sample of funded children
- the acceptability of judging the quality of teaching where most staff were not qualified teachers
- how to decide whether effective learning was happening
- how to comment on the quality of provision without inspecting leadership and management.

The result was to focus on how well the setting promoted achievement of the outcomes by the age of 5 years. The setting was not re-inspected for four years if it was found likely to promote the outcomes, but was revisited within one to two years if it had some weaknesses and within a year if it was not likely to promote the outcomes.

As with school inspections, the publication of a framework and guidance on evaluating nursery education had a positive impact on the quality of nursery provision. Continuation of businesses depended on inspection findings. More significantly, parents for the first time had access to an independent view of whether or not their chosen provider was educationally effective.

A battle for teaching and the curriculum

During the late 1990s, the tide of the national literacy and numeracy strategies was in full flood in primary schools. These highly structured programmes began in Key Stage 1. Some influential voices, not always close to nursery education, believed that what was good for 5-year-olds was also good for children aged 4 and 3: the younger the better for formal education! Such views were opposed by many working in early childhood education who believed that children's stage of development, interests and choice should have priority in determining the learning that would or would not take place. Ofsted's view, that teaching – appropriate to the age and capability of the child – is an important determinant of learning in an educational setting is supported not only by the expertise of early years HMI specialists and inspection evidence but by recent research. Findings from the Effective Provision of Pre-school Education (EPPE) project (Sylva et al., 2003b), for example, show the direct relationship between the quality of pre-school centres and the intellectual and social development of children from aged 3 and 4 years. Good quality provision, they find, is associated with:

• integrated centres, nursery schools and nursery classes
• higher qualifications of staff, especially if a good proportion of the staff are trained teachers
• pedagogy that includes 'interaction traditionally associated with the term "teaching", the provision of instructive learning environments and "sustained shared thinking" to extend children's learning'
• a balanced approach to the education and social development that regards these as complementary.

Ofsted has no formal role in determining the curriculum although it is party to national curriculum developments and provides advice based on inspection evidence. Ofsted's approaches to inspection are predicated on how well children are achieving in relation to the curriculum specified at the time. The inspection system does not therefore determine curriculum arrangements, but does provide evidence-based feedback which can influence curriculum policy.

The curriculum guidelines for the Foundation Stage (QCA, 2000) provided the first comprehensive model of a broad and balanced curriculum for the early years. The curriculum included, through 'stepping stones', the elements of progression. Its 'early learning goals' replaced the precursor 'desirable learning outcomes'. The curriculum aimed to prepare children to embark on the programmes of study from the start of compulsory schooling and did much to rebuff what some practitioners saw as the marauding downward tendencies of the national strategies. Like other new curriculum prescriptions, the Foundation Stage curriculum is probably too detailed, but it provides a carefully considered and well-received basis for early years education. The curriculum also provided a means by which the baseline assessment profiles developed by many local authorities could be reconciled as a mandatory Foundation Stage profile. It remains to be seen whether this national profile develops as a tool which aids assessment for learning and helps to inform parents or is a bureaucratic imposition designed to serve other purposes such as the development of value added measures in Key Stage 1.

Funding was extended in 1999 to include nursery places for 3-year-olds. The framework developed further at this time, to provide a greater focus on teaching and include the leadership and management of the education provided by the setting. Inspection took more of an overview of the whole setting, circumventing the perceived need to identify those children occupying funded places, using coloured ribbons, or badges, for the day of the inspection!

The transformation of Children Act inspections

In 2000, prompted by child protection issues and the wide disparity of practice in the conduct and frequency of Children Act inspections by local authorities, the government charged Ofsted with responsibility for the regulation and inspection of childminding and day care, which it assumed in 2001. Ofsted had already demonstrated its efficiency in taking on the inspection of funded nursery providers. This introduced a regulatory function that was unfamiliar in most of Ofsted's inspection work. Ofsted became responsible not only for inspection but also registration, investigation and enforcement in relation to childminders and day care providers. More centrally to the raising of standards of care and education, Ofsted was faced with the challenges of:

- reviewing an approach to inspection that was initially concerned with compliance rather than quality, and
- developing a coherent approach to the inspection of care and education across the range of early years providers,

but could not legally include nursery provision in maintained schools within the purview of early years rather than school inspection.

From compliance to quality

The National Standards for Childminding and Day Care[2] (DfES, 2000) corralled the care and education requirements into 14 standards of which 13 concerned aspects of care, and one, early learning. This signalled that those who care for children must not simply occupy them, but engage them in learning. Significantly, the standards also placed the onus on providers to demonstrate that they met the standards, thus promoting a climate of self-evaluation.

When taking on the inspection of childminding and day care, Ofsted's priority was to establish a national regulatory system. Initially, the compliance-only inspection model was a realistic and expedient measure. By April 2003, however, Ofsted had revised its Children Act inspection framework to identify providers that not only met the national standards but provided good quality care. Ofsted's 2005 review shows significant increases in the proportions of good provision in different categories of provider. The quality of registered care provision, illustrated selectively in Table 4.1, is based on the range of provision found to be good.

Table 4.1 *Children Act inspection outcomes as at 31 March 2005: England and two regions*

Type of provider	Number inspected	Quality judgements (%)		
		Good	Satisfactory	Unsatisfactory
CHILDMINDERS				
England	59,546	46.7	53.0	0.3
North East England	2,926	56.6	43.4	0.0
Inner London	2,683	38.6	60.6	0.9
FULL DAY CARE				
England	9,116	63.7	35.6	0.7
North East England	313	78.6	21.4	0.0
South West England	1,047	56.6	42.9	0.5

Source: Ofsted, 2005a.

From April 2003 to March 2005, Ofsted also inspected and made quality judgements on 19,000 non-maintained nursery education providers funded by the government to provide nursery education places for 3- and 4-year-old children. Inspectors found that 'over half the childcare provision is good; the overwhelming majority of the remainder is at least satisfactory; and a third of nursery education provision is of high quality with children making very good progress towards the early learning goals' (Ofsted, 2005a: 3). Only a very small proportion of childcare or nursery education provision was unsatisfactory.

From learning to education

The inspection of funded nursery provision, focusing on the desirable learning outcomes, and then the early learning goals galvanized into reviewing their provision closely those settings who were failing to meet the expected standards. The first complete survey of the quality of provision was published in 2005. Table 4.2 shows the position based on the previous two years of inspections using the 2003 framework with its four-point grading scale. The modal judgement for provision in every area of learning is high quality.

Table 4.2 *Quality of key aspects of nursery education*

	Judgements from all nursery education inspections from April 2003 to March 2005[1]			
	High quality	**Good overall**	**Significant**	**Unacceptable**
Areas of learning:				
Personal, social and emotional development	64	33	3	0
Physical development	56	40	4	0
Creative development	53	40	6	I
Knowledge and understanding of the world	52	42	6	I
Mathematical development	49	42	8	I
Communication, language and literacy	48	45	6	I
Aspects of management:				
Partnerships with parents	58	39	3	0
Improvements since last inspection	46	44	8	I
Leadership and management	42	51	6	I
Quality of teaching	35	57	7	I
Quality of nursery education overall	34	58	7	I
Total number of inspections[2]	5,600	9,600	1,100	100

1 Four-point judgement scale: I= high quality nursery education where children are making very good progress towards the early learning goals; 2 = good quality education overall where children are making generally good progress; 3 = acceptable provision but some significant areas for improvement, where children's progress is limited; 4 = unacceptable provision, children are making poor progress towards the early learning goals.
2 Number of inspections has been rounded to the nearest 100.

Source: Ofsted, 2005a: 32.

Provision for mathematical development and communication, language and literacy is relatively weaker than for the other areas. This is likely to reflect the greater need for qualified teaching in these areas. Table 4.2 illustrates that teaching is not as high in quality as the other 'aspects of management'. The ten-year strategy recognizes the need for each nursery provider to be led by a qualified person. It also promotes the view that working with pre-school children should have as much status as teaching in a school.

Combined inspections: towards the integration of inspection frameworks

Ever since 1997, the inspection of the educational provision of 3- and 4-year-olds in maintained and non-maintained provision has been conducted under two different inspection regimes which have defied attempts at integration. The establishment of early excellence – now children's – centres, provided Ofsted with an ideal opportunity to develop an inspection model that would cover maintained and non-maintained provision in complex settings. This work paved the way for the development of a combined framework for judging both care and education, and reporting the findings in a single report. The format brought the funded nursery education (section 122) and school (section 10) frameworks closer together, aided recently by the provisions of the 2005 Education Act (Table 4.3, Columns B, C and D).

Early excellence centres represented an innovative government initiative to provide high-quality integrated nursery education and day care for children aged 0 to 5 years, usually based on existing nursery schools. Centres combined childcare, nursery education, family support and, sometimes, adult learning in single centres. All centres were inspected and their overall effectiveness was reported in *Children at the Centre* (HMI, 2004).

Table 4.3 shows that the reporting requirements for the different sectors exhibit greater convergence than before. The strengths of the new provisions include:

- a common concern for educational quality and achievement
- an emphasis on meeting individual needs
- an emphasis on the well-being and personal development of children
- recognition that leadership and management are important determinants of effectiveness.

It is curious, however, that:

- there is little connection between the inspection requirements of the 2005 Act and the overarching 'outcomes for children'
- by including self-evaluation as one isolated aspect of quality assurance, the Act suggests a process that is

Table 4.3 *The evolution of inspection requirements for nursery education providers*

| | Education Act 2005 | | |
A. School Standards and Framework Act 1998, nursery providers	**B. Section 53, Schedule 7: Part I Inspection of child-minding and day care**	**C. Part 2: inspection of nursery education in non-maintained providers**	**D. Section 2: inspection of schools (including maintained nursery education)**
The quality and standards of relevant nursery education	The quality and standards of child-minding and day care provided in England	The quality and standards of relevant nursery education	The quality of the education provided by schools in England
	How far childminding and day care ... meet the needs of the range of children for whom they are provided	How far relevant nursery education meets the needs of the range of children for whom it is provided	How far that education meets the needs of the range of pupils at those schools
			The educational standards achieved in those schools
	The quality of leadership and management in connection with the provision of day care	The quality of leadership and management in connection with the provision of the relevant nursery education	The quality of the leadership in and management of those schools, including whether the financial resources made available to those schools are managed efficiently
	The contribution of child minding and day care provided ... to the well-being of the children for whom they are provided	The contribution of the nursery education to the well-being of the children for whom it is provided	The contribution made by those schools to the well-being of those pupils
The spiritual, moral, social and cultural development of pupils		The spiritual, moral, social and cultural development of pupils	The spiritual, moral, social and cultural development of pupils at those schools
			The extent to which those schools are developing rigorous internal procedures of self-evaluation
			The behaviour and attendance of pupils at those schools

  - set apart from the leadership and management of schools
  - by implication not expected of other providers, even though the care stan-
    dards place the onus on care providers to demonstrate that they meet the
    standards
  - the only requirement that is adjectivally defined in law ('*rigorous* internal
    procedures of self evaluation').

Despite these oddities, the statutory basis for inspection does more than before
to promote the reconciliation of inspection frameworks and approaches. The
resulting evaluation schedule for inspections of childcare and funded nursery
education (Ofsted, 2005c) successfully draws together the evaluation of
childcare and, where applicable, nursery education. The quality of teaching
and learning, central to the quality of nursery education provided, does not
feature overtly in the overarching criteria that relate to the question, how
effective is the provision? The guidance on the judgements that must be
made, however, is explicit about the evaluation and reporting of the quality
of learning and teaching as part of the quality of nursery education
(Ofsted, 2005c).

The childcare and nursery education framework can be judged an adroit compromise. The evaluation of complex settings calls for a high level of inspection
expertise, for inspectors should be thoroughly conversant with the inspection
framework and guidance, the 14 childcare standards, the Foundation Stage
curriculum and early learning goals, the framework and outcomes of *Birth to
Three Matters* (DfES, 2002) and the 2004 Children Act. They may also need to be
acquainted with the Key Stage 1 curriculum and features of quality in relation
to adult learning and child and family support. Do such paragons exist?

In contrast, the inspection of nursery and reception provision in maintained
schools is simpler, unencumbered at present by the childcare standards and the
birth to 3 years framework unless the school is a care provider. The inspection
framework, which applies to the school and further education sectors, is ren-
dered somewhat inelegant by the complexity of several of its many inspection
criteria, which could cloud judgements and distract from rigorous evaluation.
One example is the compound judgement: 'How effectively leaders and managers at all levels clearly direct improvement and promote the wellbeing of
learners through high quality care and education' (Ofsted, 2005e: 20). This
framework follows its predecessors into the trap of being too comprehensive,
which is unfortunate since the inspection visit has been greatly scaled down. Its
language in places reflects the argot of the time rather than the fundamentals of
effective schools, and it is not particularly user-friendly to small schools and
nursery schools. Ofsted proposes to 'inspect' extended schools by 'talking to key
people' about the services rather than inspecting the services directly, thus
departing from the principle of close observation. Where applicable, a Children
Act inspection will take place at the same time as the school inspection.

From inspection to self-evaluation

Self-review has been a feature of both nursery and school inspections for many years. In nursery settings, it only elicited basic operational information. In schools, including nursery schools, self-evaluation forms were piloted from 2001, developed and used to shape all inspections from 2003, and by 2005 amount to such an important part of inspection that less inspection is needed.

The process of self-evaluation and its use in promoting improvement is more important than the formal statement. The outcome of self-evaluation should be a revised and better informed improvement plan. The lack of emphasis on self-evaluation in early education inspections may be due to not wanting to put off providers. However, some early years providers, often in complex settings, already demonstrate excellent practice in this art. The report on an urban children's centre provides an example:

> The headteacher's ... judgement that the leadership and management of the Centre are good, rather than very good, reflects her desire for further improvements and does not sufficiently recognise all the things that have already been achieved. The quality of the Centre's self evaluation is particularly good ... Senior managers and co-ordinators carefully and consistently monitor and evaluate the work of the Centre. This information is used very effectively to identify training needs and helps them to reflect on the quality of their practice and how it could be improved. This is an exceptional aspect of the Centre's work. (HMI, 2004: 5)

Inspection frameworks have been very influential in promoting self-evaluation (Matthews and Sammons, 2004). There is a growing tendency for schools and other providers to ask the same questions of themselves as inspectors ask. Their perceived success in doing this has resulted in the school inspection system adapting so as to use the outcomes of self-evaluation to shape the inspection agenda. It is not clear why other providers should be precluded from this (Table 4.3).

The children's agenda

The five outcomes for children set out in *Every Child Matters* are likely to provide the theme that reconciles the different inspection frameworks. The inspection guidance for inspecting both sectors cross-references inspection criteria to the five outcomes for children. Ofsted's review of the quality of care and education (Ofsted, 2005c) demonstrated how early childhood inspections could produce the judgements needed to report on these outcomes.

Ofsted used its inspection findings to show how providers, by meeting the relevant standards (DfES, 2003c), could contribute to the first four outcomes for children; that is, how they help children to be healthy, stay safe, enjoy and achieve, and make a positive contribution. For example, the outcome for children 'enjoying and achieving' involves children enjoying play experiences that stretch and develop them and help them achieve. The relevant national standard relates to care, learning and play (Standard 3). Ofsted (2005a: 14) finds that in (the 65% of) settings where outcomes are good, children:

- are happy and settled;
- are involved in a broad range of planned activities and spontaneous events, which support their development and overall learning;
- are confident to make decisions, explore and investigate, and relate well to others; and
- respond well to adults who are interested in what they do and say.

As with the other outcomes for children, Ofsted (2005a: 31) recommended a number of actions to improve the quality of care, learning and play:

- Extend the range of planned activities and experiences for children, appropriate for their stages of development and based on their individual needs.
- Improve opportunities for children to make independent choices by using a range of resources and responding to their spontaneous interests.
- Consider ways of recording children's progress to plan the next steps for their development through play.

Turning to schools, the section on personal development in an inspection report on a small first school for children aged 4 to 9 years gives a commentary that, probably unconsciously, reflects the 'enjoying and achieving' outcome perfectly.

> The pupils acknowledge that this is a great place to learn ... and they whole-heartedly embrace school life. From the very start, young children come into nursery and reception with a smile and happily wave goodbye to parents and carers. Their expectations are high, because they associate school with exciting activities and new experiences. They delight in newfound friends and stimulating classrooms and launch into tasks with gusto. Throughout the school, pupils demonstrate an eagerness to learn; they listen attentively, persevere with tasks set and consistently produce high quality work. They are proud of their school and their individual achievements. (Peacock, 2005: 5)

The new combined and school inspection frameworks also cross-reference inspection criteria to the outcomes for children. This offers the promise that comparable reports which give an overview of outcomes for children can be generated across education and care provision. There is an opportunity for Ofsted to rise to the challenge of addressing the fifth outcome, economic well-being, in its arrangements for the future. Examples of how this may be done exist already in its archives from the HMI-led inspections of early excellence centres, for example:

The provision at the Family Centre is good and many parents would be lost without it. The staff are friendly, helpful and supportive. They achieve a good balance between catering for the needs of the adults and the children ... Parenting skills are developed well and the Centre successfully provides access to adult education. A number of parents and carers have secured jobs as a result of the skills gained at the Centre. (HMI, 2002: 4)

Joint area reviews of children's services

Under the Children Act, inspectorates will be working together for the first time to inspect and report on the quality of services for children within a local authority. Inspection reports on individual providers will contribute evidence to the area-wide inspection of children's services as described by the 2004 Children Act. Ofsted (2005e: 3) believes that joint area reviews, conducted by at least two inspectorates, will

> set out to describe the outcomes achieved by children and young people growing up in the area, and evaluate the way local services, taken together, contribute to their well-being. The reviews will seek to evaluate the collective contribution made to outcomes for children and young people by relevant services in the area. They will judge the contributions made by the council's services overall and make specific judgements about the quality, management and leadership of the council's principal education and children's social care services, and of other services where there is sufficient evidence.
>
> Joint area reviews will report on the well-being of *all children and young people* in a local area. They will cover universal, preventive and targeted services. Particular attention will be given to joint action by local services on behalf of those groups of children and young people who are vulnerable to poor outcomes. Two such groups will be covered in detail in every review: children and young people who are looked after by the council; and, children and young people with learning difficulties and/or disabilities. In the case of children and young people placed in residential establishments, this will include the duty of care that is the responsibility of the placing council, even when children and young people are placed outside the council area.

Conclusions

The arrangements for inspecting care and early education have developed considerably under Ofsted's charge. The 15 per cent increase in care places over two years indicates that providers have not been put off by the regulation they face. The transfer of Children Act inspections from local authorities to Ofsted has been managed efficiently and inspection approaches have evolved to provide evaluations of quality as well as compliance. There is now an extensive baseline against which improvements in provision can be gauged.

The majority of 4-year-old children are enrolled in maintained nursery or primary schools. Recent changes to the school inspection system will limit coverage of the quality and standards of provision in nursery and reception classes. A common inspection module could be used for the inspection of Foundation Stage provision of schools and other settings. This would give greater parity with other nursery providers. Many schools, however, would argue against the partial evaluation that would result, especially now that the foundation curriculum is part of the new national curriculum. The 2005 Act allows greater convergence of inspection arrangements for different nursery education providers. The common feature of different reports is likely to remain an assessment of provision in terms of the five outcomes for children for the foreseeable future, at least until the proposed 'single quality framework for 0 to 5 provision' has been established by 2008. The way ahead for all providers is to ensure that they have a strategy for assuring quality and making improvements based on their own appraisal of how well they are doing and what needs to be done. If this is in place, there should be no surprises from inspection, simply endorsement.

Points for discussion

❖ If there is a common inspection framework for children in the Foundation Stage, what judgements should it include that are applicable to all settings?
❖ Do the outcomes for children provide a sufficiently comprehensive basis for assessing care and education provision and safeguarding their well-being, needs and interests?
❖ Is it reasonable to expect all childcare providers regularly to evaluate the quality of their work and inspections to take account of this?

Notes

1 Later section 122 of the 2001 Education Act.
2 The standards are being reviewed at the time of writing this chapter.

5

Listening to Young Children: Respecting the Voice of the Child

Y. Penny Lancaster

Chapter contents

- Setting listening in context
- The Listening to Young Children project
- Towards respecting the child's voice
- Conclusion

Drawing on Coram Family's Listening to Young Children project, this chapter focuses on some of the issues that will need to be addressed in implementing the government's current social inclusion agenda for children and their families. First, this chapter sets Listening to Children within this significant policy context. This is followed by re-examining our 'taken for granted' assumptions about childhood and thinking about children as subjects of rights, and by exploring what it means to relate to young children respectfully. The chapter advocates that to embed genuine social inclusion for young children we need to go beyond implementation strategies. We need to develop a listening culture in early years settings.

Recent government initiatives (*Every Child Matters* [DfES, 2003b] and the Children Act 2004) have addressed to some extent the inadequacy of positioning children in the role of passive recipients in matters that affect their lives. These initiatives give practitioners permission to partner with the children they care for and work with, to include children's perspectives in planning, delivery and evaluation processes. This can be challenging as it requires a rethinking of the relationship between practitioner and children, as practitioners are expected to be willing to learn from children's perspectives of the service they are delivering.

Government policy has created a significant reform environment for social inclusion, but this on its own is not enough to ensure that the changes they promote will be implemented. For the child's perspective to be taken seriously, reflective practitioners are needed. These are practitioners who are willing to reflect on their own practice, regardless of how well they think they are already listening to children, and to evaluate whether the children they work with and care for are routinely and genuinely involved in decision-making processes. Effective implementation is dependent on practitioners working with and caring for children from a rights-based approach.

Setting listening in context

The United Nations Convention on the Rights of the Child (UNCRC) and UK legislation (primarily the Children Acts 1989 and 2004) have played and are playing a significant role in providing a legal framework for listening seriously to children's views, concerns and feelings. Embedded in these is the concept of listening to young children; of hearing the child's voice in decision-making processes that have been, traditionally, the domain of adults.

First, one of the fundamental principles of the UNCRC is Article 12,[1] which provides *all* children with the right to participate freely in all matters that affect their lives. All children have the right to have their views taken seriously according to their understanding of the issues and competence to understand the implications. Because there is no age limit it provides a very low threshold for listening to all children. The medium of expression is also not prescribed. All children capable of expressing a view are entitled to do so and have it taken into account. This includes babies and children with disabilities who express their views with a rich and diverse language repertoire of sounds, gestures, developing talk and visual representations. Article 12 states that the greater the age and capacity of the child the more weight their views should be given. It asserts the child's right to be involved in a process of participation in all matters affecting him or her, but adults retain the responsibility for the outcome (Lansdown, 2005a). The emancipatory nature of the UNCRC, of promoting children's perspectives to be taken seriously so that they can influence decisions that affect them, requires us to make a radical change in the way we think about children and childhood. It also challenges how we relate to children as we care for them and work with them within professional contexts.

Despite the emancipatory nature of the UNCRC, the responsibility of adults to uphold the best interests of the children they care for or work with is not diminished (Lansdown and Lancaster, 2001). The UNCRC is a unique provision that obligates us to respect children's capacities to be involved in decision-making processes, but it is in balance with an obligation to protect children because of their evolving capacities. Inherent in the UNCRC is the recognition that children in different environments and cultures will acquire different competencies at different ages because of their diverse life experiences and circumstances (Lansdown, 2005b). To the extent children have a rights-based entitlement to have their views taken seriously there is likewise provision for children to be protected from their unevolved capacities (Lansdown, 2005b).

The concept of evolving capacities is central to the balance embedded in the UNCRC between relating to children with respect and at the same time protecting children from being exposed prematurely to responsibilities normally associated with adulthood. While all the rights in the UNCRC extend to all children irrespective of capacity, Article 5[2] implies an ever-increasing transfer of responsibility for decision-making from responsible adults to children as the child acquires competence and, of course, the willingness to participate in matters that affect their lives (Lansdown, 2005b).

Secondly, the *Every Child Matters* (ECM) outcomes framework and the Children Act 2004 creates a significant reform agenda. They were born out of Lord Laming's report in which he revealed just how tragic consequences can be when a child is not heard. Victoria Climbié needed someone to listen to her life experiences, her concerns, her feelings and her perspective of her situation, but no one did. Her rights were overlooked and the care she received was steered by adult demand. Victoria was known to three housing departments, four social services departments, two GPs, two hospitals, an agency-run family centre and two police child protection teams (Lancaster, 2004). As Lord Laming said: 'the extent of the failure to protect Victoria was lamentable' (Laming, 2003.)

The Children Act is a legal mechanism to ensure better outcomes for children and their families. The ECM agenda promotes a step change in relating to children through a user-focus approach; through participation. They acknowledge that in order to provide effective services we need to take into account the direct views of children in addition to the perspectives of parents, practitioners and other significant adults who are usually consulted. Each ECM outcome[3] is an indicator of effective participatory practice. Together they provide a defining framework for partnering with children and their families.

All these government-led initiatives enhance the status of children. They represent a commitment to children, our youngest citizens, to have an input into their learning, health and social care. They also make a positive contribution in challenging some of society's unwritten values and norms such as children should be seen and not heard, they should do as they are told and adults know best. They acknowledge the importance of gaining understanding of the world through children's eyes so that the services we deliver are more effective. The current context is a lever to not only think about listening to children as routine, but also implementing child participation as everyday practice. As Al Aynsley-Green, England's first Children's Commissioner, said: 'we have a precious window of opportunity to embed a real change for children into our service delivery. It's the best opportunity in 50 years for children and families' (Aynsley-Green, 2004).

We can seize this opportunity to embed real change by developing a listening culture in early years provision in which listening is defined as:

- providing time, space and choice for children to make a positive contribution to their learning, social and health care
- proactively hearing and observing children's many ways of communicating their feelings, views and aspirations
- taking seriously what children express
- giving children feedback about how their perspectives have informed decision-making processes.

This definition of listening involves including children's views in decision-making processes alongside the views of other significant stakeholders (those who have a vested interest). It is not advocating that the views of others are overlooked or that we need to comply with children's wishes.

The Listening to Young Children project

Coram Family's Listening to Young Children project[4] has gained understanding of what it means to develop a listening culture within early years. The initial three-year project culminated in the development of an integrated resource pack (Lancaster and Broadbent, 2003). Since 2003 *Listening to Young Children* training courses have also been developed and rolled out nationally to early years practitioners in the education, social care and health sectors. The project was awarded the best Education and Training project in the 2005 Charity Awards.

Both the resource pack and the training courses are a timely contribution to implementing a rights based approach to working with children. They are based on the ECM outcomes framework, the Children Act 2004 and the UNCRC (Articles 5 and 12). The interdisciplinary nature of *Listening to Young Children* supports practitioners to improve listening competencies across professional boundaries. Its participatory approach translates into practice the government's commitment to young children to participate in the planning, delivery and evaluation of policies and services that are relevant to them. *Listening to Young Children* is supporting practitioners to be more effective in responding to the changes in children's lives, meeting their diverse needs, and improving care and services.

But to seize the window of opportunity that the current policy context has provided we still need to actually offer children genuine participatory opportunities to be involved in to influence their learning, social and health care. To achieve this we are going to need to understand when participation is genuine and when it is not. Genuine participation involves partnering with children in planning, delivery and evaluation processes. One of the hallmarks of participation is that it challenges the existing balance of power between adults and children. Participation calls for socially inclusive relationships in which there is mutual respect, reciprocity and sharing power between and among adults and children. They are relationships that enable children and adults to work together as partners and involve time, space and choice:

- making time for children to be involved
- allocating space to document children's views
- providing a range of material so children can choose how to express their views and choose to take part or not.

> When a group of three-four year old children commented on how boring their chairs were the practitioner took advantage of their observations to participate with children in a problem-solving opportunity. Before his involvement with the Listening to young children project the practitioner was aware that he would have quickly brushed their comments aside. He would have mentally noted that they lacked any understanding of budgetary constraints and that after all nursery chairs play a functional role rather than an aesthetic one. But this time the practitioner took their observations seriously. During circle time he offered the children four chairs. This gave them the opportunity to solve the problem that they had identified. The children organized split into four groups and with the support of the practitioner and a parent, as facilitators, creatively turned the chairs into anything but boring artefacts – a throne, butterfly, mirror, and a castle (in *Creative Design and problem-solving*, pp 4–5, Lancaster and Broadbent, 2003).

Drawing on the Listening to Young Children project the rest of this chapter explores some of the issues that need to be addressed in developing an environment in which children are enabled to routinely express their perspectives and have them taken seriously.

Towards respecting the child's voice

Research has shown that even when the notion of giving participation is accepted (Prout, 2001), it is not a given that this will result in the child's voice being heard. Others (Bronfenbenner, 1979; Rogoff, 1990) have shown that our assumptions, about what children can or cannot do at any given age, and our values inform the way we relate to children. Moreover, the way we view childhood determines the expectations we have of the children we work with and or care for (James and Prout, 1990; Lansdown, 2005b). Regardless of our willingness to meet, for instance, the ECM standards, our taken for granted views about children and childhood have the potential to hinder children from actually achieving the outcomes we are working towards.

Re-examining our view of childhood

Embedded in the current policy context (UNCRC, ECM and the Children Act 2004) is the assumption that children are stakeholders. They have a considerable interest in the services we deliver. However, the evolving nature of children's capacities tends to give rise, in particular within Western cultures, to a construction that perceives children as 'in training'; in process of becoming a person, learning and practising to exist for the future (Quortrup et al., 1987). This view masks children's ability to express their understanding of their particular experiences (Lansdown, 2005b), and constructs children in deficit terms while they are actually coping with their experiences, acquiring language and accomplishing physically, emotionally, socially and cognitively (Quortrup et al., 1987; Alderson, 2000). Viewing children as participants, as stakeholders, as users of service delivery involves making their contributions visible. Yet, adults are still often perceived as more reliable to express the child's view, rather than the child directly. This is often the case when a child has a disability, language delay, is pre-verbal or who does not understand or speak English. This can lead, as in the case of Victoria Climbié, to tragic consequences. A view of childhood that limits children from making a contribution to decision-making processes and from influencing matters that affect them denies them the opportunity to reach their potential and blinds the adult world to the reality of what children are capable of achieving (Lansdown, 2005b)

> Milo[5] (16 months old) was experiencing widespread gross motor delay. He was unable to crawl, stand or walk. His mother was becoming increasingly concerned over her child's condition and Milo was becoming very frustrated, especially when he was around other children. His family health worker and mother decided to observe Milo, to tune into his likes and dislikes in order to understand his needs, feelings and preferences. They noticed he loved music and movement sessions. Subsequently, with Milo setting the pace, Milo's mother began mirroring his movements in music and movement sessions. His confidence grew and before too long he began to walk, climb and run and make friends. Tuning into Milo, through music and movement, gave Milo the time, space and choice to imagine and explore in his own way. It also gave both the mother and the family health worker the opportunity to support him to enjoy good physical and mental health because they knew what interested him.

Children are significant stakeholders in educational, social care and health services, whose views can benefit service delivery. They are competent in expressing their views in a range of ways (Alderson, 2000; Delfos, 2001). They are people already, and like all people, they are continually evolving their capacity to communicate how they are making sense of their lives. They are also like us in that their preferences and views are constantly evolving.

Children are stakeholders, no matter how young they are. While the weight given to their views needs to reflect their level of understanding not one child should be overlooked or excluded from any decision-making process that affects them.

> At a baby massage class a first time mother arrived with her 6 months old baby boy. The class had been recommended to her because she was finding it difficult to build a relationship with her child, *'he is so fractious and will not settle. I feel such a failure – I don't think he likes me'*. She was returning to work within the next three months and was not happy that she had not built a loving relationship with him. With her consent I videoed their 'baby massage' experience which included time in which she gave her son his bottle. Afterwards the mother and I viewed the footage at slightly slower than normal speed. It was only at this speed that we saw that while she held him close to her he was calm and for the most part intently gazing at her. For the first time this mother, to her delight, 'heard' her son interacting with her. The mother was transformed. Her face beamed with pleasure and her whole demeanour changed. Her child's expression of love for her built a confidence and self esteem as a mother that was not present when she arrived at the baby massage session (Lancaster, 2004: 150–1).

Using a video camera in this way helps us to listen to all children; babies, toddlers, children with disabilities, and children who do not have English as their first language. In particular when observation involves 'slow motion replay' we can gain a keener awareness of how children are making sense of their lives and expressing their needs, preferences, concerns, wishes and views.

Children as subjects of rights

Listening to young children fits a rights-based approach in relating to children. It promotes a move towards viewing children as subjects of rights, and advocates a move away from viewing young children as passive recipients of adults' decisions, where choices and decisions need to be made on their behalf. While the current policy context is a lever that is raising children to this status in decision-making processes that affect them, it is not an approach that devalues or disregards the rights and responsibilities of significant adults in their lives. Inherent in the current policy context, because of children's evolving capacities, there is a balance of emancipation and protection. Children are not ascribed the status of having the sole expertise of their lives. We are obligated to listen to children's views and take them seriously in addition to listening to all the other stakeholders (Lancaster, 2003).

A rights-based approach involves providing children with opportunities to participate in all actions and decisions that affect their lives. One of the ECM outcomes (making a positive contribution) requires practitioners to offer children opportunities to express their views. Article 12 obligates adults, in their capacity as parents and professionals, to ensure that children are enabled to and encouraged to contribute their views in all relevant matters and to provide age-appropriate information which helps them to form their views (Lansdown, 2005a). Most young children, however, are unaware that they have this entitlement and subsequently are dependent on adults to fulfil their obligation. For children to be heard they need not only sensitive listeners, but also listeners who support them to access decision-making processes.

Practitioners at a children's centre[6] involved children in planning a garden for their new outside area. They initially observed that children were designing a garden in the sand tray. They took advantage of this by having a number of small and large group discussions to identify how they could partner together to develop ideas for the garden and to list the materials they would need. In the process, the children used digital cameras to record the things they liked and disliked about the garden. Once these were printed, they were ranked with happy and sad faces. Children also drew garden designs on paper about what they would like in the garden. Seed catalogues were provided for ideas which led to children wanting to plant the seeds themselves. A three-dimensional map and model of the garden was also developed, using salt-dough and paint. This helped them to think about the design and to locate where everything should go. The children were very happy with the outcome of the project and felt that they had made a genuine contribution to the new outside area. The participative nature of the project has since inspired a number of other projects.

A rights-based approach is dependent on parents, carers, practitioners and policy-makers proactively partnering with young children in decision-making processes. Their perspectives need to be proactively and sensitively sought.

Involving children in decision-making processes is analogous with 'pulling up another chair' (Lancaster, 2003). It involves ensuring that the child's voice is represented, either directly or indirectly. According to the nature and location of the decision-making process children's views can be tabled either by them directly or via drawings, audio recordings, photographs, writing, models or other visual-based documents that represent the direct voice of the child (rather than changing their voices to fit the adult context). In addition to this it is important that any documentation drawn on, to communicate children's perspectives, needs to reflect the time, space and choice (of materials and methods) that children have had to express their views. Pulling up another chair in this way promotes inclusion and counters exclusion.

At a supervised Child Contact Centre I provided an opportunity for children to 'have their say' about their experiences of contact. I ensured there was a range of materials that was appropriate for children to choose how they wanted to express their views. One seven year old child came to me and said, with much emotion and conviction, *'I don't ever want to see my dad again'*. He then took some paper, wrote some of his thoughts and attached it to one of the 'have your say' signs. Inside I panicked – *'what have I done? What do I do now'?* When I told him that I did not know how to respond he said *'just listen, let me say it, I know you can't do anything, just listen to me'*. Even though he knew he had to see his dad again, he needed to be heard and to have space so that he could express his view and feelings about the court order that imposed the visits he did not want. A few weeks later, I met with him and two other children, who also experience supervised visits with a non-resident family member. Together, we brainstormed about ways in which their voices and the voices of much younger children could be heard in the midst of problems and difficulties. The most important message I learnt from these children had nothing to do with the creative medium that could be offered to support children express their feelings and wishes. Rather it was about how we as adults need to give them time and space to express their feelings and their views, no matter how uncomfortable it makes us. They said – *'We know you cannot always change things for us; but we want you to know how we feel and what we think about things, we want you to hear us!'* (Lancaster, 2003: 35–6)

Rethinking the way we relate to children

Together the UNCRC, ECM outcomes framework and the Children Act 2004 are a significant reform agenda. They provide a platform to think seriously about involving children in decision-making processes, in assessing their own learning and being involved in developing the services that they use. They also give permission for practitioners to partner with the children they care for and work with. However, government policy on its own is not enough to ensure implementation. While Article 12 is a right for all children to express their views, in matters that affect them, children are not obligated to participate if they are not willing.

Central to listening to young children and participatory processes is respect. Respect involves making time in our schedules to listen to children routinely, allocating spaces to document their perspectives, choice of media that children can draw on to express their views, and valuing the many languages children (Malaguzzi, 1993) use to express themselves. It also involves providing 'feedback loops' so that children understand how their views were considered – they need to be informed, accompanied with explanations, how their views have, or have not, influenced decision-making processes.

There is no doubt that decision-making processes tend to be at their best when the views of all those involved in a matter are tabled and where the process of gathering perspectives is inclusive rather than exclusive (Lansdown, 2001). But, because we all gain understanding of our experiences through a particular social and cultural lens (Guba and Lincoln, 1989; Sparkes, 1992) we can inadvertently hinder children while endeavouring to be inclusive. The values, beliefs and assumptions that are embedded in our home, social networks, education, workplace and faith community experiences have all influenced the development of a unique lens through which we make sense of our experiences (Lancaster, 2003). Its unique nature, however, has a weakness – it can only ever offer us a partial and tentative insight. Our lens can only render one perspective of what the experience might be like. We are unable to capture our experiences in order to 'see and tell it' like it is (Eisner, 1992).

One nursery that worked with the Listening to Young Children project now gives each new child a camera to record their views on this transitional experience from home to school. One of the children took a photo that for the most part illustrated the sensory garden. The nursery teacher, on seeing this responded by saying how delighted she was that he liked the sensory garden, but the child said 'it's not a picture of the sensory garden, I took a picture of the mud, I don't like it, I don't like the mud'. The mud could be clearly seen, but to have his meaning count, for it to be significant the child had to first challenge the nursery teacher's interpretation. (Lancaster, 2004: 152)

Our perspectives are at best social constructions. They are interpretations rather than a captured reality. Their partial nature means that our understanding of our experiences is tentative. Like the above example, they can often be inaccurate. When the child is not sufficiently assertive, as this child was, or there is no 'checking process', there is the potential that we represent children's views inaccurately. Respecting the child's voice involves checking with children that we have understood how they have made sense of their experiences. This strategy prevents their perspectives from being excluded or, to put it another way, from our interpretation hijacking the child's.

Our culturally specific values and norms also define what is appropriate in different social contexts. These are not only physical locations, but also include interactions. Together they shape not only *what* is appropriate to express, but also *how* to express our views, feelings, concerns, aspirations and experiences. While we still have agency to 'go along with, or not' with what is expected in a particular setting or person, they influence what we say and do and what we do not say or do. Subsequently, what children express, or do not, has the potential to reveal their understanding of the ground rules or expectations when they are in particular service delivery settings, or with different practitioners.

In one nursery I sought to understand children's perspectives of the unwritten ground rules. To do this I introduced the children to two pairs of lifelike dolls, one small and one large pair.[7] After making a list of the children who wanted to participate I began working with the children individually. Each child selected one of the dolls and named it. They were then asked to pretend that, for instance, 'Jessica' was starting nursery today. What was important for her to know? Some children only wanted to take part for a short time, while others became immersed in the project for more than half a day. One child immediately took 'Jessica' to the toilet and then told her to wash her hands. Jessica also learnt that at apple time you were expected to offer the fruit to others before taking a piece for yourself. Another child felt it was important that 'Abby' knew where to play and what they could do. Throughout this process I added each important ground rule to a list. By the completion of one week the list of 'important' things was substantial. So much so that the practitioners were more than just a little surprised at just how many 'ground rules' the children had identified, far more than they were aware of.

How, where and from whom had the children learnt all these ground rules? We are sending all kinds of messages to children throughout any given day. These are not only the explicit messages that we send through our direct talk, but also the messages that we are sending through our implicit 'talk'; for instance, our body language, our gestures, tone of voice, silent expectations, disappointments, excitement and our schedule. These messages can be based on an agreed set of values and practices laid out, for instance, by the nursery, the health clinic or the family centre, but each set can likewise be peppered with the individual home values and practices of each practitioner. Our own social and cultural lens, together with our talk, whether implicit or explicit, has the potential to devalue and inhibit children's contributions. Being a reflective practitioner provides a strategy to critically analyse our practice; to self evaluate and to evaluate our practice with children.[8] It supports us to check that we are actually enabling children to participate in decision-making processes rather than hindering them.

Conclusion

The ECM outcomes framework, the Children Act 2004 and the UNCRC have opened a window of opportunity. They provide children with an entitlement to participate in decision-making processes that affect them. They obligate us to provide direction and guidance in participatory processes. They give us permission to implement social inclusion strategies and changes in our practice. This gives us a real opportunity to 'pull up a chair' for all children, to raise their status in participatory processes. But for children to experience genuine social inclusion we need to reflect, consider and proceed in seizing this window of opportunity more broadly – by developing a listening culture within early years settings.

We will know we have succeeded in embedding real change for children when all children are routinely influencing their learning, social and health care. We will know we have succeeded in taking advantage of the best opportunity we have had for children and families in 50 years when all children's views impact on the way we manage and organize the services we provide. We will also know that we have developed a listening culture when we are relating to all children as positive contributors in matters that affect them, routinely, and when every child does matter.

Points for discussion

❖ Participation involves creating a culture of listening in which adults and children are working respectfully together within decision-making processes. Think about the following questions as you discuss what it will take to develop a listening culture in your setting. How, with examples, are we involving children? What comments have we overlooked or brushed aside that we could have taken advantage of to support children learn how to make decisions and problem solve? What decisions have we made this past week that children could have contributed towards, or perhaps made instead?

❖ Listening to children promotes partnering with children so that service delivery is more effective. This implies that children's perspectives can support our own professional development; that we can learn from children. Apart from the following questions, how else could you reflect on your practice with children? What did you like today and why? What didn't you like and why? How could we have made today better? What could we change? What could I have done differently? What shall we do next? What else could we do?

Notes

1 Article 12:

• States Parties shall assure to the child who is capable of forming his or her own views the right to express those views freely in all matters affecting the child, the views of the child being given due weight in accordance with the age and maturity of the child.

• For this purpose, the child shall in particular be provided the opportunity to be heard in any judicial and administrative proceedings affecting the child, either directly, or through a representative or an appropriate body, in a manner consistent with the procedural rules of national law.

2 Article 5:

• States Parties shall respect the responsibilities, rights and duties of parents or, where applicable, the members of the extended family or community as provided for by local custom, legal guardians or other persons legally responsible for the child, to provide, in a manner consistent with the evolving capacities of the child, appropriate direction and guidance in the exercise by the child of the rights recognised in the present Convention.

3 Can be remembered as SHEEP (source unknown).

• **S**tay safe: protected from harm and neglect and to grow up to look after themselves.

• Be **H**ealthy: enjoying good physical and mental health and living a healthy lifestyle.

• **E**njoy and achieve: getting the most out of life and develop broad skills for adulthood.

• Achieve **E**conomic well-being: overcoming socio-economic disadvantage to achieve their full potential.

• Make a **P**ositive contribution: to the community and society.

4 With the support of the Esmée Fairbairn Foundation, Bernard van Leer Foundation, SureStart Unit (DfES) and Safeguarding Children and Families (DfES).

5 Kindly submitted to the Listening to Young Children project as part of the Listening to Young Children training course by Cardiff SureStart.

6 Kindly submitted to the Listening to Young Children project as part of the Listening to Young Children training course by Grove House, Ealing, London.

7 Based on the Daycare Trust 'Teddy' idea.

8 See Points for discussion above.

PART 2
PRACTICE

6

The Curriculum from Birth to Six

Bernadette Duffy

Chapter contents

- What is the curriculum
- Current curriculum frameworks and other key documents
- The issues
- What next?
- Conclusion

I first read *Contemporary Issues in the Early Years* as a Master's student and when I was asked to write this chapter the first thing I did was reread the excellent curriculum chapter Tricia David had written in that 1992 edition. What immediately struck me was how many changes there have been since then – the introduction of the *Curriculum Guidance for the Foundation Stage*, the *Birth to Three Matters* framework, the Primary National Strategy, the Every Child Matters agenda, to name only a few. But what also struck me was how many of the questions that Tricia raised remain the same. So in this chapter I will be building on Tricia's original questions and asking:

- What is the curriculum?
- What are the current curriculum frameworks and key documents?
- What are the issues surrounding them?
- Where does the curriculum need to go next?

What is the curriculum?

There continues to be much debate about how the curriculum should be defined. Does it include the 'hidden curriculum', that is, the things children learn through the way in which the setting or school is planned and organized, and the materials provided, for example such things as identity? Does it include the 'planned' and 'received' curriculum, that is, the experiences the practitioner has planned and what the child actually understands or receives, which as we all know are not always the same? Does it include the 'formal' and 'informal', that is, the elements that are seen as part of the 'school' day and those that are seen as extra-curricular? Does it only include 'school'-aged children and those in receipt of public funding, or does it also include the youngest children, the babies and young children up to 3 who are increasingly part of early years settings?

All these elements seem too important to leave to chance, and the early years curriculum needs to include all the learning that goes on, whether explicitly planned and intended or that which happens as a by-product of our planning and practice. As more school and early years settings offer longer hours, it is becoming increasingly important to think carefully about what children are experiencing during these times and to ensure that the provision offered is what they actual need.

Current definitions of the term show that the curriculum is much more than a body of knowledge to be transmitted, subjects to be delivered, formal learning contexts or schooling. The *Curriculum Guidance for the Foundation Stage* already includes a definition of curriculum that is broad. 'The term curriculum is used to describe everything children do, see, hear or feel in their setting, both planned and unplanned' (QCA, 2000: 2). According to Kelly the curriculum is 'the totality of the experiences the pupil has as a result of the provision made' (Kelly, 2004: 8). The *National Curriculum Handbook for Primary Teachers in England* (QCA, 1999: 2) defines the curriculum as 'all the learning and other experiences that each school offers'. Drawing on these definitions I use the term curriculum in this chapter to describe all the experiences the child has in their setting.

Using the term curriculum with reference to the age range from birth to 3 raises particular questions. For many years the idea of producing a framework to support those working with the very youngest children was greeted with anxiety. Practitioners and the wider public have been concerned that such a framework would lead to formalized learning and introduce pressure for children to conform too early to targets for their development (Abbott and Langston, 2005). I would argue that using the term 'curriculum' to describe frameworks for this age group is giving the youngest children the same status as older children. It is showing that the learning and development of a 1-year-old is as important , if not more important, than that of a 15-year-old.

But why do we need an early years curriculum at all? Increasingly, children are experiencing provision outside the home at a younger age. Most 3- and 4-year-olds now attend early years settings and an increasing number of children under 3 attend some form of provision and this is likely to continue (HMT, 2004). Children are born with the desire to learn and make sense of the world around them. Fortunately, adults are usually keen to help them to do this (Gopnik et al., 2001). At home, parents are supporting babies and young children they know extremely well and are in tune with. However, adults outside the home may not share this level of understanding; indeed, they are unlikely to when we consider the diverse backgrounds that children entering our provision come from. These adults need guidance to help them fulfil their role, to understand what is important for children at different ages and how best to support children from a range of backgrounds. Education is not just about what goes on in the school or setting; it is about the child as part of the community and society, and the curriculum should reflect the child's culture.

Wood and Attfield point out that 'all curriculum models reflect a set of beliefs and values about what is considered to be educationally and developmentally worthwhile in terms of children's immediate needs, their future needs and the wider society' (Wood and Attfield, 2005: 138). As a society we need to agree what is important for children, based on evidence from research and experience, and make sure that children get what they need to ensure their well-being, learning and development. This requires a curriculum framework to support practitioners and answer the questions:

- What do we believe is important for the youngest children and why do we believe this? These are the values, aims and principles that our curriculum is based on.
- When do we think it is best to focus on particular learning experiences and how should we do this? This includes our understanding of children's likely patterns of development and our understanding of the processes involved in learning and teaching, sometimes referred to as pedagogy.

We also need a curriculum that can grow and evolve. The curriculum must be able to develop in response to changes in society and our understanding about how children learn – neither stands still, and nor should the curriculum.

Current curriculum frameworks and other key documents

Birth to Three Matters: A Framework to Support Children in their Earliest Years

Birth to Three Matters (DfES, 2002) (*BTTM*) signalled an acceptance that practitioners needed guidance for their work with the very youngest children. This has not always been the case, as is explained above. Happily the introduction and reception of *BTTM* has shown that practitioners have welcomed this guidance (Abbott and Langston 2005). While the framework does not use the term 'curriculum' it does reflect the definition of curriculum used above. The guidance is underpinned by the principles and organized into four aspects: a strong child; a skilful communicator; a competent learner; and a healthy child. Each of these aspects is further divided into four components. For example, a strong child includes: me, myself and I; being acknowledged and affirmed; developing self-assurance; and sense of belonging.

Curriculum Guidance for the Foundation Stage 3–5 years

The *Curriculum Guidance for the Foundation Stage (CGFS)* was introduced in 2000. In 2002 the Foundation Stage was made a statutory part of the National Curriculum to ensure that it had the same status as the curriculum for older children. The guidance has been warmly welcomed by most practitioners (QCA, 2004). Like *BTTM* the *CGFS* is underpinned by principles. The guidance is divided into six areas of learning: personal, social and emotional development; communication, language and literacy; mathematical development; knowledge and understanding of the world; physical development; and creative development. The areas of learning are further divided into aspects, for example, mathematical development includes numbers as labels and for counting, calculating and shape, space and measure. Each aspect outlines the 'stepping stones' that show the knowledge, skills, understanding and attitudes that children need to learn during the Foundation Stage. The early learning goals form the final stepping stones and indicate the child's likely attainment by the end of the reception year.

The new agenda

As well as the curriculum frameworks described above, there are a number of other key documents which are already influencing curriculum development and will continue to have an influence in the future. These include the day care standards (DfES, 2000; 2003), and the interface between these and curriculum guidance, especially in integrated services, is addressed in Chapter 4. I will briefly look at two other key documents: *Every Child Matters* (DfES, 2003b) and the ten-year childcare strategy *Choice for Parents, the Best Start for Children* (HMT, 2004). One of the key implications of these documents is that learning is, and increasingly will be, taking place in a multi-agency context and curriculum guidance will need to reflect this.

Every Child Matters

As Gillian Pugh explains in Chapter 1, the 2004 Children Act builds on the Green Paper *Every Child Matters*. The aim is to ensure that each child has the opportunity to fulfil their potential and that no child slips through the net. *Every Child Matters* sets out five outcomes for children which services should work towards: being healthy; staying safe; enjoying and achieving; making a positive contribution; and economic well-being. The outcomes framework published with *Every Child Matters: Change for Children* (DfES, 2004b) shows how services are to be judged on the contribution they make. Early years is included under the outcome 'enjoy and achieve' and will be judged on how well provision promotes children's development and well-being and helps them meet early learning goals. While it is good to see a specific reference to early years it is perhaps disappointing to see it only mentioned under one outcome, though of course its contribution to all the outcomes can be implied. The introduction of *Every Child Matters* and the five outcomes is already having an impact on curriculum development as more agencies incorporate these into their work. For example, as Ofsted is now using the five outcomes as the basis for their inspections, schools and early years settings are addressing these in their self-evaluation forms and starting to look at the curriculum in this context.

The ten-year childcare strategy

The ten-year childcare strategy, *Choice for Parents, the Best Start for Children* (HMT, 2004), builds on *Every Child Matters*. Its vision is to ensure that every child gets the best start in life and to give parents more choice about how to balance work and family life. The factors that influence child development have informed the strategy, as has recognition that experiences in the early years can have lifelong consequences. The strategy's rationale is underpinned by evidence from research such as the Effective Provision of Pre-school Education project (Sylva et al., 2004; and see Chapter 12). The earliest years are recognized as the most formative stage, and the importance of giving children a better start in life is stressed. There is recognition that currently the quality of provision can vary, which undermines parents' confidence and, at its worst, can have a harmful impact on children's development. The strategy's view is that good quality early education experiences can transform children's lives, and this includes the important role that parents and the home learning environment can play.

The strategy announces the introduction of a single quality framework for services from birth to 5. The framework will strengthen links between *BTTM* and the *CGFS*. It will also incorporate elements of the national standards for day care and childminding. The framework will be based on an integrated approach to care and education and will be underpinned by a play-based approach to promoting children's development and learning. It will also help with earlier identification of special needs, leading to earlier referral. Proposals will be put forward in 2006 and there will be wide consultation with practitioners and experts to ensure that the framework is based on clear understanding of what works in practice.

The strategy also includes a proposal to increase the number of hours of early education children are entitled to and give parents greater flexibility to support their employment needs. Traditionally the Foundation Stage has been linked to a pattern of two and half hours per day, five days per week attendance due to funding arrangements. The increased flexibility will have an impact on the way in which the curriculum is viewed.

The issues

Let us look at the issues surrounding the current frameworks. How well is the curriculum for the early years working? Both documents, *BTTM* and *CGFS*, have been warmly welcomed by practitioners (QCA, 2004; Abbot and Langston, 2005) and the Foundation Stage as a distinct phase in education is seen as a success (HMT, 2004). Each has helped to show that working with the youngest children requires knowledge, skill, insight and commitment, and that those who work with this age group are to be valued. However there are differences between the two and concerns about the frameworks in practice which need to be explored.

Status and continuity

At the moment while there is a statutory curriculum for the age range from 3–6-year-olds, the framework for 0–3-year-olds – *BTTM* – remains as guidance, which gives it a different status. While the Qualification and Curriculum Authority is responsible for the maintenance and development of the *CGFS* and Key Stage 1, the DfES Sure Start Unit is responsible for *BTTM*. The Foundation Stage advisers in the Primary National Strategy do monitor the implementation of *BTTM* but, as it is not statutory, it is up to each setting to decide how they will work with children in this age group.

There also is a lack of continuity between the principles, aims, pedagogy and content of the two frameworks. *Birth to Three Matters* focuses on what we want the child to be and the experiences that will promote this, while the *CGFS* focuses on what we want children to achieve. 'This guidance is intended to help practitioners to plan to meet the diverse needs of all children so that most will achieve and some, where appropriate, will go beyond the early learning goal by the end of the foundation stage' (QCA, 2000: 5). The principles for *BTTM* stress the importance of relationships, whilst in comparison the Foundation Stage principles focus on what practitioners should do in order to work effectively – there are a lot more 'shoulds', 'musts' and 'requires'! The tone is different and shows the different periods in which the two were written. Although there is only two years between them, *BTTM* reflects a move to person-focused approaches that is more in tune with *Every Child Matters*. It also uses a format and language which are more accessible to the multi-agency teams who are increasingly working in early years settings and a more flexible approach to promoting learning and development which works well in integrated settings.

The Foundation Stage in practice

As explained above, the Foundation Stage is monitored by QCA, which produces a yearly monitoring report. The latest report highlights that what practitioners like most about the Foundation Stage is the approach to the curriculum, especially the emphasis on play (QCA, 2004). However it also highlights concerns about the status that practitioners give to the six different areas of learning. More priority is given to personal, social and emotional development, communication, language and literacy and mathematical development. Though few settings claim to give low priority to any area of learning, a significant minority gives less priority to physical development, knowledge and understanding of the world and creative development. Those practitioners working with 4- to 5-year-olds give greater priority to communication, language and literacy and mathematical development, with greatest emphasis placed on the literacy aspects within communication, language and literacy. According to the QCA, in many reception classes the national literacy and numeracy strategies teaching frameworks often take precedence over the guidance for the Foundation Stage. Despite the evidence that priority is most often given to literacy, this very area is most often deemed to have early learning goals that are not achievable, especially by practitioners in settings for 4- to 5-year-olds. Practitioners believe they are not achievable as children are not developmentally ready and the curriculum is too challenging. One of the reasons for the pressure to achieve these particular goals appears to be the 'standards agenda' having a strong impact on practice in reception classes, and 'top-down' pressure on reception class teachers from head teachers and Key Stage 1 (KS1) colleagues to prepare children for statutory testing at the end of KS1 and the publication of school results. This is restricting the breadth and range of curriculum experiences, particularly for part-time children, exerting significant pressures on curriculum balance and teaching approaches in reception classes, and can lead to more formal, adult-directed teaching (QCA, 2004).

Continuity with Key Stage 1

There are a number of discontinuities between the Foundation Stage and KS1. While principles are the staring point for *BTTM* and the *CGFS*, the National Curriculum did not include aims and principles in its early version and these were only introduced when it was reviewed in 1999 (QCA, 1999). Also, while personal, social and emotional development are statutory in the Foundation Stage, they are not statutory in KS1.

In May 2004 Ofsted published the results of an evaluation of the transition from reception to year 1 (Ofsted, 2004). They found a lack of continuity between the curriculum and assessment frameworks for the Foundation Stage and KS1. This is partly due to the transition between the Foundation Stage curriculum organized around six areas of learning, and the ten-subject National Curriculum for KS1. Increasingly Foundation Stage practitioners and teachers in KS1 consider that discontinuities in the curriculum frameworks could be significantly reduced by extending into KS1 a curriculum-model based on the pedagogy promoted in the *CGFS* (QCA, 2004).

Overload and focus

The *CGFS* is 128 pages long and includes over 300 stepping stones. Many practitioners tend to focus on the stepping stones and the early learning goals rather than the principles and guidance on teaching and learning. In recent seminars and workshops, I have asked groups of practitioners what the Foundation Stage curriculum consists of. All list the six areas and stepping stones – so far none have mentioned the principles and the rest of the guidance. The reasons given for this focus included practitioners' belief that Ofsted requires them to track children learning against every stepping stone, the view that as the Foundation Stage Profile is based on the stepping stones it makes sense to focus on these, and a lack of confidence. The stepping stones were designed to help practitioners to identify next steps and aid their planning and assessment, they were not designed as a curriculum to be covered, yet too often this is how they are being used. A focus on predetermined goals can lead practitioners to miss the learning that is actually occurring and underestimate the children's knowledge and understanding.

Where next?

In the early years we have moved from a situation of no guidance to a plethora of guidance. It may be time to review the guidance we are providing for practitioners to help them focus on what is most important for children; indeed, there may well be a strong argument for doing less but doing it better.

The introduction of the Early Years Foundation Stage

As previously stated the ten-year childcare strategy included the proposal to create a unified framework from birth to 6, to be known as the Early Years Foundation Stage (EYFS). The Childcare Bill published in November 2005 indicates that there will be a fundamental restructuring of the existing quality frameworks, *BTTM* and the *CGFS*, to create the EYFS guidance. The new framework will contain a set of principles which will underpin ethos and practice. It will take as its starting point the five outcomes set out in *Every Child Matters* and the Children Act 2004. Elements of the 14 national standards for under 8s day care and childminding will also be included. There will be guidance on how the four aspects of *BTTM* link to the six areas of learning and examples of the framework in action in integrated settings.

There is much to welcome in the proposed new framework, including recognition of the importance of the early years and the key role of parents. Bringing the existing frameworks together to create a unified phase consistent with the five outcomes of *Every Child Matters* is also to be applauded. However, there are also concerns. The Childcare Bill will remove the Foundation Stage from the National Curriculum, though it will still have the same legal status. This could lead to the Foundation Stage becoming detached from the rest of the education system and we may lose the opportunity to move the ethos of the Foundation Stage into Key Stage 1. The terms 'education' and 'curriculum' are rarely used in the proposals for the new framework. Again this has the potential to distance the early years from the rest of the education system and to reduce the status of early year's provision. The new framework will reflect the new emerging national literacy and mathematics strategies frameworks. It is to be hoped that this will mean addressing the unrealistic goals in these areas of learning which we looked at earlier in this chapter. The concern is that, instead, this could lead to a greater emphasis on these areas of learning and a narrowing of the curriculum.

On the information currently available there is a danger that the new framework will not mark a fundamental change in the way the curriculum for the youngest children is conceptualized. If this is the case, we will have missed an opportunity to create a curriculum that is focused on the right elements. At the same time as the Early Years Foundation Stage framework is being devised, the curriculum for older children is also under review and there seems to be a move away from an emphasis on subject-based curriculum to, hopefully, one that is focused on the learner.

The move away from subject-based curriculum

In October 2005 the QCA published the 'Futures' paper (QCA, 2005a) which recognized that we are living in a rapidly changing world. We need people who can be more enterprising, adaptable and flexible, and the curriculum needs to change to ensure that this happens. 'Education only flourishes if it successfully adapts to the demands and needs of the time' (QCA, 2005a: 1). Certain subjects have been part of the curriculum since the eighteenth century and came from the desire to understand the nature of God by dividing knowledge into discrete units or subjects. These are now so familiar and well established that often they are not questioned. But knowledge is changing fast and we cannot hope to give children all the knowledge they need to know for their future lives. Instead, we need to help them to develop supple and nimble minds to cope with real life in a complex world (Claxton, 2005). A continued focus on knowledge is likely to fail both children and us. We need to move to a person-centred approach. One has only to look at the increase in cross-curriculum frameworks, for example the Primary National Strategy framework, *The Key Aspects of Development and Learning* (DfES, 2004), to see that dividing the curriculum into discrete subject chunks is not making sense and there is a need to reintegrate the curriculum.

While the term 'area of learning' rather than subject is used in the Foundation Stage it is clear in the introduction to each section that most areas of learning are based on subjects. For example, knowledge and understanding of the world are described as the foundations for later work in science, design and technology, history, geography and information and communication technology, and the aspects are clearly laid out to reflect this. Subjects do have a role to play in the curriculum. The EPPE study (Sylva et al., 2004) found that practitioners' subject knowledge was a key element in outcomes for children. The subjects provide the 'stuff', the content to explore. But they should not be centre stage; they are there to promote what we believe is important for children.

We need to be able to hold the curriculum in our head if it is to truly influence our day by day, minute by minute work with children. That is why the six areas of learning have been held on to by practitioners – they are easy to remember even if they are not the most important parts of the guidance. However, now is the time to reconsider our approach, to move away from areas of learning as the focus and look to research to identify the elements that should be at the heart of our curriculum.

Messages from brain research

The Researching Effective Pedagogy in the Early Years (REPEY) project found 'that for most practitioners the declared priorities in the early years were the development of positive dispositions to learning, safety, confidence and independence' (Siraj-Blatchford et al., 2002: 10; see also Chapter 12). This view is reflected in research. In recent years we have learned more and more about what works for children. Gopnik et al. (2001) show how brain research has revolutionized our ideas about childhood, the human mind and the brain. Babies' brains are designed to enable them to make sense of the world around them. Babies and young children think, draw conclusions, make predictions, experiment and look for explanations. The reason they can do so much so early is because they have the help of the people who care for them (Gopnik et al., 2001). Gerhardt (2004) points out that love is essential to brain development in the early years of life as a baby's earliest relationships shape their developing nervous systems. We need to use this information to ensure that all children, but especially the youngest, experience warm loving relationships that nurture them in our settings.

For the brain to develop effectively it is important that babies and young children have a secure and steady source of positive emotion, a nutritious diet and stimulation of the senses (though not all at the same time!) in an atmosphere free from stress but with a degree of pleasurable intensity. There needs to be a series of novel challenges that are neither too hard nor too easy, social interaction and active participation rather than a passive observation (Diamond and Hopson, 1998). Again this information must feed into our curriculum.

Blakemore (2001), in his paper 'Early learning and the brain' argues that we have much to learn from cognitive psychologists about the kinds of things that appear to emerge at particular stages of development and how we can act on this knowledge in our work with children. Our sense of being an individual emerges between 6 to 8 months and 2 years, and between 1- to 4-years-old we are developing a sense of our selves and our beliefs in relation to others. For Blakemore these are the things that our brains are set up to develop in the early years – learning about ourselves, others, co-operation and collaboration – all the things society needs and which, if we combine them with creativity, enable us to respond to the challenges we face as individuals and as a society (Duffy, 2006).

The crucial role of the practitioner

The curriculum is only as good as the people who offer it to the children. Practitioners are a key element in the curriculum and the experience of the child will depend on them; they have a make or break role. It is not possible to 'practitioner proof' the curriculum; it is impossible to provide schemes of work or support materials that practitioner will use the way the planner intended (Kelly, 2004).

The EPPE project (Sylva et al., 2004) identified the importance of a form of interaction between children and adults they call 'sustained shared thinking' in promoting children's learning and development. Sustained shared thinking is when practitioners and children work together in an intellectual way to solve a problem, clarify a concept, evaluate an activity or extend a narrative. Sustained shared thinking contributes to thinking and develops and extends the child's understanding. Each setting is unique and the curriculum offered needs to reflect this. This requires every practitioner to be reflective, to be able to use underpinning theory, research and evidence from practice to develop the curriculum that works best for the children in the setting they are in. This is a highly skilled role. It requires the practitioner to differentiate, to understand each child as an individual and to personalize the curriculum content to match their needs and interests.

What do we need from the curriculum?

What we need from the curriculum today depends on who we think children are, what we believe they need now, how we think they develop and learn and what we want for children in the future. I would argue that while there are many things that children can be doing in the early years, we need to focus our curriculum on what is most important for them, the things they need to be doing at this particular stage of their development. It seems to me that, looking at research and practice, the most important things are:

- *Being social* – making attachments; being with others and sharing experiences; being flexible and independent; showing care for one's self, others and living things; understand that people have different needs, views, cultures and beliefs that need to be treated with respect.
- *Being positive* – developing positive dispositions and attitudes; a willingness to try new things; showing confidence and enjoyment; displaying high levels of involvement and persisting for extended periods; having a sense of pride in one's own achievements.
- *Being a communicator* – enjoying using words/gestures to communicate; speaking to others about wants and interests; interacting with others; listening and taking account of what others say; using talk to resolve disagreements, negotiating and taking turns; listening with enjoyment and responding to stories, rhymes, and so on; exploring sounds and letters; finding out about books and writing.
- *Being creative* – being curious, investigating, exploring and experimenting; questioning; noting similarities and differences; seeing patterns; pretending and imagining, constructing, combining ideas and materials, making connections, representing, responding to comments and questions
- *Being healthy and safe* – developing understanding of healthy practices with regard to eating, sleeping and hygiene, dressing/undressing and personal hygiene; handling tools, objects, construction and malleable materials safely with increasing control; moving with control and coordination; feeling safe and secure, demonstrating a sense of trust and belonging, having a positive self-image and being comfortable with themselves, standing up for their own rights.

None of this is new – all these things are already in the current guidance and appear in all aspects and areas of learning. The only problem is that, for many practitioners, at the moment they are hidden by the words that surround them.

Conclusion

In this chapter we have looked at:

- What is the curriculum?
- What are the current curriculum frameworks and key documents?
- What are the issues surrounding them?
- Where does the curriculum need to go next?

The curriculum needs to link theory with practice. It needs to develop from a theoretical underpinning which informs the practitioners' work and helps them to grow the curriculum with the child to reflect children's changing interests and developing abilities (Goldschmied and Jackson, 2004). Focusing our attention on what is most important is not about lowering standards but about expecting high standards from the right things, the things that will make most difference for children. We do not have to do everything in the early years, after all there are 11 more years of statutory schooling to follow. But we must do what we do to the best of our ability to ensure that we promote each child's learning development and well-being.

Points for discussion

❖ What do you consider to be the values which should underpin the curriculum in the early years?
❖ Where do they come from?
❖ Why do you hold these values?

7

Watching and Listening: the Tools of Assessment

Cathy Nutbrown

Chapter contents

- What is assessment?
- Why assess young children's learning and development?
- Values and vision
- National policy and early assessment of learning
- Assessment for teaching and learning
- Key aspects in assessing young children
- With due respect ...

This chapter focuses on how early childhood educators can understand young children's capabilities and learning needs. It asks what is assessment and why assess young children's learning and development? It considers values and vision underpinning assessment, and discusses current national policy on early assessment of learning in England. In discussing assessment for teaching and learning the chapter emphasizes the importance of observation as one of the most effective 'tools of the trade'; it discusses some key aspects of assessing young children and the importance of assessing with due respect for young children.

What is assessment?

The word 'assessment' is used in different contexts and taken to mean different things. It refers to at least three different purposes, and there is no single shared understanding in policy or practice. Nutbrown (2006) has suggested three different purposes for assessment in the early years, arguing that different tools are needed for different purposes. *Assessment for teaching and learning* is the process of identifying the details of children's knowledge, skills and understanding in order to build a detailed picture of a child's development and subsequent learning needs. *Assessment for management and accountability* prefers scores over narrative accounts of children's learning. Such assessments included the Baseline Assessment system which measured children's progress in predetermined objectives (SCAA, 1997) and allowed the 'value added' by the school to be calculated. *Assessment for research* includes those assessments (and often tests of 'scales' involving numerical outcomes) which are used specifically in research projects where quickly administered measures are needed and where uniformity of approach is necessary. One such example is the Sheffield Early Literacy Development Profile (Nutbrown, 1997), which was developed to measure aspects of early literacy of 3–5-year-olds. Table 7.1 summarizes the characteristics of these three purposes of assessment.

Assessment of young children raises a number of concerns in relation to their well-being and self-esteem. Roberts writes:

> Assessment and recording arrangements carry a world of hidden messages for children and parents. Is a positive model used, one which identifies children's special strengths as well as areas for support? Is there accurate and detailed information about children? Do adults make sure that children share their successes, both with their parents and with each other? These questions raise some of the issues which have a direct bearing on how children learn to see themselves. (Roberts, 1995: 115)

Why assess young children's learning and development?

This is a fundamental question in teaching young children. Children's learning is so complex, so rich, so fascinating, so varied, so surprising and so full of enthusiasm that to see it taking place every day, before one's very eyes, is one of the greatest privileges of any early childhood practitioner. The very process of observing and assessing children's learning is, in a sense, its own justification. Watching young children can open our eyes to the astonishing capacity of young children to learn, and shows us the crucial importance of these first few years in children's lives. But there is much more to say about assessing children's learning. Watching young children learn can, at times, make us marvel at their powers to think, to do, to communicate and to create. But observation points to more that our awe at young children's capacities. There is also an important piece of work for early childhood practitioners to understand, to really understand what they see.

Several pioneers (Froebel, Piaget, Vygotsky and Isaacs) and more recent figures such as Donaldson (1983), Athey (1990), Elfer et al. (2003) and Nutbrown (1997) have illuminated children's learning and development and provided practitioners with strategies for reflecting upon and interpreting their observations of

Table 7.1 *Some characteristics of the three purposes of assessment*

Assessment for teaching and learning	Assessment for management and accountability	Assessment for research
Focus on individuals	Focus on age cohort	Focus on samples
Concerned with details about each individual learner	Concerned with a sample of group performance	Concerned with performance of the sample
Is ongoing	Occurs within specific time frame	Takes place at planned points in a study
'Takes as long as it takes'	Is briefly administered or completed from previous assessment for teaching	Can be brief, depends on assessment and ages
Needs no numerical outcome to be meaningful	Numerical outcome provides meaning	Numerical outcomes often essential
Is open-ended	Often consists of closed list of items	Often consists of closed items
Informs next teaching steps	Informs management strategy and policy	Informs research decisions, and findings – measures outcomes
Information relates primarily to individuals	Information relates primarily to classes, groups, settings or areas	Information relates to the sample, not to individuals or schools
Assessments required for each child	Some missing cases permissible	Some missing cases permissible
Main purpose is teaching	Main purpose is accountability	Purpose is to add to knowledge
Only useful if information is used to guide teaching	Only useful when compared to other outcomes (of other measures of cohorts)	Only useful as evidence of effectiveness of research study
Requires professional insight into children's learning	Requires competence in administration of the test	Requires competence in administration of the test
Depends on established relationship with individual children to be effective	Can draw on Information derived through interaction with individual children, but not dependent on relationship	Often requires no previous relationship, but the ability to establish a rapport with the child at the time of the assessment
Requires ongoing professional development and experience	Requires short training session, learning the test and practice	Requires short training session, learning the test and practice.

Source: Nutbrown, 1999: 127

children. The rich resource of research and commentary opens up to educators the meanings of children's words, representations and actions. Educators' personal experiences of individual children's learning can help them to see more clearly the general principles that other researchers and educators have established as characteristic of that learning. For example, those who work with babies and young children under 3 can draw on the work of Elfer, Goldschmied and Selleck (2003), Goldschmied and Jackson (2004), Abbott and Moylett (1997) and the *Birth to Three Matters* framework (DfES, 2002) in order to embellish their own understanding of the children with whom they work. When early childhood educators hold up the work of others as a mirror to their own, they can see the essential points of their own work reflected more clearly and better understand the learning and development of the children with whom they work.

The published observations of some of the earlier pioneers can be useful to educators now as tools for reflection on children's processes of learning and as a means of moving from the specifics of personal experiences to general under-standings about children's thinking. Susan Isaacs, for example, ran an experi-mental school, The Malting House, in Cambridge from 1924 to 1927. Her compelling accounts of the day-to-day doings of the children in the school show clearly how her analysis of children's intellectual development is the product of a mass of detailed anecdotal insights. For example, she describes (Isaacs, 1929) the development of the basic concepts of biology, change, growth, life and death, and illustrates the process with a rich body of observational evidence as the following show:

18th June 1925
The children let the rabbit out to run about the garden for the first time, to their great delight. They followed him about, stroked him and talked about his fur, his shape and his ways.

13th July 1925
Some of the children called out that the rabbit was dying. They found it in the summerhouse, hardly able to move. They were very sorry and talked much about it. They shut it up in the hutch and gave it warm milk.

14th July 1925
The rabbit had died in the night. Dan found it and said: 'It's dead – its tummy does not move up and down now'. Paul said, 'My daddy says that if we put it in water it will get alive again'. Mrs I said 'shall we do so and see?' They put it into a bath of water. Some of them said. 'It's alive, because it's moving.' This was a circular motion, due to the currents in the water. Mrs I therefore put a small stick which also moved round and round, and they agreed that the stick was not

alive. They then suggested that they should bury the rabbit, and all helped to dig a hole and bury it.

15th July 1925
Frank and Duncan talked of digging the rabbit up – but Frank said, 'It's not there – it's gone up to the sky.' They began to dig, but tired of it and ran off to something else. Later they came back and dug again. Duncan, however, said, 'Don't bother – it's gone – it's up in the sky' and gave up digging. Mrs I therefore said, 'Shall we see if it's there?' and also dug. They found the rabbit, and were very interested to see it still there.

Isaacs's diary entries about the play and questioning of young children formed the basis of her analysis of children's scientific thinking and understanding, and offer rich evidence of the development of children's theories about the world and the things they find in it. Isaacs was able to learn about children's learning through her diligent and meticulous study of her own detailed observations of their play and other activities. Observation as a tool for assessing children's learning is not new, though for some who have not had the opportunity to continue to practise their skills of observation or had time to reflect with colleagues on those observations, these tools may have become a little blunt and may need to be sharpened and polished. However, many researchers and practitioners have followed Isaacs's observational practices; indeed, my own work on young children's learning has been informed by my daily journal jottings (made while working with young children) of children's words, actions and graphic representations (Nutbrown, 1999). Similarly, the pioneering practice of Reggio Emilia in northern Italy is developed largely through careful documentation which includes observations, notes, photographs and reflections upon the children's work as it unfolds in their learning communities (Filippini and Cecchi, 1996; Abbott and Nutbrown, 2001).

Goldschmied's (1989) work with babies illustrates the importance of close observation. Watching babies playing with the Treasure Basket can give the adult valuable insights into their learning and development and interactions with others. The following extract from an observation of Matthew shows the fine detail of this 9-month-old's persistent interests:

Kate places Matthew close enough for him to reach right into the basket. He immediately reaches in with his right hand and selects a long wooden handled spatula. 'Oohh, ahh,' he says and looks directly at his mother. She smiles at him in approval. Still holding the spatula he proceeds to kneel up and lean across the basket in order to reach a long brown silk scarf. He pulls at the scarf and squeals in delight as he pulls the fabric through his fingers, 'oohh, ahh' he repeats. He lets go of the spatula and abandons the scarf to his side, his eyes rest on a large blue stone, he picks up the large stone with his right hand and turns it over on his lap using both hands. Still using both hands he picks the stone up and begins to bite it, making a noise as his teeth grind against the hard surface. He smiles; looking at his mother as he repeatedly bites the stone over and over again. He stops, holds the stone up to his face and looks at it intently then puts it to his mouth once more. He then picks up the wooden spatula again and whilst holding it firmly in one hand, he turns the contents of the basket over with his other hand, squealing loudly with delight as he discovers the matching long handled fork. Matthew looks at his mother and waves both items in the air smiling and rocking on his knees saying 'oohh, ahh'. He turns away from the basket and waves the long handled implements up and down in his hands, first one then the other then both together. He turns back to the basket with a puzzled expression and for a few seconds stops waving the items. He drops the fork and reaches back into the basket and randomly picks up items one at a time, looks at them and then discards them on the floor beside him. He continues this pattern for several seconds until he comes upon a long handled brush. He picks up the brush, pauses and then waves it in his left hand, all the time continuing to hold the wooden spatula in his right hand. For several seconds he proceeds to bang the long handled items together, smiling as the two wooden items make a sound as they came together. He then spots the wooden fork he had disposed of earlier and letting go of the brush picks up the wooden fork and bangs it together with the spatula. 'Baba, baba, da, da, da' he says, then a little more loudly he repeats 'baba, baba, da, da, da'. (Nutbrown, 2005: 153)

Elfer et al's sensitive (2003) observations of babies in day care also show how so much can be learned about babies' interests and needs if observations are made and reflected upon.

Other reasons for observing and assessing young children centre around the adults' role as a provider of care and education. Young children's awesome capacity for learning imposes a potentially overwhelming responsibility on early years practitioners to support, enrich and extend that learning. When educators understand more about children's learning they must then assume an even greater obligation to take steps to foster and develop that learning further. The extent to which educators can create a high-quality learning environment of care and education is a measure of the extent to which they succeed in developing positive learning interactions between themselves and the children such that the children's learning is nurtured and developed.

'Quality' is often culturally defined and community specific (Woodhead, 1996) but whatever their setting and wherever they are located, where educators watch the children they teach with a view to using those observations to generate their own understandings of children's learning and their needs, they are contributing to the development of a quality environment in which those children might thrive. Where educators observe young children they are using a tool that plays an important part in achieving high-quality pre-school experiences, shaping their present, daily learning experiences – whatever the type of setting. The evaluative purpose of assessment is central for early childhood educators, for they cannot know if the environments they create and the support they provide for children as they work are effective unless they watch and unless they learn from what they see.

- *Observation can provide starting points* for reviewing the effectiveness of provision and such observational assessments of children's learning can be used daily to identify strengths, weaknesses, gaps, and inconsistencies in the curriculum provided for all children.
- *Assessment can be used to plan and review* the provision and teaching as well as to identify those significant moments in each child's learning which educators can build upon to shape a curriculum that matches each child's pressing cognitive and affective concerns.
- *Observation and assessment can illuminate the future* as well as provide information with which to improve the quality of the present. This forward-looking dimension of assessment is the means by which early childhood practitioners can explore the possibilities offered through the provision they create in the settings in which they work. Curriculum, pedagogy, interactions and relationships can all be illuminated and their effectiveness reviewed through close observation of adults' work with children. Despite the introduction of the Foundation Stage and the Foundation Stage Profile, formal assessments continue to be used routinely to diagnose children's abilities and there is a danger that over-formalized assessment at the age of 4 can limit the opportunities children are offered rather than opening up a broad canvas of opportunity for learning. It is important, however, to use the active process of assessment to identify for each child the next teaching steps so that learning opportunities in the immediate future are well matched to the children for whom they are offered.

This focus on the next steps in teaching and learning takes us into the 'zone of proximal development' – a concept developed by Vygotsky (1978) who argued that assessment does not end with a description of a pupil's present state of knowing, but rather begins there. Vygotsky (1978: 85) wrote: 'I do not terminate my study at this point, but only begin it.' Effective assessment is dynamic, not static, and can be used by educators as a way of identifying what s/he might do next in order to support children's learning. Assessment reveals learning potential as well as learning achievements.

Observation and assessment are the essential tools of watching and learning with which practitioners can both establish the progress that has already taken place and explore the future – the learning that is embryonic. The role of the adult in paying careful and informed attention to children's learning and reflecting upon that learning is crucial to the enhancement of children's future learning.

Values and vision

Against the backdrop, in England, of the Foundation Stage Profile, and an emphasis on the acquisition of some identified elements of knowledge, skills and understanding, it remains the case that early childhood educators can assess children in ways which are appropriate to their age and learning stage. As devolution gathers pace around the UK, it is possible to see the way in which different policies are being developed to allow, to varying degrees, a freedom of practitioners to decide how and what to assess. Whatever the national policy, practitioners' own personal and professional values underpin their assessment practices. Those who work with young children bring to the processes of assessment their implicit values and their beliefs about children. Whatever the framework for national assessment, the ways in which adults assess children depend upon their views on the nature or childhood, children's behaviour, children's feelings, and their personal approaches to living and learning. Whenever, wherever educators observe, assess and interpret young children's learning, they are influenced by personal beliefs and values.

Policy documents since the early 1990s show a shift in the language about children and childhood and the purposes of early education and care which perhaps indicate a change in the dominant political view of childhood. The language in policy documents of the 1990s suggested that 'childhood' had been reconstructed for policy (or perhaps *through* policy) with very young children becoming 'pupils' and early 'experiences' designed to promote learning gave way to 'outcomes' (Nutbrown, 1998). In 2000, there was a re-emergence of a more appropriate language within early education with talk of 'foundations', 'play' and 'children'. However, target-driven assessment dominated until 2002 when the Foundation Stage Profile held out the hope of a more flexible approach to ongoing assessment of young children's learning and needs through observation. It is crucial that early childhood educators are supported in the appreciation and articulation of their own personal vision of early experiences for children (how things might be) as such vision derives from the values they hold, their own constructions of childhood. It is important, too, that early childhood educators challenge the language of policy when it is at odds with a holistic and developmental view of children's early learning. Target oriented assessment remains but such targets are only useful if they match children's learning and development needs.

National policy on early assessment of learning

The Foundation Stage Profile (QCA/DfES, 2003) brought a further shift in the language of early education and policy. The following example is taken from this Profile and illustrates how one of the items on the assessment scale for Knowledge and Understanding of the World is assessed, through indirect observation, for a number of children.

Item 6 Finds out about past and present events in own life, and in those family members and other people s/he knows. Begins to know about culture and beliefs and those of other people:

After a visit by her grandmother, Grace talks to a group about the old toys she has brought for display and explains how they were used by her grandmother when she was a girl.

Zara and Helen lay out the laminated pictures in the correct sequence – baby, toddler, child, adult. Then they sort the basket of objects (keys, baby bottle, picture book, lipstick, etc.), putting them next to the appropriate picture.

Sanjay takes Toby (the diary dog) home for the weekend. In circle time on Monday he describes what he did with Toby and his family during his stay.

Sally explains to her mum that her friend is having a special family dinner because her uncle is going to Australia. (DfES/QCA, 2003: 47)

Assessment for teaching and learning

Effective and meaningful work with young children which supports their learning must be based on appropriate assessment strategies to identify their needs and capabilities. The fine mesh of learning requires detailed, ongoing and sensitive observations of children as they play.

Observation is crucial to understanding and assessing young children's learning. The following example demonstrates the importance of involving parents in assessing their children's learning.

Sean was three and a half years old. He attended a nursery class each morning, where he spent much of his time playing outdoors, on bikes, in tents, climbing, gardening and running. His nursery teacher was concerned that he did not benefit from the other activities available indoors – painting, writing, drawing, construction, sharing books, jigsaws and so on. Even when some of these opportunities were placed outside, Sean still seemed to avoid them. The nursery teacher spoke with Sean's mother who said: 'We don't have a garden and there's nowhere for Sean to play outside – he hasn't got a bike and there's no park for climbing, or swings around here, or a space to do outside things, but we have lots of books and jigsaws, Lego, playpeople, we draw and make things.' Sean was balancing his own curriculum but the adults involved needed to share what they knew in order to understand his learning needs and current capabilities. (Nutbrown, 1996: 49)

Key aspects in assessing young children

Several aspects need to be addressed if assessment is to work for children (Box 7.1).

Box 7.1 Issues in assessment

- *Clarity of purpose* – why are children being assessed?
- *Fitness for purpose* – is the assessment instrument or process appropriate?
- *Authenticity* – do the assessment tasks reflect processes of children's learning and their interests?
- *Informed practitioners* – are practitioners appropriately trained and supported?
- *Child involvement* – how can children be fittingly involved in assessment of their learning?
- *Respectful assessment* – are assessments fair and honest with appropriate concern for children's well being and involvement?
- *Parental involvement* – do parents contribute to their child's assessment? (Adapted from Nutbrown, 2005: 14)

Respectful assessment can include the development of inclusive practices which seek to allow children to 'have their say' in the assessment of their own learning. Critchley (2002 – Box 7.2) explored ways of including children in the assessment of their achievements.

Box 7.2 Including children in assessment of their own learning

Critchley (2002) carried out a study in the United Arab Emirates, to explore 4–5-year-old children's abilities to assess their own learning. She talked to 18 children in their classrooms, some in small groups, others on an individual basis. Some children were Emirate with Arabic as their first language, others were children of expatriate families with English as their home language. Some children spoke both English and Arabic. The first interview focused on their progress and the second on their reasons for learning. Children were asked to review their own work and to comment on what they 'thought they were better at now'.

One child compared two similar pieces of work and, because she saw progress in terms of visual data such as neatness of letter shape, perceived the neater work to be of better quality. In another instance where a child compared his two pieces of writing, he declared that the earlier piece was better because he thought it looked neater – it did – but the earlier work had been copied from a slip of paper and the later piece had been written independently and had clearly been concentrating more on words and meaning than letter formation. That the independent effort did not represent progress in his eyes can be a problem for teachers, and they need to ensure that their views do not dominate children's opinions when they select work to represent children's progress.

When asked, 'What have you learnt this year that you're pleased about?' one child answered 'Doing work like adding' and when asked 'Is there anything you need to practice more?' he replied 'Take away'. Another child expressed her progress in terms of playground activity and swimming, 'I can now open my eyes under water' – rather than the adults' perspective of the distance she could swim. Most children, however, viewed their progress in terms of drawing, as the following, fairly typical, conversation illustrates:

DC: What have you learnt this year that you're pleased about?
Danny: Drawing zebras.
DC: Anything else?
Danny: [drawing] Jumping rabbits.
DC: Anything else that's not drawing?
Danny: Colouring clowns.
DC: Is there anything you need to practise more?
Danny: [drawing] beds!

The children's perspective suggested that for them progress in drawing was important and desirable – often forming part of their classroom and out of school experience and being also something they could see and feel – so progress was immediately visible.

The mismatch between the child's perspective and the adult's perspective represented by the school report is stark. The fact that the child's view is neither elicited nor considered in many such situations could lead a child to abandon his or her view of progress and achievement in favour of the accepted, adult view of progress – and this would not be because of reaching mutual ground but because the child's view had gone unnoticed.

With due respect …

This chapter has considered why early childhood educators should observe and assess young children in the context of assessment policy in England. Answers to remaining questions depend upon the principles on which early education and assessment are based. The principle of respect is crucial. Assessment must be carried out with proper respect for the children, their parents, carers and their educators. Respectful assessment governs what is done, what is said, how relationships are conducted and the attitudes which practitioners bring to their work. Those who watch young children – really watch and listen and reflect on their learning – will know that time to watch and reflect is essential to really understanding what young children are doing. Observations which are never reflected upon are wasted effort. It is only when practitioners seek to understand the meanings behind what they have seen that the real worth of observational practices is realized.

Whatever the future of the Foundation Stage Profile and future policies and practices, two things are essential: the involvement of parents and practitioners in generating respectful understandings of children's learning, and professional development for educators which is worthy of children's amazing capacity to learn. The Reggio Emilia model of documentation and reflection shows the benefits of practitioners talking together about children's learning and their role in it.

Time for teaching and assessment, *confidence* in educators' capabilities, *recognition* of the judgements practitioners make, can create the important climate of *respectful early education*. The concept of respect can underpin and inform the way adults work and how policies are developed and implemented, but the notion of respect in education can be misunderstood (Nutbrown, 1996; 1997). 'When advocates of respect for children are accused of being "idealistic", of "romanticizing early childhood" – their meaning is misunderstood. Respect is not about "being nice" – it is about being clear, honest, courteous, diligent and consistent' (Nutbrown, 1998: 14).

In 2005 Prime Minister Tony Blair announced his desire to see respect restored to the classroom. A clear way to ensure that children respect their teachers is for them to experience respect in their early years. The concept of respectful assessment and respectful teaching could be dismissed by some as an over-romanticizing of early education. Therefore, the careful articulation of meanings is important, as is the examination of what the concept of respectful work with children might mean. Table 7.2 suggests what might constitute respectful approaches to teaching, and identifies the characteristics of the opposite – *desrespectful* approaches to teaching (who would want to endorse such a term!).

Teaching young children requires clarity, honesty, courtesy, diligence and consistency. It means identifying what children *can* do, what they *might* do and what their educators need to do next to support and challenge them in their learning. Despite repeated policy attempts to keep it simple teaching young children can never be other than complex. Watching young children as they learn, and understanding their learning moments, is complex and difficult work and places the highest of demands upon their educators.

Table 7.2 *What is a respectful educator? What is respectful teaching? What is respectful assessment?*

Respectful approaches	Disrespectful approaches
Taking account of the learner – 'children as as participants' in learning	Ignoring the learner – 'children as recipients' of knowledge
Building on existing learning	Disregarding/unaware of existing learning
Based on tuning into learners' agenda	Based on predetermined teaching
Responsive/adapted to learners' needs interests	Unresponsive/unadaptive to learners and needs and interests
Informed by children's developmental needs	Informed by targets/key stages/ages
Curriculum based on children's identified needs	Curriculum based on external definitions of needs
Includes/embraces issues of children's rights	Ignores/disregards issues of children's rights
Clarity for learner	Lack of clarity for learner
Authentic assessment to inform teaching	Contrived assessment used to track progress of cohort
Challenge	Unchallenging
Opportunity for extension and diversity	Little or no extension and diversity
Holistic	Compartmentalized
Involves parents	Excludes parents
Evaluative	No evaluation
Revision in the light of experience	'Carrying on regardless'
Recognizes all achievement	Values achievement of specific, prespecified goals
Purposeful	Lack of purpose
Knowledgeable practitioners	Practitioners with limited knowledge
High-quality professional development for practitioners	Lack of/limited professional development opportunities
Appropriately qualified early childhood educators	Unqualified/poorly trained/qualified early childhood educators
Every learner matters uniquely	The cohort/group/majority is the main focus
Equality for *all* children	The 'same' for all children
Inclusive practices	Segregated/exclusionary practices
Sufficient and appropriate equipment and resources	Insufficient and inadequate equipment/ resources
Sufficient/appropriate space and access to learning areas/experiences	Insufficient/inappropriate space and limited access to learning areas/equipment
Key workers	No key worker system

Points for discussion

❖ Consider the purposes of assessment detailed in Table 7.1. Which is the most helpful in working with young children?

❖ What steps might be taken in your setting to further develop children's involvement in their assessment?

❖ Consider the elements of respectful and disrespectful practices in Table 7.2. How might these relate to your own practices?

❖ In your assessment practices, how do you ensure the development of positive self-esteem in young children?

❖ What part might parents play in the assessment of their children's learning?

❖ How might your setting further develop the use of observation to enhance the development of each child's Foundation Stage Profile?

8

Diversity, Inclusion and Learning in the Early Years

Iram Siraj-Blatchford

Chapter contents

- Multiple identities
- Diversity and achievement
- Diversity and learning
- Promoting positive self-esteem
- Social competence
- Involving parents

In modern, diverse societies, it is essential that children learn social competence to respect other groups and individuals, regardless of difference. This learning must begin in the earliest years of a child's education. In this chapter I identify groups who are often disadvantaged due to the poor understanding that some early years staff have of them. I argue that there is a need to challenge the hidden assumptions which oppress particular individuals and groups. While most early childhood settings appear to be calm and friendly places on the surface, I argue that there may be a great deal of underlying inequality. This may occur through the implementation of differential policies, adult interactions, the use of displays, or through variations (or lack of variation) in the planning, curriculum or programme that the staff offer to individuals or groups. These are especially important issues to be considered because they concern the early socialization of *all* children. In the early years children are vulnerable and every adult has the power to affect each child's future actions and behaviour, as well as their intentions, learning outcomes and beliefs.

Children can be disadvantaged on the grounds of diversity in ethnic background, language, gender and socio-economic class in both intentional and unintentional ways. Children with special educational needs are also commonly disadvantaged in early childhood and this is an important area of equity education, but beyond the scope of this chapter (though see Chapter 9). The structures through which social inequality can be perpetuated and measured are related to aspects such as employment, housing or education. For instance, we know that women earn less than men as a group, and that working-class people live in poorer homes and have relatively poor nutrition, health and education. It was in response to these grim social realities that the Sure Start programme was introduced in the UK, which has been developed to support poor families and children under 4.

Although I am concerned with the structural inequalities which create an over-representation of some groups in disadvantaged conditions, I have cautioned elsewhere (Siraj-Blatchford, 1996) against the assumption that all members of a structurally oppressed group (for example, all females) are necessarily oppressed by those members of a structurally dominant group (for example, all males). Because of the interplay between social class, gender, ethnicity and dis/ability, our social experience and identities are multifaceted. I therefore argue that children can hold contradictory individual positions with respect to the structural position that their 'group' holds in society. Interactional contexts are also often highly significant.

Multiple identities

Identity formation is a complex process that is never completed. The effects of gender, class and other formative categories overlap, often in very complicated ways, to shape an individual's identity. While I do not attempt to discuss this complexity in detail , it is important for practitioners to be aware of the nature of shifting and changing identities. Because no group of children or any individual should be treated as having a homogeneous experience with others of their 'type'.

A number of publications related to the development of children's personal, social and emotional education provide very useful strategies for supporting the positive development of children's personal identities (Roberts, 1998), yet few writers relate this work specifically to ethnicity, language, gender or class.

There is now a great deal of research evidence of racial, gender and class inequality at a structural level in education (MacPherson, 1999). Concerning racial identity, culture and 'agency' (the interactions between individuals and groups) there is only an emerging literature, and most of this is about adolescent school children. This is particularly interesting because issues of gender and class identities have received more attention over the years, but again with regard to older children.

Working-class and minority ethnic children's poor academic performance has been well documented, and so has girls' performance in particular subjects (Lloyd, 1987). The link between racism, sexism, class prejudice and underachievement has also been thoroughly established (Ladson-Billings and Gillborn, 2004). However, if those who work with young children are able to undermine children's self-esteem (however unintentional this might be) through negative beliefs about children's ability due to their gender, religion, socio-economic status, language or ethnicity, then we have to evaluate these actions very carefully.

A child may be classed, gendered or 'racialized' (language status is also important here) in more than one way. Stuart Hall (1992), for example, discusses not only the discourses of identity but also those of difference *within* ethnic groups. In the very act of identifying ourselves as one thing, we simultaneously distance ourselves from something else. In terms of race and ethnicity, Hall argues that there are often contradictions within these categories as well as between these and other categories such as sexuality, class, dis/ability. The way we perceive identities is very much shaped by how they are produced and taken up through the *practices* of representation (Grossberg, 1994).

Making use of the metaphor of a kaleidoscope in understanding identity based on a range of inequalities, Bailey and Hall (1992) argue that there will be individual differences within any identity-forming category, such as race, language, gender and social class. For instance, in Britain, an Indian woman who is a first-generation immigrant, and working class, will have a different identity to her daughter who is second-generation British-Indian, and has become a teacher. Their experience will vary because of how others perceive the combination of ethnic background in relation to their gender, socio-economic status, dress, language, even age and so forth. Mother and daughter will certainly not be treated by others in the same way but they might have some shared experiences.

Staff also need to find resources and a shared language with which to work with dual-heritage children and their parents to support a strong identity. But it would be even better if staff worked with all children to make them aware that they all have an ethnic/racial identity and that they all have a linguistic, gendered, cultural and diverse identity. Surely this is the way forward? In being sure of one's own identity as multifaceted, it must be easier for children to accept that others are exactly the same – even when the combinations are different!

In their early childhood, children inevitably identify closely with a range of individuals and groups; from an early age they develop multiple commitments and solidarities. In addition to the 'sense of cultural belonging' that they develop in terms of their language and faith group, their gender and social class, educationalists support children in progressively accepting the social and moral responsibilities, and the community involvement associated with national and international (global) citizenship.

The UK has never been a monocultural society, and calls for the development of any single 'national' identity have therefore always been misplaced. Citizenship, just like identity, must be recognized as a multifaceted phenomenon. Contradictions and controversies are an inevitable consequence of diversity. They are also grist to the mill of progress and creativity. In any event, democracy requires something more than simply an orientation towards common values. From the earliest years we should be preparing children to participate, critically engage and constructively contribute to local, national and global society. An appropriate aim may be to develop the sort of 'cosmopolitan citizenship' that has been identified by Osler and Starkey (2005). In doing so, we should also recognize that:

> Cosmopolitan citizenship does not mean asking individuals to reject their national citizenship or to accord it a lower status. Education for cosmopolitan citizenship is about enabling learners to make connections between their immediate contexts and the national and global contexts. It is not an add-on but rather it encompasses citizenship learning as a whole. It implies a broader understanding of national identity. It also requires recognition that British identity, for example, may be experienced differently by different people. (Osler and Starkey, 2005: 27)

As the Advisory Group on Citizenship (DES, 1998: 216) suggested: 'The ethos, organization, structures and daily practices of schools have a considerable impact on the effectiveness of citizenship education'. A few early childhood settings, particularly those influenced by Dewey (O'Brien, 2002), Frinet (Starkey, 1997) and Niza (Folque and Siraj-Blatchford, 2003), are already providing young children with significant opportunities to learn how to participate. A good deal more could be achieved in this direction.

The sexism, racism and other inequalities in our society explain why at a structural level certain groups of people have less power while others have more. But at the level of interaction and agency we should be critically aware of the danger of stereotyping and should focus on individuals. This is not to suggest that we should ignore structure, far from it, we need to engage in developing the awareness of children and staff through policies and practices, which explain and counter group inequalities. I will turn to the point of practice later. What I am suggesting is that educators need to work from a number of standpoints to empower fully the children in their care. Children need to be educated to deal confidently and fairly with each other and with others in an unjust society, in this way our values will be reflected in our children (Siraj-Blatchford and Clarke, 2000).

The experiences and values of children can come from parents' views, media images, and the child's own perceptions of the way people in their own image are seen and treated. In the absence of strong and positive role models children may be left with a negative or a positive perception of people like themselves. This bias can start from birth. In the Effective Provision for Pre-school Education (EPPE) project, the largest project on early years education in the UK, we have found some marked differences in equity issues. For instance, we know that most providers create a poor environment for children in terms of diversity (Sylva et al., 1999) with the exception of combined centres and some nursery schools (see also Chapter 12). The EPPE study also found that the provisions for diversity were associated with as many as five of the nine attainment outcomes measured. This was higher than for any of the other Early Childhood Environmental Rating Scale sub-scales that were applied to evaluate the quality of the learning environment that was offered. The EPPE study also showed that minority ethnic workers were better represented in social services-type day care and combined centres, and very few were employed in other sectors (Taggart et al., 2000). Managers and staff in settings need to be challenged by such data and think about how this has come about and, indeed, how it might be changed.

Many parents and staff conclude from children's behaviour that they are naturally different, without considering their own contribution to the children's socialization, or considering the impact of role-modelling. Difference, therefore, is also a matter of social learning, as well as physiology. This has implications for practice and the kinds of activities that we should make sure all children have access to, regardless of their gendered or other previous experiences.

Diversity and achievement

Cultural identity should be seen as a significant area of concern for curriculum development and values education (Siraj-Blatchford, 1996). All children and adults identify with classed, gendered and racialized groups (as well as other groups) but what is especially significant is that some cultural identities are seen as less 'academic' than others (often by the staff and children). We know that children can hold views about their 'masterful' or 'helpless' attributes as learners (Dweck and Leggett, 1988). Dweck and Leggett (1988) therefore emphasize the importance of developing 'mastery' learning dispositions in children. There is evidence that children who experience education through taking some responsibility for their actions and learning become more effective learners. They are learning not only the content of the curriculum, but also the processes by which learning takes place (Siraj-Blatchford and Clarke, 2000). Roberts (1998) argues that the important area of personal and social education should be treated as a curriculum area worthy of separate activities, planning and assessment.

The 'helpless' views adopted by some children can be related to particular areas of learning and can lead to underachievement in a particular area of the curriculum. Children construct their identities in association with their perceived cultural heritage. Recently we have heard a good deal in educational debates about (working-class) boys' underachievement. The results from the school league tables suggest that some boys do underachieve in terms of basic literacy, but it is important to note that this is only certain groups of boys and not all boys. In the UK working-class white boys and African-Caribbean boys are particularly vulnerable (Siraj-Blatchford, 1998). Similarly, children from some minority ethnic groups perform poorly in significant areas of the curriculum while other minority ethnic groups achieve particularly highly (Gillborn and Gipps, 1997).

It is apparent that certain confounding identities, for instance, white/working class/male, can lead to lower outcomes (in the UK and some other societies) because of expectations held by the children and adults. In asserting their masculinity, white working-class boys might choose gross-motor construction activities over reading or pre-reading activities. Similarly, some girls may identify more strongly with home-corner play and favour nurturing activities over construction choices. Class, gender and ethnicity are all complicit here and the permutations are not simple but they do exist and do lead to underachievement. The answer is to avoid stereotyping children's identities but also requires educators to take an active role in planning for, supporting and developing individual children's identities as masterful learners of a broad and balanced curriculum (Siraj-Blatchford, 1998).

As previously suggested, in the active construction of their identities, children distance themselves from 'others' (Siraj-Blatchford and Siraj-Blatchford, 1999). As one little boy was overheard in a playgroup saying to another boy 'Why do you just sit reading? Girls read, boys play football!' The issue is therefore to show children that they are mistaken in associating these 'others' with particular areas of learning. We have to extend children's identity as learners and break down the stereotypes. Boys need to disassociate literacy from 'girls' stuff', and be presented with strong male role models that value literacy. Work with fathers is particularly relevant here.

Diversity and learning

Children need to be in a state of emotional well-being, secure and to have a positive self-identity and self-esteem. The curriculum must be social/interactional and instructive and children need to be cognitively engaging (Siraj-Blatchford and Clarke, 2000).

It is widely recognized that an integrated, holistic and developmental approach is needed to learning, teaching and care with children from birth to 7. They learn not only from what we intend to teach but from all their experiences. For example, if girls and boys, or children from traveller families, are treated differently or in a particular manner from other people, then children will learn about the difference as part of their world view. To deny this effect is to deny that children are influenced by their socialization. The need for emotional, social, physical, moral, aesthetic and mental well-being all go hand in hand. This is also true of our youngest children, hence the references to equal opportunities in *Birth to Three Matters* (DfES, 2002).

The early years curriculum should therefore incorporate work on children's awareness of similarities and differences, and to help them to see this as 'normal'. Some children can be limited in their development by their view that there are people around them who do not value them because of who they are. This would suggest that early years staff need to offer *all* children guidance and support in developing positive attitudes towards all people. A focus on similarities is as important as dealing with human differences (see Siraj-Blatchford and Siraj-Blatchford, 1999). The early years are an appropriate time to develop this work with young children.

Children in all types of early childhood settings might have similar experiences. Students, teachers, childminders and playgroup workers have often asked how they can deal with class, gender and ethnic prejudice. It would be a great mistake to assume that this is only a 'problem' in largely multi-ethnic settings. Strategies which allow children to discuss, understand and deal with oppressive behaviour aimed at particular groups, such as minority ethnic children, girls, the disabled and younger children, are essential in all settings. I suggest that educators should always make opportunities for stressing similarities as well as differences.

Promoting positive self-esteem

Early childhood educators have an instrumental role to play in this development. Staff need to help children learn to guide their own behaviour in a way that shows respect and caring for themselves, other children and adults, and their immediate and the outside environment. Values education goes hand in hand with good behaviour management practices. The way that adults and children relate to each other in any setting is an indication of the ethos of that setting. To create a positive ethos for equity practices, staff in every setting will need to explore what the ethos in their setting feels like to the users, for example, parents, children and staff. Staff need to explore what behaviours, procedures and structures create the ethos, which aspects of the existing provision are positive and which are negative, and who is responsible for change.

Children need help from the adults around them in learning how to care for each other and to share things. To help the children in this respect, the educator must have the trust of the children and their parents. Young children's capacity to reflect and see things from another person's point of view is not fully developed. Most small children find it difficult to see another person's view as equally important. Children need a lot of adult guidance to appreciate the views and feelings of others. This can be learnt from a very early age. In her research on the relationship between mothers and their babies, and relationships between very young siblings, Judy Dunn (1987: 38) suggests that mothers who talk to their children about 'feeling states' have children who themselves 'become particularly articulate about and interested in feeling states'. Consideration for others has to be learnt.

Of course educators cannot expect children to behave in this way if they do not practise the same behaviour themselves. If children see us showing kindness, patience, love, empathy, respect and care for others, they are more likely to want to emulate such behaviour. For many educators the experience of working actively with children in this way may be underdeveloped, especially when it comes to dealing with incidents of sexism or racism. Each setting, as part of their equity policy, will need to discuss the issue of harassment and devise procedures for dealing with it. In earlier writings I have shown how staff can take some of the following actions in dealing with incidents of name-calling:

Short-term action
- If you hear sexist, racist or other remarks against another person because of the ethnicity, class or disabilty you should not ignore it or you will be condoning the behaviour and therefore complying with the remarks.
- As a 'significant' other in the child's life, she/he is likely to learn from your value position. Explain clearly why the remarks made were wrong and hurtful or offensive, and ask the abused child how she/he felt so that both children can begin to think actively about the incident.
- Do not attack the child who has made the offending remarks in a personal manner or imply that the child as a person is wrong, only that what was said is wrong.
- Explain in appropriate terms to the abuser why the comment was wrong, and give both children the correct information.
- Support and physically comfort the abused child, making sure that she knows that you support her identity and that of her group and spend some time working with her on the activity she is engaged with.
- At some point during the same day, work with the child who made the offending remarks to ensure that she knows that you continue to value her as a person.

Long-term action
- Target the parents of children who make offensive discriminatory comments, to ensure that they understand your policy for equality and that you will not accept abuse against any child. Point out how this damages their child.
- Develop topics and read stories which raise issues of similarities and differences in language, gender and ethnicity, and encourage the children to talk about their understandings and feelings.
- Create the kind of ethos that promotes and values diverse images and contributions to society.
- Involve parents and children (depending on the age of the children) in decision-making processes, particularly during the development of a policy on equality.
- Talk through your equality policy with all parents as and when children enter the setting, along with the other information parents need.
- Develop appropriate teaching and learning strategies for children who are acquiring English so that they do not get bored, frustrated and driven to poor behaviour patterns (adapted from Siraj-Blatchford, 1994).

A positive self-concept is necessary for healthy development and learning, and includes feelings about gender, race, ability, culture and language. Positive self-esteem depends on whether children feel that others accept them and see them as competent and worthwhile.

Social competence

One of the most important challenges for early childhood workers is to help children develop the skills to interact with others. Developing the social skills that assist children to get along with their peers and adults will have a significant impact on their lives. Even at this level, language is a major tool. Social skills involve the strategies we use when interacting with others. They cover awareness of the feelings of others. Social skills are used to enter and maintain interactions, to engage others in conversation, to maintain friendships and to cope with conflict. Non-verbal skills involve smiling, nodding, eye contact and the development of listening skills. All of these non-verbal strategies form foundations for language interactions.

All babies and toddlers in childcare and nursery settings need opportunities for warm interactions with adults. Young children need consistency in the care provided, and those children who come from language backgrounds other than English need support on a consistant basis from staff who speak their first or home languages. The children need to receive messages that say they are important to their caregivers. They need to develop a feeling of trust in their new environment. Staff need to respect all the children in their care. This means taking particular care to understand and acknowledge the different cultural and socio-economic backgrounds of the children and to make special efforts to work with families to assist the children to settle into a new environment (Siraj-Blatchford and Clarke, 2000).

Boys and girls can have different language experiences within the same household. Dunn (1987) studied the relationship between mothers' conversation styles with their children aged 18–24 months. She states:

> The analysis also showed marked and consistent differences in the frequency of such conversations in families with girls and with boys. Mothers talked more to 18-month-old daughters about feeling states than they did to their 18-month-old sons. By 24 months the daughters themselves talked more about feeling states than did the sons. (Dunn, 1987: 37)

In multicultural or diverse societies there is a great variety of family values and traditions and it is important that children are brought up to balance the tensions and handle the adjustments of being reared in one way and being educated in another. Children need to become socialized into the new practices and society. Early childhood staff need to be patient, caring, tolerant, flexible and need to be able to communicate effectively with parents and other staff about their work.

Effective early childhood curriculum and programmes provide children with a range of first-hand experiences that promote interactive learning, foster children's self-esteem and support individual children in their construction of knowledge. They also recognize the key role of play in young children's development and learning. Central to this is the role of the early childhood staff in establishing the learning environment, structuring interactions and supporting learners in their development.

Young, developing children do not compartmentalize their learning, so an integrated environment suitable for the development of cognitive, social, emotional, aesthetic, linguistic/communicative and physical dimensions needs to be created. Therefore, the approaches highlighted in this chapter must go across the whole of the curriculum.

All children have the right to an early childhood curriculum that supports and affirms their gender, cultural and linguistic identities and backgrounds. From an early age, young children are beginning to construct their identity and self-concept and this early development is influenced by the way that others view them and respond to them and their family. Within today's society, the prejudice and racist attitudes displayed towards children and families can influence their attitudes towards themselves and others (MacPherson, 1999). Early childhood educators need to examine their own values, attitudes and prejudices, and learn to deal with them in positive ways.

All early childhood programmes should reflect multicultural and equity perspectives regardless of whether they are developed for exclusively English-speaking children or for children from a range of diverse backgrounds and languages. A culturally responsive curriculum and staff who understand and respect the cultural and linguistic backgrounds of the children in their care can make a difference. Children can grow up with the ability to retain their home language and culture, and to have pride in their gender and class identity as well as adapting to the new cultures and languages of any early childhood setting they enter.

Curriculum for children in the early years should:

- foster children's self-esteem
- acknowledge the cultural and linguistic backgrounds of all children
- actively maintain and develop the children's first or home languages
- promote the learning of English as an additional language
- value bilingualism as an asset
- value what boys and girls can do equally
- support families in their efforts to maintain their languages and culture
- foster an awareness of diversity in class, gender, ability and culture
- promote respect for similarity and difference
- challenge bias and prejudice

- promote a sense of fairness and justice
- promote principles of inclusion and equity
- support the participation of the parents in the children's learning (Siraj-Blatchford and Clarke, 2000).

All those working with young children need to learn about the family and community lives of the children they teach. They can keep contact with the families, with community centres, with ethnic associations and community-based organizations. They can discuss with parents and community members issues which concern both parents and staff. The following list covers some of the aspects of family and community life which should be explored and so enhance understanding:

- family history
- religious beliefs and practices (including important cultural events)
- children's everyday life at home
- language practices
- parents' theories about learning
- parents' views on schooling and early education
- community events and contacts.

Involving parents

Reference has already been made to the data that was collected in the EPPE project (Sylva et al., 1999) on early years provisions for 'diversity'. The EPPE project also looked particularly closely at the quality of the home learning environment (HLE) (Melhuish et al., 2001) that was provided by parents. Although the parents' socio-economic status and levels of education were found to be related to child outcomes, the quality of the home learning environment was found to be even more important. At the age of 3 years and onwards a strong association was found between poor cognitive attainment and less stimulating HLEs. By comparison there was only a moderate, positive association between the HLE and parents' socio-economic status and qualifications ($r = 0.3$). For example, the children of parents who reported that they regularly taught/played with the alphabet had pre-reading scores 4.5 points higher than children whose parents did not teach/play the alphabet. This could be compared to the impact of social class where the difference between lowest class (IV and V) and highest (I) was only 2.4 points. In other words, EPPE found that it is what parents did that is more important than who they were (Melhuish et al., 2001).

Research on pre-school education in five countries evaluated by Sylva and Siraj-Blatchford (1996) for the United Nations Educational, Scientific, and Cultural Organisation (UNESCO) also considered the links between home and school. The authors report the importance of involving parents and the local community in the construction and implementation of the curriculum. When they begin school or early childhood education, children and their parents 'bring to the school a wealth of cultural, linguistic and economic experience which the school can call upon' (Sylva and Siraj-Blatchford, 1996: 37).

Sylva and Siraj-Blatchford (1996: 37) conclude that: 'It therefore becomes the responsibility of the teacher to localise the curriculum and to enlist the support of the local community and families in framing school policy and practice and making the school and educational materials familiar and relevant to the children's experience'.

Parents need to be given information about the curriculum and learning outcomes and about the achievement of their children. They may also require support in improving their home learning environment. Sharing information of this kind demands a shared understanding of what children are learning. Early years practitioners will need to establish a dialogue with parents that is meaningful to them. Observations of children can be exchanged between staff and parents in an informal way, and showing any assessments that have been done as part of the routine record-keeping processes can provide a more formal means of developing mutual understandings (Moriarty and Siraj-Blatchford, 1998). To achieve values of true inclusiveness, everyone has to be part of the process of education and care.

Points for discussion

❖ When was the last time an audit of equity issues (SEN, gender and racial equality and so on) was conducted in your setting and what were the outcomes?
❖ How can the *Curriculum Guidance for the Foundation Stage* and the Early Years Foundation Stage be truly inclusive to all children – and their parents?
❖ How are parents involved in informing your inclusive practice and how do they remain partners in its implementation?

Further reading

Siraj-Blatchford, I. (2004) 'Educational disadvantage in the early years: how do we overcome it? Some lessons from research', *European Early Childhood Education Research Journal*, 12(2): 5–20.

Siraj-Blatchford, I. and Clarke, P. (2000) *Supporting Identity, Diversity and Language in the Early Years*. Buckingham: Open University Press.

9

Meeting Special Needs in the Early Years: an Inclusive Stance

Sheila Wolfendale and Mary Robinson

Chapter contents

- Contextualizing and realigning special needs in the early years
- The placing of special needs in the early years on the educational and social agenda
- Promoting partnership with parents in special needs and early years
- Collective responsibility for children with special needs in early years
- Inclusion in the early years
- Judging quality and effectiveness of provision for young children with special needs
- Case study

This chapter tracks a number of recent developments in the area of special needs in the early years within the context of *Every Child Matters*. A case study of a pre-school child highlights current and emerging practices in meeting special needs in early years within inclusive contexts.

Contextualizing and realigning special needs in the early years

Recent developments have done much to erode the hitherto disparate world of special needs and mainstream early years provision. Historically and until recently the early years and special needs domains were largely separate – this proposition was examined in Wolfendale (2000) and a realignment was proposed. Along the same lines, a diagrammatical depiction of the overlapping and interlocking local worlds of early years and special educational needs (SEN) was shown in Wolfendale and Robinson (2004) which has been updated and is reproduced in Figure 9.1. Some of the more recent initiatives on the diagram are mentioned in this chapter.

Figure 9.1 promotes an inclusive view of early years policy and provision, a philosophy which is expounded by Ruth Wilson (2003) who points out that, traditionally, early childhood education and special education have followed separate and differing paths and that the contemporary merging of these disciplines is to be welcomed by all early years practitioners.

These sentiments accord with

- the overarching outcomes for children framework which is a universal and inclusive set of goals towards which children's services, in partnership with parents, strive to achieve
- moves to extend children's centres to be accessible for all young children
- extended schools – the prospectus for extended schools states 'children with disabilities or SEN must be able to access the new services' (DfES, 2005b: 8).

Underpinning such inclusive approaches is a core philosophy which states that all children have primary and secondary needs, most attain competence in key cognitive, physical, affective, social, linguistic areas of development, and for those children whose life-path contains learning and developmental challenges (vulnerable children and those with special needs and disabilities), it is society's responsibility to offer them and their families maximum support and resources to surmount and cope with these challenges (Abbott and Langston, 2005). This philosophy informs the rest of the chapter.

The placing of special needs in the early years on the educational and social agenda

Significant landmarks with reference to special needs in the early years since the seminal and influential Warnock Report (1978) have included the:

- 1981 Education Act on special educational needs
- 1993 Education Act, Part 3 (which subsumed the 1981 Education Act)
- 1994 *Special Educational Needs Code of Practice* (replaced by the 2001 *Special Educational Needs Code of Practice*, see below)
- *Special Educational Needs Programme of Action* (DfEE, 1998b) outlining plans by the newly elected Labour government
- SEN Tribunal, now called the SEN and Disability Tribunal (SENDIST)
- Early Years Development and Childcare Plans/Partnerships
- creation of Sure Start (see below and Chapter 1).

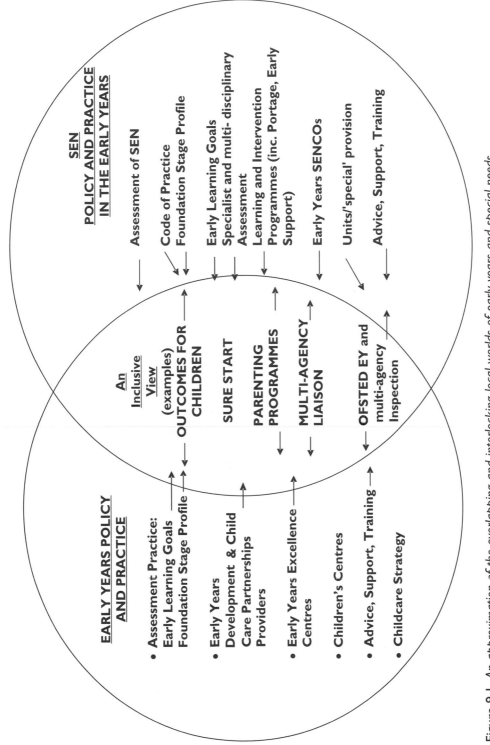

Figure 9.1 An approximation of the overlapping and interlocking local worlds of early years and special needs

Since the beginning of the new millennium the special needs/early years profile has continued to rise, with the landmarks listed above acting as building blocks for recent and current developments, several of the most important of which are highlighted below to illustrate practice as well as the growing and pervasive ideology that meeting children's special needs is an indivisible part of a childrens' services agenda, applicable to all children.

2001 Special Educational Needs Code of Practice and Special Educational Needs and Disability Act

The 2001 *Special Educational Needs Code of Practice* (DfES, 2001) replaced the 1994 *Special Educational Needs Code of Practice* (DfEE, 1994) and goes hand in hand with the 2001 Special Educational Needs and Disability Act (SENDA) which replaced the 1993 Education Act in respect of special needs.

Chapter 4 of the 2001 *Special Educational Needs Code of Practice* deals with identification, assessment and provision in early years education settings, all of which are expected to have regard to the Code of Practice. They are also expected to identify a member of staff to act as the special educational needs co-ordinator (SENCO), a post that can be shared between individual childminders or playgroups and the co-ordinator of that network. The responsibilities vary from liaising with parents and professionals to organizing a child's individual education programme (DfES, 2001: 34, para. 4.15).

The Code outlines two action points, School Action and School Action Plus. For the early years, these are designated Early Years Action and Early Years Action Plus. This approach is described as a 'graduated response so as to be able to provide specific help to individual young children' (DfES, 2001: 34, para. 4.10) and 'once practitioners have identified that a child has SEN ... the provider should intervene through Early Years Action' (DfES, 2001: 33, para 4.11) and if further advice and support are needed, then Early Years Action Plus is triggered, leading to statutory assessment.

Following the 2001 *Special Educational Needs Code of Practice*, designated early years SENCO provision has increased, as has the supply of learning support assistants for children with special needs (Vincett et al., 2005).

Sure Start and children's centres

A cornerstone of the present government's drive to tackle child poverty, social inclusion and early learning is the ambitious, long-term early years Sure Start programme. The programme's aims are to improve the health, well-being and therefore life-chances of children before and after birth, offering services such as family support, advice on parenting, increased and better access to health care and other services (see Chapter 1).

Each Sure Start programme has to make a clear statement on special needs and there is also a commitment to the early identification of special educational needs and social inclusion. Each programme has to set out:

- the different provision and services available to young children with SEN and their families
- arrangements made by existing service providers for early identification, assessment and support for young children with SEN
- details of specialist provision and services.

The government's current agenda is to incorporate Sure Start within an expanded nexus of children's centres (3,500 by 2010) which will offer a range of educational, health and social services for young children and their families (see Learner, 2005, for a description of two areas, the London Borough of Newham and Manchester, where 'mainstreaming' Sure Start is already occurring).

Outcomes for children: linking philosophy to practice

Five core 'outcomes' for children were first identified in the Green Paper *Every Child Matters* (DfES, 2003b), and these were subsequently given expression in *Every Child Matters: Change for Children* (DfES, 2004b). In brief, the five outcomes for all children of all ages are: be healthy, stay safe, enjoy and achieve, make a positive contribution, achieve economic well-being (for a full list of the 25 specific aims associated with these five outcomes see page 9 of *Every Child Matters: Change for Children*).

The five outcomes for children represent the conceptual-philosophical framework within which practitioners and policy-makers are beginning to operate and will do so in the future. The link between the outcomes for children as first espoused in 2003 (DfES Green Paper, *Every Child Matters*) and their relevance to children with special needs is expressed within the government's strategy document for SEN, *Removing Barriers to Achievement* (DfES, 2004a). Particularly relevant is Chapter 1 on 'early intervention', which focuses on present and proposed provision for meeting special needs in the early years. Linkages between *Every Child Matters*, the five outcomes for children and the later (2004) Children Act are made explicit in the chapter, which outlines plans to, for example, implement a new strategy for children with SEN and disabilities, encourage local authorities to extend SEN advice and support services to early years settings, and develop early years staff skills in this area.

One proposal contained in that chapter was to 'implement a new strategy for childcare for children with SEN and disabilities, promoting an integrated approach to early education and childcare and improving information for parents' (DfES, 2004a: 10). This 'promise' presaged forthcoming legislation on childcare. At the time of writing, the government is consulting on its plans for the Childcare Bill (DfES, 2005a). There is an emphasis in the bill upon childcare for low-income families and families with young disabled children, and the legislation will require local authorities to have specific regard to these groups.

The outcomes requirements for under 5s will be supported by a statutory duty to set up proactive and integrated early years teams. The rationale for the proposed Childcare Bill is summarized thus: 'Delivery that is focussed on the outcomes for children, achieved through services that seamlessly provide for their needs, will create the best chances for all children' (DfES, 2005a: 10).

This brief historical account of early years and special needs in wider contexts indicates clearly that the profile has risen on the educational and social agenda, in tandem with an evolving, inclusive ideology which itself drives a moral imperative to ensure that:

- special needs and disabilities are identified as early as possible in a child's life
- appropriate intervention is in place to meet these identified needs so that they are not overlooked nor neglected in a system where every child matters.

This chapter goes on to single out a number of related areas of significance to early years and special needs.

Promoting partnership with parents in special needs and early years

Paralleling the rising profile of early years/special needs, the involvement of parents and carers in their children's development, learning and education has commensurately increased over the years, as a number of texts have chronicled (cf. Wolfendale and Einzig, 1999; Hallgarten, 2000; Wolfendale and Bastiani, 2000; Edwards, 2002; Quinton, 2004; Moran et al., 2004).

The area of special needs and the involvement of parents has been particularly active over the years. Some of the landmark developments in this area include:

- a chapter devoted to partnership with parents contained in the 1978 Warnock Report on Special Educational Needs
- a number of parental rights to be involved in (SEN) statutory assessment were enshrined in special needs legislation (1981 and 1993 Education Acts and the 2001 Special Educational Needs and Disability Act [SENDA])
- partnership with parents principles outlined in the 1994 *Special Educational Needs Code of Practice* and the 2001 *Special Educational Needs Code of Practice*
- continued growth of Portage, the early years/special needs intervention partnership between parents and professionals (White, 1997)
- advent of local, regional and national parents' groups, lobbying for special needs/inclusive provision (Wolfendale, 1997)

- creation in 1994 of local SEN Parent Partnership Services (PPSs): these were designed to provide parents with information about SEN provision and assessment procedures, and to offer support during and after statutory assessment (see Wolfendale, 2002, for a national overview of developments and accounts of several local SEN PPSs).

Within the Every Child Matters and outcomes for children agendas, parents are seen as integral partners in service provision and delivery. Within the vision of extended schools (DfES, 2005b) and children's centres (DfES, 2004b) advice and information for parents and parenting support are seen as key to the realization of the outcomes for children.

A government innovation that epitomizes partnership working is Early Support, initiated in 2002 and planned to be a four year, DfES-funded, rolling programme. It is designed to offer a co-ordinated service to families with babies and very young disabled children, key features of which include:

- co-ordinated assessments
- key worker support and the notion of the 'team around the child' (Carpenter and Egerton, 2005)
- parents as partners in assessment and provision planning and delivery
- provision of practical toolkits for families and for practitioners
- Early Support – localized training for parents/carers and practitioners to work in partnership ways (for further information refer to the Early Support website: www.espp.org.uk).

There is an increasing evidence-base for the impact and effectiveness of parental involvement (Desforges and Abouchaar, 2003) that goes hand in hand with the growing commitment by central and local government to *actively* involve parents in assessment and decision-making.

That parents have a wealth of first-hand experience of and accumulating expertise about their children is now being acknowledged. Beveridge states the view that 'because parental perspectives on their children are holistic, they are well placed to integrate the individual concerns of all the professionals who are involved' (2005: 104).

Collective responsibility for children with special needs in the early years

The significant shift towards multidisciplinary agency working with and on behalf of children has already been alluded to. For many years practitioners subscribed in principle to the tenets of multi-agency working but few implemented in practice the exhortations contained in a raft of government circulars, including the 1994 and 2001 SEN Codes of Practice. The endemic barriers to joint working on the part of statutory and voluntary agencies (Sloper, 2004) as well as the perceived benefits (Tomlinson, 2003) have been addressed by government directives and legislation (see above).

Figure 9.2 illustrates the many areas of shared responsibility for meeting special needs, within schools, early years settings and other local services.

The government intends to change the children's services landscape over time by changing working practices. Two fundamental areas of change are briefly mentioned below, as they will have profound implications for those working with and on behalf of young children with special needs.

The Children's Workforce Strategy

The DfES consultation document, *Children's Workforce Strategy* (DfES, 2005f), sets out an ambitious medium- and long-term vision for restructuring training and working practices for the many thousands of people working with and on behalf of children, including meeting the highly specific needs of young children identified as having special needs (see Chapter 13).

Toolkit for multi-agency working: challenges for multi-agency working

To support the increasing amount of multi-agency working, the DfES published on its website between May and August 2005, several guides, for example, tool-kits for managers of integrated services (DfES, 2005c), for practitioners, for managers of multi-agency teams. Essentially these are good practice pointers, designed to facilitate teamwork and enhance confidence in joint working.

Via all these measures and reforms the government is intent on fostering an ethos of collective responsibility for the planning and delivery of children's services. From the early years perspective, this focus on the management of multi-agency teams and sharing of information has diverted attention from one of the more challenging aspects of the proposed changes in service delivery – that of maintaining and extending knowledge and expertise in providing for the needs of children in this age group.

For some groups of children, for example, those with the most complex needs and those whose behaviour can lead to them being excluded from provision, this specialization has implications for breaking down barriers and fostering good practice at all levels, including regional and national. The proposal to create small local teams has within it the danger of the possible loss of specialist knowledge to all but a few 'lucky' areas. While some of the developing Children's Trusts have included plans for team training to raise the level of knowledge in all areas, concerns exist that there is unlikely to be funding available for widespread training in these more specialist areas.

Inclusion in the early years

A major change in the way that the needs of our youngest children are met has come about through the shift in educational philosophy that emphasizes including children with special educational needs within mainstream educational and care settings. This philosophy, which embraces both equality of opportunity and the valuing of difference, has followed on from the recognition of the need for universal education and a redefinition of 'education' to mean the way in which we learn to adapt to and interact with our environment (National Children's Bureau, 2004). The broadening of the concept of 'education' fits well with the social model of special educational needs which places an emphasis on the person first and then considers the needs arising from the disability.

This approach contrasted with the medical model of disability, with its focus on early identification of need, high-quality diagnostic procedures and recommendations for the most appropriate placement, management and monitoring. The social model questions the implication that there is only one way in which the identified need can be met in educational terms. For parents and those supporting the child at this early stage, this is often where the first battles for inclusion are staged. Once the expectation is established that the options for the child include mainstream education with support, it becomes imperative to focus on what is needed rather than describing the deficit, and this opens the door to discussion and negotiation around what is most appropriate for the individual child.

The placement of children with special educational needs depends on local as well as national agreements and practices. Department for Education and Skills guidance indicates the assumption of mainstream education, with any other alternative needing justification and discussion (DfES, 2001). Even where it is agreed that segregated education may be the appropriate long-term option, many parents request an inclusive early years experience for their child. One of the reasons given for the success of inclusion in the early years is the flexibility of the Foundation Stage curriculum with its emphasis on exploration and the sensory aspects of learning (QCA, 2000). The focus on social and emotional development and the acquisition of play skills highlights the importance of peer group interaction and the discovery of what is shared rather that what discriminates between children.

The inclusion of children at this early stage has a pragmatic as well as a philosophical impact on parents and providers. Parents are likely to take a wider view of 'education' and see their child in terms of developing abilities, rather than disabilities; staff are empowered by experiencing how well many such children manage the mainstream environment and flourish within it; and society's expectations shift with each positive experience. While special schools are likely to continue to be necessary for some children and popular with some parents, the automatic assumption of special schooling has been replaced by a consideration of what is best for each child and this is most evident at the point of diagnosis within early years.

128

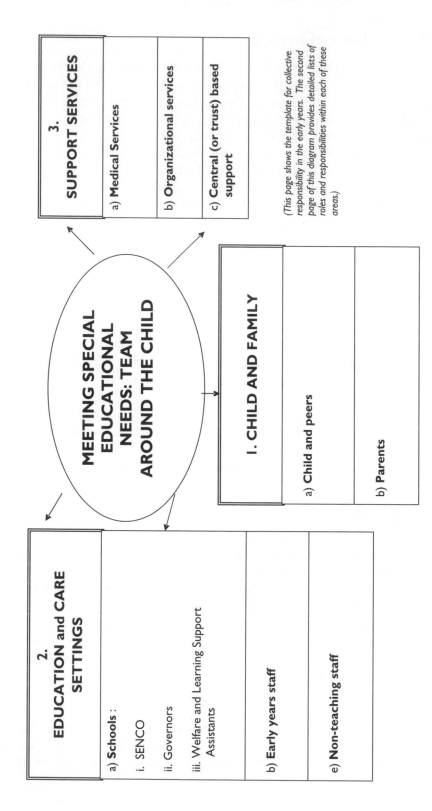

3. SUPPORT SERVICES

a) Medical Services

b) Organizational services

c) Central (or trust) based support

(This page shows the template for collective responsibility in the early years. The second page of this diagram provides detailed lists of roles and responsibilities within each of these areas.)

MEETING SPECIAL EDUCATIONAL NEEDS: TEAM AROUND THE CHILD

I. CHILD AND FAMILY

a) Child and peers

b) Parents

2. EDUCATION and CARE SETTINGS

a) Schools :

i. SENCO

ii. Governors

iii. Welfare and Learning Support Assistants

b) Early years staff

e) Non-teaching staff

Figure 9.2 *Collective responsibility for special educational needs*

129

Central (or Trust) based support 3c
- System of links with and between schools and teaching collaboration
- Procedures for assessment and school support at COP Stages
- Reporting to schools, parents, agencies
- Review systems
- INSET and guidance for teachers
- Enabling access to National Curriculum for all pupils
- Assist schools to implement whole-school policy
- Providing (lending) specialist equipment

Child and peers 1a
- Self-assessment (pupil profile)
- Self-recording, for example, of IEP
- Peer tutoring/co-operative learning
- Participation in own review
- Views on policy and provision
- Be assisted to support other children (empathy, tolerance, acceptance, valuing)

Organizational services 3b
- Implement Code of Practice
- Mandatory provision for children on statements
- Support and advisory services (co-ordinate)
- Special/mainstream links and inclusion
- INSET

Medical services 3a
- Post-natal and infant care
- Assessment of possible needs/difficulties
- Co-ordination of Health Visitor/School Nurse services
- Speech and Language Assessment therapy
- Physio, and occupational assessment and therapy
- Hearing and vision checks
- Liaison with parents, schools, hospitals, and so on
- Review and care conferences

Parents 1b
- Contribution at COP Stages
- Contribution to assessment and record-keeping
- Contribution to child's review
- Home-based learning programmes
- Receipt of written progress reports } Response to Individual Education Plans or programme reports
- In receipt of curriculum plans
- Involvement in policy setting and review
- Parental representation
- Parents' pressure and support groups
- Responsibility for primary needs
- Planning for the future

MEETING SPECIAL EDUCATIONAL NEEDS

TEAM AROUND THE CHILD

Non-teaching staff 2c
- Supporting learning and behaviour programmes outside the classroom
- Informing and liaising with teaching staff about out-of-class events, for example, dinner time
- Contribution to INSET
- Secretaries frequently liaise with parents
- Contribution to advice for statements
- Part provision for children with statement
- PR function

Early years staff (in consultation with SENCO) 2b
- Observation/assessment
- Child care
- Parent liaison
- Liaison with other staff and support services
- Child support with learning/behaviour programme
- Key workers
- Early years specialists (development and care)
- Record-keeping
- Implement Code of Practice
- Implement SEN Policy

Schools (via SENCO) 2a i
- Implement Code of Practice (COP)
- Set policy and implement (special needs, discipline, pastoral, equal opportunities)
- Links with parents
- Links with support services and schools
- National Curriculum arrangements
- Assessment and record-keeping
- Learning and behaviour programme/IEP
- Classroom organization
- INSET
- Organizing review
- Fulfilling statements

Governors 2a ii
- Check on implementation of Code of Practice
- Statutory duties to ensure pupils' special educational needs are identified and met
- Monitor school policy, provision and resources
- Monitor assessment procedures
- Monitor INSET and staff support
- Links with other schools and parents
- Teacher appointment
- Keep special educational needs on agenda
- Ensure full access to a suitably differentiated National Curriculum for pupils with SEN

Welfare assistants 2a iii
- Observation/assessment
- Record-keeping
- Child support: with programme: practical care, progress review
- Involvement in policy review
- Self-evaluation and professional development
- Supporting teachers
- Regular liaison with all involved

Figure 9.2 *continued*

Judging quality and effectiveness of provision for young children with special needs

From April 2005 Ofsted has changed the way it carries out inspections of child-care and nursery provision (Ofsted, 2005b). Inspectors will assess performance and quality against a set of 14 standards, one of which (Standard 10) is 'special needs, including SEN and disabilities'. Thus Standard 10 is embedded within an inclusive framework.

From September 2005 and for the following three years, all local authority services for children and young people and the wide range of services from other agencies and organizations will be subject to a Joint Area Review (JAR) (Ofsted, 2005d; and see Chapter 4). These JARs will focus on the five outcomes for children, and among other areas of inspection will 'report on the well being of all children ... Covering universal, preventative and targeted services, paying particular attention to children and young people who are vulnerable such as those looked after by the council and/or those with learning difficulties or disabilities' (Ofsted, 2005d: 2). By these means service providers are held accountable for the quality of their provision.

Another means of exploring quality is to search for evidence that provision 'works', that is, meets young children's developmental and learning needs by offering sound, proven practice. A performance and evidence-based approach to service delivery is increasingly taking hold, on pedagogical as well as ethical grounds, as Macdonald and Roberts (1995: 3) stated: 'Children and their families have a right to expect that our interventions in their lives will be based on the best available knowledge'.

Bodies of knowledge about 'what works' and what is good or best practice in early years and special needs services are beginning to accumulate (see McNeish et al., 2002) and see Thomas and Pring (2004) for a broader introduction to evidence-based practice in education.

The DfES has drawn upon the findings of research that it commissioned. The longitudinal Effective Provision of Pre-School Education (EPPE) study, funded by the DfES between 1997 and 2004 (see Chapter 12), includes SEN as one of its main areas of study.

From complex data, using a variety of analyses, Sammons et al. (2002: 59) report that 'higher quality pre-school provision is significantly associated with greater movement out of "at risk" status for cognitive measures, whereas poorer quality is associated with more movement into "at risk" status by entry to primary school'. Another related EPPE study (Taggart et al., 2004: 38) looking into the perspectives of parents of young children with SEN concluded that 'promoting active parental involvement in learning and play activities, is likely to play a significant role in providing children with a better start to school and reducing the risk of later SEN'.

These studies provide a sound empirical basis for organizing and operating provision for young children with special needs and such investigations act as a powerful model of research evidence informing practice.

Case study

We have chosen a case study format to illustrate some of the themes and issues raised in the chapter, particularly those of early intervention and collaborative working. Natasha (not her real name) lives in an Outer London Children's Services area where one of the authors works.

Background

Natasha is the second child in her family, born at 32 weeks and identified as having Down's syndrome at birth. Parents now recall being told that she had Down's syndrome very soon after she was born and thinking, initially, that this was related to the prematurity.

Early support

Follow-up services from the hospital ensured that the family was visited regularly, initially by the health visitor and a member of the local Down's Syndrome Support Group. At the age of 15 months, following regular appointments at the local children's centre, Natasha was referred to the Preschool Liaison Group (PSLG) by the health visitor. This is a multidisciplinary group which meets every two weeks to consider new referrals and to discuss issues of continuing support for children in the pre-school age range. The group was established to co-ordinate early response to the identification of difficulty and to ensure that intervention is planned effectively from the earliest involvement with families. The PSLG consists of an educational psychologist (chair), head of the Pre-school Support, Early Years Support Service, Pre-School Learning Alliance, health visitors, early years development and childcare co-ordinator, with occasional attendance by speech therapist, physiotherapists, and so on. At this point it was agreed that a referral to the home-visiting team was most appropriate and a schedule of two-weekly visits was set up.

Pre-school experience

At the age of 2 years Natasha was again discussed at the PSLG and a request made for educational psychologist involvement. A part-time place had been secured at the local playgroup and it was agreed that she would have support from the Preschool Learning Alliance for two mornings each week. This was to be extended to three sessions per week by the age of 2 years 9 months and continued following transfer to a new playgroup when the family moved house within the children's services area. A place in nursery within the local primary school became available when Natasha was 3 years 3 months.

The nature of support

Priority concerns and the focus of support during the early months in playgroup were the development of communication and the management of behaviour. Support staff worked with the playgroup and parents to ensure that clear expectations and boundaries were set and that Natasha could not avoid or charm her way out of following instructions. As Natasha settled and gained confidence, the focus of support shifted to encouraging social interaction and introducing her to a range of play materials. At the point of transfer to nursery, Natasha was a well-integrated member of the group, enjoying the contact with other children and beginning to show real interest in observing and copying others.

Early education

Natasha entered the nursery attached to the school her brother attended and where her name was already registered. At this point, a pre-school planning meeting included a discussion of the timing of the statutory assessment of Natasha's special educational needs. It was agreed that a period of at least six months of multidisciplinary involvement was needed prior to initiating the assessment. This would allow the various agencies involved to gain information of the most effective level of support that would facilitate Natasha's full inclusion in the Foundation Stage curriculum. She began to attend at the beginning of the autumn term and by the end of that term was attending five mornings a week, sharing support with another pupil for four of those mornings and being supported by nursery staff on the fifth. The major focus of support was now on developing expressive language, and Makaton signing was introduced to support the development of speech. Both parents and staff in nursery attended Makaton training courses, and signs were gradually introduced to all aspects of Natasha's life.

Assessment and intervention

While in playgroup and nursery, Natasha had a Pre-School Support Plan, outlining the targets agreed between staff and parents and suggesting the most effective learning strategies. These plans were reviewed twice yearly and Natasha's progress was also reviewed at the children's centre. Information from both sources formed the basis for advice for the statutory assessment and helped to provide a picture of the optimal learning environment for Natasha to the Special Educational Needs Panel whose job it was to consider the need for a Statement of Special Educational Needs and agree the support required. A statement of SEN was issued which planned for both the final term in nursery and the transition to the infant school. An enhanced level of support was proposed for the first year in school to ensure that a positive start was made and that any transition issues could be dealt with effectively. Support was specifically targeted on group interaction skills and the development of attention to less preferred activities.

Team around the child

In their report for statutory assessment, Natasha's parents spoke of their feelings of pride in what she had achieved and their belief that they shared this pride with all those who had supported her since her birth. When asked to reflect on the way in which that support was organized, they mentioned in particular the central organizing role played by their pre-school home visitor and the importance of the contact that had been maintained through attendance at the opportunity group. They felt very positive about the involvement of the many health and educational agencies involved and commented that 'somehow these seemed to be introduced at just about the time Natasha needed them'. As Natasha was about to begin full-time schooling they felt that support would be centred more around school now and were looking forward to sharing the co-ordination of this with the SENCO, whom they had already met.

Summary comments

This case study exemplifies the benefits of joint planning and shared information in supporting children with special educational needs from the earliest involvement. It demonstrates the effectiveness of active parental involvement and the benefits of access to a mainstream educational environment and peer group. Longer-term planning is facilitated by the focus on targeting support to meet need, rather than accessing placement or support.

Points for discussion

These areas are suggested as being suitable and relevant for discussion and debate between early years practitioners, policy-makers and researchers.

❖ How to best promote inclusive education
❖ How to ensure quality early years/SEN services
❖ What are an effective means of recognizing, identifying and assessing SEN?
❖ What are the professional skills needed to work with early years and SEN?
❖ What are the hallmarks of good practice in working with families?

10

Working in Multidisciplinary Teams

Trevor Chandler

Chapter contents

- Integration
- Leadership
- Multidisciplinary work
- Examples of multidisciplinary work
- Conclusion

The real magic of discovery lies not in seeing new landscapes, but in having new eyes. (Marcel Proust)

Working in multidisciplinary teams is a complex process and is subject to many levels of influence in terms of how effective they may be. In this chapter I will explore some of these influences and identify some of the challenges and benefits of multidisciplinary and multi-agency work. This will include the integration of services and the role of leaders. I will give examples of practice in one integrated centre through the experience of Pen Green Centre in Corby.

Integration

Working in multidisciplinary teams is a key feature of integrated services to children and families. Four important aspects were identified in the initial start-up guidance for children's centres:

- A shared philosophy, vision and principles of working with children and families at all levels and by all partners.
- A perception by users of cohesive and comprehensive services. This is the real test of whether we are succeeding or not.

- A perception by all members of the staff team of a shared identity, purpose and common working practices.
- A commitment by partner providers to fund and facilitate the development and delivery of integrated services (DfES, 2003d: 11).

This presents a real challenge for local authorities, who will have the primary duty and responsibility for the delivery of integrated services to children and families. 'Each change and expansion brings new dimensions of complexity in which uncertainties are increased, confusions compounded and comforts compromised' (Whitaker, 2002: 2).

In their research on leadership issues in integrated centres, Thorpe and Gasper interviewed 20 leaders of well-established integrated centres. In response to the question 'what leaders found difficult/problematic about their role', there was one common, recurring theme: 'The lack of understanding or appreciation of what an integrated centre is and represents was identified by most interviewees, who identified frustrations in dealing with LEAs – particularly the lack of flexibility of personnel and finance sections' (Thorpe and Gasper, 2003: 9).

If integrated services are to be delivered successfully and effectively it is critical that this agenda is understood and championed at every level of the organization and in every agency involved. Few people would argue against the idea of integrated services and there is important research evidence that supports the efficacy of integration, for example, the EPPE study (Sylva et al., 2003b) and the Early Excellence Centre evaluation (Bertram et al., 2002). The evaluation of early excellence centres identified the general benefits of providing integrated services as:

- services being more easily available to parents if they are on one site – especially in poor and disadvantaged areas
- breaking the cycle of poverty
- providing diversity and more choice of services in a non-judgemental way
- early years is now recognized as a critical learning phase and for learning to take place the child needs social and emotional stimulation
- social cohesion is more likely to be achieved where levels of social and psychological capital are high, that is, where there are:
  - dense and complex relationships
  - accessible and informative networks
  - clear cut norms and sanctions about behaviour
  - perceived opportunities for advancement
  - perceived stability in the community.

Benefits for children included:

- enhanced social and emotional competence
- enhanced cognitive development, particularly in language skills
- early remediation of special needs and improved rates of inclusion in mainstream settings

- a reduction in the rate of Child Protection Orders and 'looked after' children
- improved physical well-being
- well-planned, rich and stimulating experiences across all areas of learning offered from birth
- regular and extended access to centre sessions from an early age (Bertram et al., 2002: 77).

However this programme for change brings with it real challenges to established working practices. Risks need to be taken and assumptions challenged if the rhetoric is to be translated into reality.

Some of the challenges that have been identified at Pen Green Centre are:

- target-driven services within longer-term outcomes
- conditions of service – integrated services are difficult to achieve where pay and conditions vary significantly across the private/voluntary/maintained sectors and between health, social services and education
- commissioned services that work within a value base of early years services
- offering targeted services within universal provision
- catchment areas and targeted populations
- providing a range of services that parents can access and not be confused by
- sustainability of services within targeted areas of social and economic disadvantage.

A shared philosophy, vision and principles of working with children and families at all levels and by all partners

In order to have a clear and meaningful vision of integrated services for children and families we need to ask ourselves some fundamental questions. What do we want for our children? What should be the relationship between children, parents and society? How do we understand early childhood? What are the purposes of early childhood institutions?

> The early childhood institution is also a place where people seek to deepen their understanding of many issues related to children and childhood ... not through workers educating parents, but by all concerned working together to make meaning of the work. The early childhood institution is a place for the inclusion of young children into a civic society, and a place for making local democracy meaningful through participation and dialogue. (Moss, 1997: 9)

Values in practice at Pen Green Centre

The purposes of early years institutions advocated by Moss have been core values of Pen Green Centre since it opened in 1983. Pen Green is

A Centre in which all the adults, parents and staff are rigorous thinkers, focussed and analytical, and yet aware of the rhythms of the organisation and their personal lives; where the work is rooted in the local community but staff also reach out and make their views known ... It would be a centre in which children's rich emotional lives were acknowledged and supported, where they were encouraged and cognitively challenged and their learning was promoted. (Whalley, 1999: 336)

Pen Green Centre opened in 1983 and was jointly funded and managed by social services and the LEA. The health authority provided health workers' time with health visitors co-leading groups and offering advice to parents. General practitioners provided clinics at the Centre. The Centre opened with six staff and nursery provision for children 2–5 years old. The vision for the Centre was to provide integrated services to children and their families. The successful services were and are developed according to identified need through a variety of evaluation methods, including an ongoing dialogue between staff and parents at their core. Additional funding was secured through various schemes that were short term but enabled the Centre to establish family support, community education and voluntary sector services such as a playgroup and a Homestart scheme. Funding of the Centre remains complex with funding from the local authority, central government and income generation including parent fees. The Research Base at the Centre is entirely self-funding. The nursery is based in an old secondary school and the Centre expanded its provision and eventually secured more and more of the premises. A detailed historical account of the development of Pen Green Centre is given in *Learning to be Strong* (Whalley, 1994).

With the election of the Labour government in 1997 the Centre experienced a rapid expansion of services. It was one of the first to be designated an Early Excellence Centre (1997), a trailblazer for the Sure Start Local Programme (1999) and early designation as a Children's Centre (2003).

Building on the work of MA students at Leicester and Humberside Universities, Pen Green Centre has used a community development model as a paradigm:

• Parents have the right to expect high-quality, flexible services that respond to the changing needs of their families.
• Staff need to believe in parents' deep commitment to supporting their children's learning. They need to encourage parents to increase their competence.
• Parents and staff both need to have high expectations of the children. They need to work together to get children the best possible deal.

The Centre aims to

• develop the individual's capacity to be self-directing
• help individuals to gain more control over their lives
• raise self-esteem
• promote learning as a lifelong experience

- actively promote equal opportunities
- encourage and support constructive discontent – not having to put up with things the way they are
- encourage people to feel they have power to change things
- work towards self-fulfilment (Whalley, 1999: 24).

The Centre also constructed principles for the community education programme that is strongly influenced by Paolo Freire (Freire, 1970; Freire and Macedo, 1998):

- Groups arise in response to community need.
- Groups are concerned with the individual capacity for self-direction.
- Groups should encourage people to have the power to change things.
- Groups should enable constructive discontent.
- It is vital to understand and acknowledge people's learning journey to enable self-fulfilment.
- Education is through learning, discovering and uncovering – self-discovery.
- We will start to understand what prevents people from feeling able to learn.

There is not the space here to detail all of the services that the Centre provides, but the core services offered on site are:

- nursery provision for children up to 2 years
- nursery provision for children 2–4 years – local authority maintained
- nursery provision for children 2–4 years – voluntary sector
- crèche provision for parents and carers attending groups at the Centre
- community education
- adult learning with nationally accredited courses such as Open College Network, basic skills, National Vocational Qualifications (NVQs), childminders, GCSE and A levels, degree courses
- e-learning
- support groups, for example, lone parents, young parents, English for speakers of other languages (ESOL), fathers, parents who have children with special needs, mothers who were sexually abused as children
- parent and children groups, for example, infant massage, 'growing together', messy play and community drop-in
- after-school club and holiday playschemes; summer playscheme for children with additional needs
- family support through home visiting, counselling, groupwork, outreach
- research, training and dissemination. This includes an MA in Integrated Provision for Children and Families, piloting the National Professional Qualification in Integrated Centre Leadership and supporting the roll out programme, and providing international conferences.

Leadership

The critical concept for successful integration is a shared philosophy, vision and principles of working with children and families at all levels and by all partners. This can only be achieved through clear and strong leadership. Effective leaders are 'aware and articulate human developers concerned with the people in the organisation in which they work and able to recognise and support the emotional lives of their organization' (Whalley, 1999: 24). Effective leadership and management of integrated services are vital. Professor João Formosinho from the University of Braga makes the distinction between the two roles and argues that integrated services need to have both good leadership and effective management (Formosinho, 2003). Leadership is essential if the integrity of the organization is to be maintained with strong ethics, and a clear, meaningful vision and value base. Good management structures and systems need to be in place for the organization to run effectively. Management without leadership can lead to a mechanistic delivery of services, and organizations that are run in this way have been shown to have a compliant workforce and children who are compliant. A mechanistic approach can also be an inhibitor to providing effective services when it is target driven and out of context with the broader vision.

Handy (1994) identifies two types of organization (Figure 10.1) and argues that the organization with the strong vision and clear principles is likely to be more responsive and effective. This type of organization will also include the belief of shared leadership and subsidiarity. As early years institutions such as children's centres develop, organizations based on these principles are more likely to meet the challenges of the complexity of integrated, multidisciplinary work with the child firmly based at the centre.

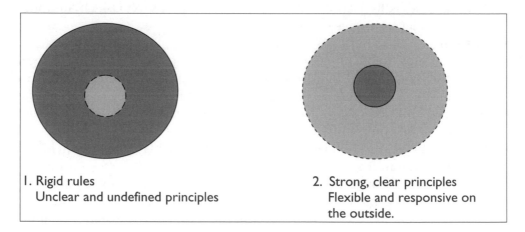

| 1. Rigid rules | 2. Strong, clear principles |
| Unclear and undefined principles | Flexible and responsive on the outside. |

Figure 10.1 *Two types of organization (adapted from Handy, 1994)*

Subsidiarity depends on mutual confidence. Those in the centre have to have confidence in the unit, while the unit has to have confidence in the centre and members of the unit have to have confidence in each other ... when mutual confidence exists there is no need for the production of procedures, the manual, inspections, performance numbers and counter signatures which clutter up large organisations. These are signs of distrust ... (Handy, 1994: 122)

The multidisciplinary team at Pen Green Centre

The senior management team at Pen Green is a multidisciplinary team representing the various aspects of the Centre's work: nursery education, adult learning, family support and professional development and research. The frank and honest exchanges that we have can at times be difficult, but these are important if we are to work creatively together in the interests of families and the staff team. Handy points out that 'organisations based on subsidiarity are full of ambiguity and argument and conflict, but if it is an argument among friends, united by a common purpose, then it is a useful argument' (Handy, 1994: 126).

The leadership and management of the Centre has had to adapt to the growth of the organization and the increasing complexity of continuing to provide integrated services. This has included the use of external consultants to help us step outside our daily practice to examine and gain a deeper understanding of what we are doing and how we can do it better.

The operational values and principles have remained the same and provide an important anchor in this sea of change. But how we lead and manage services has had to change. We have always aimed for a shared leadership model rather than a hierarchical structure. Fullan supports this idea of shared leadership: 'Leaders provide the vision and context and design of learning experiences – solutions have to be found by coalface workers – everyone and everything is affected. Leadership will not be judged by your effectiveness, but by what leadership you produce in others' (Fullan, 2001: 137).

Old structures need to be revised, for example, staff meetings with 25 workers are possible, but not with 85 workers. Staff meetings are now broken down in to team meetings and there is the need to work across teams if we are to challenge and inform our own practice. Regular integrated staff meetings have been introduced. These are theme based rather than task focused, for example, inclusion, team-building, Birth to Three Matters.

Given the complexity and range of services that children's centres are expected to provide, it is very difficult for one person to hold in mind every aspect of the Centre's work. At Pen Green Centre the senior management team decided to identify the various domains of work of the Centre and each member of the team would then be accountable for and hold the group accountable to the area for which they are the guardians. In this way the overall values and value of each domain would be held in mind when the group met to discuss and debate service delivery. We constructed three components to every domain:

- *development* where all staff have the right to be all they can be through working to their strengths and passion, and working on their areas of discomfort
- *delivery* of service through taking responsibility
- *discovery* through research and evaluation – identifying how we will know when we have achieved our goals.

A domain can be either an area of service, for example, nursery provision, family support, adult education, or a defined group such as children with additional needs, children within a certain age group, fathers, professional development of staff, enhancing children's life chances, and so on. The five outcomes defined in *Every Child Matters* (DfES, 2003b) will run through every aspect of the work. Within the senior management team the appropriate senior management team member leads each domain according to their field of expertise. Margy Whalley has developed these ideas in the *National Professional Qualification in Integrated Centre Leadership Rollout Training Guidance* (Whalley, 2005).

The internal management structures have changed as the organization has grown. The structure in Figure 10.2 (highly simplified) has been created to ensure that the vision and principles of the Centre are adhered to, that there are clear lines of accountability and that ethical decision-making can take place.

Multidisciplinary work

For any worker, whether they are an educationalist, health worker, social worker or volunteer, there are three levels that will influence their practice within multidisciplinary teams.

1 Their personal life history and what has motivated them to work in their chosen profession.
2 Their professional background, training and experience.
3 The agency in which they work and what the beliefs, values, aim and objectives of the agency are.

What and how the worker presents within the multidisciplinary team they are working with will be strongly affected by these influences. There may be times when these three levels need to be explored by the team in order to make explicit what is implicit, particularly when the team is not working well together.

The more deeply embedded the values of the Centre are in the worker, the more effective the worker is. For example, a value that is central to our work is

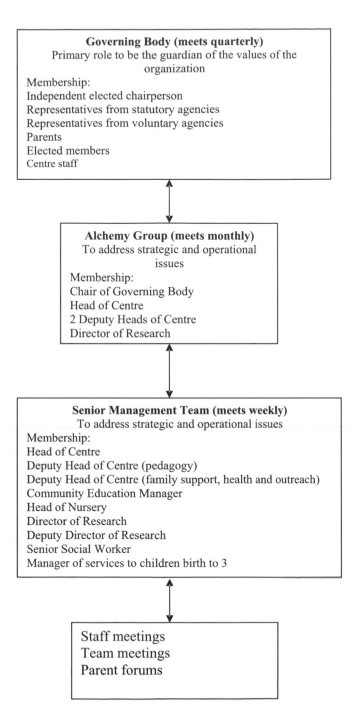

Governing Body (meets quarterly)
Primary role to be the guardian of the values of the organization
Membership:
Independent elected chairperson
Representatives from statutory agencies
Representatives from voluntary agencies
Parents
Elected members
Centre staff

Alchemy Group (meets monthly)
To address strategic and operational issues
Membership:
Chair of Governing Body
Head of Centre
2 Deputy Heads of Centre
Director of Research

Senior Management Team (meets weekly)
To address strategic and operational issues
Membership:
Head of Centre
Deputy Head of Centre (pedagogy)
Deputy Head of Centre (family support, health and outreach)
Community Education Manager
Head of Nursery
Director of Research
Deputy Director of Research
Senior Social Worker
Manager of services to children birth to 3

Staff meetings
Team meetings
Parent forums

Figure 10.2 *Management structure of Pen Green Centre*

that parents, as co-educators of their children, have a critical role to play and we must work in an equal partnership with them. The degree to which we agree with this can range on a continuum from a superficial rhetoric that is dutifully acknowledged in meetings, to a deeply held belief that you feel passionate about with every fibre of your being.

The degree of success in working in a multidisciplinary team or with workers from external agencies is not so much about their professional background, but the level of synergy there is in the beliefs and values that are appropriate to support children and families' development. The health visitors, social workers, paediatricians and mental health workers who have been drawn to Pen Green Centre have worked very effectively because they feel an affinity with the principles, aims and working practice of the Centre.

To bring about change in working practice, staff need to be supported. Bringing about change is not easy. It is not a sequential trajectory from A to B. Rather it is an iterative process. In order to support the change process:

- there needs to be effective support structures – this would include regular supervision and support, team meetings and mentoring
- as leaders and managers we need to be sensitive to the staff's ability to change and at their own pace
- staff need to feel confident in their own abilities and confident enough to be open to different perspectives from professionals in other fields. High-quality staff training and professional development play a key role in achieving this.

Pen Green Centre has always had a multidisciplinary team of early years educators, social workers and health professionals. We recognized very early on that we needed to value our professional backgrounds and recognize that we bring specialized knowledge to our overall understanding of families and young children.

David Panter, former chief executive of Brighton and Hove Council who facilitated a number of team-building days for the whole Pen Green staff group, talks about the idea of the 'integrated professional'. We need to extend and broaden our knowledge. For example, nursery workers not only have to develop their understanding of pedagogy but, if they are to work effectively with families, they need to understand family structure and family dynamics, psychoanalytic theories and to develop counselling skills. Effective pedagogy is about understanding the emotional lives of children and carers as well as children's cognitive development and how children learn.

Similarly, social workers and health workers need to realize the importance and effectiveness of the role of education in supporting and empowering children and families. Health visitors have consistently been involved in providing services at Pen Green and have readily taken up training provided at the Centre or through the Centre, for example, counselling courses, infant massage training, groupwork, and so on. Providing joint training for workers from different disciplines and agencies is an effective way of developing working practice and a sense of common purpose.

Examples of multidisciplinary work

Developing universal services

The work of the Research Base at Pen Green Centre involves a multidisciplinary team approach with the research team, and practitioners at the Centre such as psychotherapists, teachers, parents, social workers, family workers from Pen Green nursery and Sure Start workers working together.

As part of the research study on parent–child relationships with children from birth to 3 years, a number of groups were set up called 'Growing Together' (Tait, 2004). These groups run on a weekly basis and a team of four workers work with and support parents who attend with their children. The team of workers consists of a research worker, a worker from nursery, a psychotherapist and an early years specialist. The groups are open to parents on a drop-in basis and are very well attended, attracting families from all walks of life. The multidisciplinary team works effectively together with a common purpose, offering different perspectives and a wide range of skills and knowledge on parent–child interactions.

The elements that have ensured the success of the groups are as follows:

- The groups were set up out of an identified need.
- The workers involved agreed a common purpose that was to 'support and promote helpful attachment patterns through focusing closely with parents on their infant, and on their patterns of relating with her or him, and through modelling ways of tuning in to babies and young children' (Woodhead, 2001: 3).
- The aims of the groups were clearly identified as
    - to give parents a chance to play with their child
    - to help parents to understand more about their relationship with their child
    - dialogue with parents about their child's development
    - to encourage reflective parenting
    - to facilitate parent to parent support
    - to validate the feelings women are experiencing when they are suffering from postnatal depression
    - to reinforce helpful attachment experiences through modelling, video feedback and discussions
    - the workers used and developed common theoretical frameworks that included psychodynamic theories of 'holding' (Winnicott, 1965), 'containment' (Bion, 1962) and 'attachment theory' (Bowlby, 1988).

By discussing these theoretical concepts with parents we are able to develop a dialogue; we can have conversations about the children we are watching and develop a shared understanding. The parent is able to bring their specialist knowledge about their own child into the conversation, and the worker is able to offer their theoretical understanding (Easen et al., 1992). The parent and worker develop a shared language with which to think about the child (Tait, 2004).

- Workers make time for reflection after each group. This is essential since workers need containing too.
    - Babies have raw, primitive feelings, which get inside those who are caring for them.
    - Feelings may also arise about ones own infancy and experience of being parented.
    - This is a time to make sense of the experience and to process one's own emotional responses.

'In naming and discussing these feelings, we mirror the work done in the groups ... ' (Woodhead, 2001: 10).

The name 'Growing Together' has several layers of meaning. It refers to the purpose of the group to support the parent and the child in their relationship of attachment. It also refers to the relationship between workers, parents and children. The group is run within the overall values and ethos of the Centre as part of a learning community where staff and parents share their learning journeys.

A project as an example of targeted services within universal provision

In 2004 Pen Green Centre began a project to support parents who were involved in the misuse of drugs and/or alcohol. A project team was formed including external agencies such as probation officers, health workers, social workers and specialists in drug and alcohol addiction. Preparation work included joint training with specialists in this area of work, consultation with parents and staff to explore the possible barriers to the work, and a consultant for the group workers was engaged. The group workers included a social worker employed at the Centre and a family visitor from the Sure Start Local Programme. The purpose of the group was to support parents to manage their addictions and to be better able to support their children.

An evaluation of the first group, with the group members, led to the establishment of a second group that would focus on self-esteem. The aims of the group became more parent focused:

- To provide a safe, supportive, confidential and non-judgemental space.
- To encourage self-expression, creativity and exploration, while maintaining boundaries and respect.

- To encourage women to find and use their voice, to explore, find, redefine and welcome a sense of self.
- To create an atmosphere of validation, belief, courage, sharing and under-standing at each person's pace.
- To create a safe place to explore addiction, recovery, relapse and abstention.

Referrals were taken from external agencies and clear contracts were drawn up with parents, Pen Green staff and external agencies. It was important that there were clear boundaries concerning confidentiality and information that would be shared between agencies. Some families were involved in court proceedings, so clear parameters were essential. The group workers also offered individual support to families attending the group through home visits, so it was impor-tant for parents and staff to be clear about what was shared in the group and what remained confidential.

The crèche team that provided the childcare for the group work were involved in the planning of the group. They were actively involved in the group through providing feedback to the parents about their children's development and learn-ing. The crèche workers provided an added and important dimension to the work of the group and felt more valued as a consequence.

Working within the principles of the group work programme the group workers were sensitive to the parents' needs and had to be flexible in how they worked. The work continued for 12 months and developed through dialogue with the parents attending the group and included discussion with some of the older children. As a consequence of this way of working, the group remained well attended and tackled some important issues. The group workers found that they had to address the needs of the parents themselves before they were able to explore their role as parents. For some parents this was a very painful, and ulti-mately rewarding, journey.

Street (2005: 22) concludes:

> We believe that the time spent in communication with all workers in the Centre ... and with other agencies has been invaluable in generating an enabling, pos-itive environment throughout the organisation within which the first group could succeed. A small project, specifically targeted to the needs of a small number of families, has been successfully integrated into a large, complex organisation providing universal services to hundreds of families each week.

Conclusion

For multidisciplinary teams to work effectively, commonly held philosophy, beliefs, values and ethos must be firmly established. Policies and structures within local authorities and health trusts need to be in place to support front-line workers to deliver integrated services to children and families within their communities. For all the work that is done at Government and Local Authority level it is the daily interactions with parents and children that really matter. This is the only place where services are meaningful and where we can positively affect people's lives: 'it is people, in their communities, organisations and institutions, who ultimately decide what it all means and why it matters' (Brown and Duguid, 2000: 14).

The examples given in this chapter, of multidisciplinary work both from workers within the Centre and the involvement of external agency workers, have common elements of how to provide successful services that are child and family centred. These elements are as follows:

• Services are created in response to identified local need.
• A shared philosophy, vision and principles of working with children and families is established.
• Services have clearly defined and agreed aims and purpose.
• Identification of additional training needs to enable and empower workers.
• A clearly defined theoretical framework is shared with parents so that a common language is used to further dialogue and understanding.
• A reflexive and responsive approach includes supervision and mentoring as well as ongoing evaluation of the work.

The agenda for change is complex on many levels, but it is also very simple. As long as we remind ourselves of the vision and the values upon which our work is based then we can cut through much of the complexity of interdisciplinary and multi-agency work.

Jackson Pollock describes the process of his painting as follows:

When I am in my painting, I am not aware of what I am doing … I have no fears of making changes, destroying the image etc., because the painting has a life of its own. I try to let it come through. It is only when I lose contact with the painting that the result is a mess. Otherwise there is pure harmony, an easy give and take and the painting comes out well. (Emmerling, 2003: 65)

Working in communities is very similar. Pollock talks about creating a mess when he loses contact with his painting. As practitioners, if we lose contact with our beliefs and values and we lose contact with our local communities, then we will create a mess. If we are in tune with parents, children and staff, then there is a synergy and creative energy from which we all benefit. It is vital that we establish high-quality services now. We owe it to children and families in our communities to get it right. The quote from Proust, at the beginning of this chapter, seems particularly pertinent. Many of us have worked in our own domains with children and families for years. The landscape has not changed but the challenge is how able are we to see the landscape in different ways?

Points for discussion

❖ What are the vision and values of your organization and how do they concur with your own?

❖ What do you feel most passionate about and will not compromise on?

❖ What structures are in place to ensure that the values are adhered to? What are the decision-making processes in your organization and how much influence do you have?

❖ What joint training would be useful to further multi-agency work?

11

Working with Parents

Lucy Draper and Bernadette Duffy

Chapter contents

- Why is partnership important?
- What are the benefits and challenges of working in partnership with parents?
- Thomas Coram Children's Centre
- Conclusion

> Partnership with parents should be a key aspect of provision. Parents should be recognised as children's first and enduring educators, and should be seen as key partners in supporting children's learning and development. (DfES, 2003d: 10)

In this chapter, we draw on our work in Thomas Coram Children's Centre in London to look at the central importance of parents and practitioners working in partnership together in early years settings.

We ask *'Why* is it important that we work in partnership with parents?' and 'What are the benefits and challenges of working together?'. We then describe our work at Thomas Coram and some of the lessons we have learnt about different groups of parents and what partnership means to them. While using our own centre as an example, we hope that this chapter will have relevance to practitioners working in a wide range of settings.

When we use the term 'parents' we are referring to all those who take on this role in children's lives, whether or not they are the child's biological parent. When we use the term 'practitioner', we are referring to the wide range of adults who support children's learning and development, whether paid or unpaid.

Families are changing, as they always have done. Parents are not a homogeneous group; their views and beliefs will be diverse. Our views about what constitutes a family and the roles these different individuals take, need to reflect this and, in turn, will influence the way we work with parents.

Why is partnership important?

There is a long tradition of working with parents in early childhood settings. At the beginning of the twentieth century, Margaret Macmillan included lectures for parents and parent groups as part of the nursery schools she established. However, by the 1960s, parent involvement programmes tended to focus on parents whose children's achievements seemed low, and parental involvement was seen as a way of compensating for the limitations of home. In recent years, models of parental involvement have moved from being largely compensatory to participatory (Whalley and the Pen Green Centre, 1997).

Today, working in partnership with parents is interpreted in a number of ways. These can include parents working with staff in settings, practitioners visiting families in their own homes, parents as governors or on management committees, parents attending workshops and courses, and parents running services such as toy libraries.

For the past 20 years, government legislation and guidance has strongly encouraged working in partnership with parents. The Education Reform Act 1988 emphasized schools' accountability to parents and parental choice, while the Children Act 1989 introduced the concept of parental responsibility.

The Sure Start programme, launched in 1998 and now integrated into the rapidly expanding national programme of children's centres, recognized the centrality of parental involvement from the start. Both the *Birth to Three Matters* framework (DfES, 2002) and the *Curriculum Guidance for the Foundation Stage* (QCA, 2000) emphasize that effective practice involves using the knowledge and expertise of parents and other family adults, while the *Every Child Matters: Change for Children* framework (DfES, 2004b) stresses the importance of parents, carers and families in meeting the desired outcomes for children.

What are the benefits and challenges of working in partnership with parents?

Benefits for children

There is growing evidence of the long-term benefits of preventive work with parents and young children within mainstream open access services (Pugh, 1999). In the USA, the High Scope Project found that high levels of parental involvement were one of the keys to a successful early years programme (Schweinhart and Weikart, 1993). Projects such as Peers Early Education Partnership (PEEP) in Oxford demonstrate the significant and lasting benefits of working with parents and children from babyhood onwards (Evangelou and Sylva, 2003), while Flouri and Buchanan (2004) looked specifically at the role of fathers and showed that a greater level or frequency of fathers' interest and direct involvement in their children's learning and education is associated strongly with better educational outcomes for children. The Effective Provision of Pre-School Education (EPPE) research project (Sylva et al., 2004) has identified the key role of home learning environments in children's achievements.

Many of these findings were cited in a review of research carried out for the DfES by Desforges and Abouchaar in 2003, which confirmed the view that both parental involvement in the early years setting and the educational environment of the home have a positive effect on children's achievement and adjustment, even after other factors (such as social class) have been taken into account.

In a survey of parents we carried out at Thomas Coram on parents' views of their children's transitions into nursery, it was clear that their main worry was whether the nursery staff would *understand* their child in the way that the child had up until then taken for granted that they would be understood. They listed their worries:

- 'Will my child be able to go to the toilet?'
- 'Will they give extra time to the new children?'
- 'Are there any other children from my ethnic background?'
- 'Will there be someone who speaks my child's language?'
- 'He asked if they'd cook him pasta if he doesn't like the dinner!'

It is important to children that the adults in their lives share an understanding of who they are, what matters most to them and what they are capable of. They mind very much about whether the adults they care about – first their parents and, later in their lives, their nursery workers – seem to like and respect each other. Continuity between home and setting benefits children's learning. Parents and staff who are focusing together on the child's learning are able to share insights and to understand the child more fully. This involves the practitioners going to some degree of trouble to get to know the family and in showing an interest (without being off puttingly intrusive) in a child's home circumstances and life history to date, in their interests and achievements, hopes and fears, likes and dislikes. It will also entail staff sharing with parents the details of a child's life in the nursery, and the sometimes familiar and sometimes entirely new facets of a child's personality that reveal themselves in the early years setting.

Benefits for parents

Parents' first and most important motivation to have a good relationship with staff in their child's early years setting is that they can see that the better the practitioner understands their child, the happier their child is likely to be. They are also intrigued to know about what their child is doing and learning during the hours they are apart from them, and children, frustratingly, are not always able (or willing) to explain this themselves. ('What did you do at nursery today?' 'Played.') Parents may also welcome a different (and less intense) perspective on the rewarding, but often challenging, experience of bringing up a child. Practitioners bring a broader view of the different developmental stages young children go through, what is 'normal' and, perhaps, what really is concerning, and parents are grateful to learn from this. They are often fascinated to find out a bit more about the ways in which early years settings provide learning opportunities and the particular ways in which their own child responds to these.

Some parents also welcome the chance to develop themselves as individuals; if they are asked to contribute their particular ideas, knowledge or skills to share with children in the setting, they will feel respected and valued. Involvement of this kind can release untapped potential – many early years practitioners have started out this way. Other parents have got involved in courses, which have led on to further and higher education. Involvement in management committees and governing bodies empowers parents and gives them a voice in their community, as well as ensuring that their perspective informs the thinking of the setting. Programmes designed to bring practitioners and parents together also bring parents together, reducing parental isolation and helping to build support networks in the wider community.

Benefits for practitioners

Parents and practitioners need each other and have useful differences in their approach that can complement each other. Parents are experts on their own individual child and their family culture, and practitioners offer expertise in this stage of children's development and learning. By combining these, the best opportunities can be provided for each child. For many staff, the opportunity to work closely with parents adds a new dimension to their work. Practitioners can assume that their experience of family life is the only way it can be, and working with parents from diverse communities widens their views on families and family life. Differences can be shared, respected and explored. The children's life at home provides many opportunities for learning, on which the setting can build.

At Thomas Coram, we have tried to make our partnership focus include all these elements and thus benefit children, parents and practitioners. We believe that, though there are different roles and responsibilities, there is not such a great separation between staff and parents. Many practitioners *are* parents, and all have been children. Everybody shares a concern for the welfare of the children, and this is also true of the wider community.

The challenges of partnership

Studies looking at parental involvement from the point of view of the parents (for example, Ghate and Hazel, 2001; Quinton, 2004) show that parents want to have their views taken seriously, to be listened to, to be respected and to be treated as partners in the upbringing of their children.

However, working together in partnership is not always easy for either parents or practitioners, and partnerships are not necessarily equal. Both may have anxieties about the relationship; for example, if practitioners have a view of themselves as the experts on children's learning they may find it difficult to value the parents' views. Often, practitioners who feel confident in their work with children feel less confident in their work with parents, or with parents who are very different from them. On the other hand, parents may have negative memories of school, or may have questions about some aspect of the curriculum, but find it hard to find the courage to express this.

Settings may find it harder to work in partnership with some groups of parents than with others. Our discussions about so-called 'hard to reach' parents made us question who it was that was having the difficulty in 'reaching'. Exciting work has taken place at Thomas Coram with both very young parents and with fathers, both groups who are as keen to support their children as any other parent, but who may want to get involved in different ways.

A lack of shared language (both literally or metaphorically) can make communication harder. Family circumstances (lack of time, pressures of work, no crèche facilities for younger children) may make it difficult for parents to participate in programmes or events organized by the setting. Practitioners are often busy, and where children are transported long distances to attend, or where there is a rapid turnover of children, opportunities to build relationships can be limited.

Such situations bring constant challenges to good partnership working. However, none of these problems is insurmountable and, in the following section, we will be describing some of the ways in which we have tried to put partnership into action at Thomas Coram.

Thomas Coram Children's Centre

Our centre is situated in the King's Cross area of London and is a partnership between Camden Local Education Authority, Coram Family – a children's charity – and the local King's Cross Sure Start programme. Already having to think about working in partnership as different professionals, we draw on many of the same understandings in our work with parents. The centre is part of Coram Community Campus, which houses a wide range of providers from the maintained and voluntary sectors. It consists of the Early childhood centre – often referred to as 'the nursery' – which provides 106 places for children from 6 months to 5 years; and (adjoining it in the same building) the Parents Centre, which provides support and training for parents from the nursery and the wider community, health and mental health services, as well as a drop-in centre, crèches and out-of-school childcare. The activities in the Parents Centre are accessible to both the parents of children attending the nursery and to families in the wider community. Potentially, therefore, a family can have a connection with the whole centre for many years, spanning the child's transition from home to nursery to school. The centre as a whole offers a training and dissemination programme, including training for practitioners in working with parents.

When we are thinking about partnership with parents, we need to think about what we wish to achieve in our particular setting. What are the characteristics and needs of the community we serve and how will we reflect this in what we offer? At Thomas Coram, we have tried not to assume that the practitioners' agenda for partnership is necessarily shared by parents (Henry, 1996), but that trust, sharing information, sharing decision-making, sharing responsibility and accountability are all important.

A successful partnership involves a two-way flow of information, and flexibility and responsiveness are vital. We want to create a centre that reflects our ethos that everyone is welcome, that parents can express their views and feelings, that diversity is valued and that the centre is seen as part of the wider community.

In the following section, we will be giving examples that highlight different aspects of our work with parents:

• working with parents around children's learning
• support for parents
• access to further training
• parental involvement in management.

Working with parents around children's learning

In any early years setting, the 'settling-in' process is a crucial arena for the establishment of a good partnership between parents and practitioners. We know from attachment theory that if a child feels securely attached to their parent or carer, they will also have more confidence to be able to learn from new experiences. The Parents Centre gives the opportunity for parents and children to 'practise' small amounts of separation, without the stress that is sometimes felt when a child is starting nursery full time and a parent perhaps needs to get back to work. In the drop-in, which parents and children attend together, a child may start by taking a few small steps away from his or her parent or, sitting on their lap, simply start to show an interest in an activity in which other children are involved. Later, parents may attend groups or classes, while the children stay in the crèche for an hour or two. In the nursery, some children will already have visited from the Parents Centre drop-in before they are offered a place, but our first contact with others is during weekly visitors' mornings, when prospective families come to look at the centre.

Once children are offered a nursery place, the family is invited to join our induction programme, which consists of visits to the centre, home visits by the key worker, and a settling in period. During this time, we get to know the family and they get to know us. Part of this process is a detailed parent conference during which parents tell us about their child in a semi-structured interview. The information we get from this covers all areas of the child's development and learning, and provides the foundation for our planning for the individual child. At the same time, parents and children are starting to make a relationship with the key worker – if they feel that they like and trust them (which often comes from feeling that the key worker has a genuine and open interest in the child), this is a sound basis for good communication in the future.

Feedback from parents – what do we look for in a practitioner?

- Listening very carefully.
- Being understanding.
- Not quick to judge.
- Giving time for us to explain.
- Finding a way out of turmoil – a chance to calm down.
- Never say 'you are not doing it right'.
- Take time – get to know the children. If our children like you, we will like you.
- Don't compare the children unfavourably to others – say 'some children do this, some children do that'.
- It's important to discuss cultural and religious issues in parenting.
- Understand that it's hard for us when one worker leaves, but you can slowly build up trust in a new person.

(Comments from parents contributing to a practitioner training programme.)

Arrival and collection times are crucial for communication between parents and practitioners, though in a nursery as large and busy as ours, they can also be quite pressured. We organize the sessions to ensure that staff, especially key workers, are free at these important times of day to welcome families and exchange information. As well as daily informal contacts, there are regular times for parent and key worker to meet and review the progress of individual children. As part of this review, parents and key workers jointly decide the next priorities for learning and discuss how they can work together to support the child. Key workers in each base room also hold regular meetings with parents to discuss what is going on in the room and possible new developments.

As our work with parents developed, it became clear that being available for parents was a priority. In a review of the nursery management structure, it was decided that we should free up one of the deputies specifically to work with parents and to encourage involvement and inclusion. This has proved to be particularly important for, and valued by, the parents of children with special needs.

The centre makes full use of video footage to share children's nursery experiences with parents; parents love to come in and talk about their children's lives in more detail. While key workers have been privileged to learn a little more about the child's family life from the home visit – perhaps seeing a child they have thought of as quiet showing confident fluency in their home language –

parents watching a video of the child's day in nursery will often be struck by the ways in which their children are different in this other setting – passing food around at lunchtime, for instance, might be something they've never done at home. In this way the child's two worlds are brought together, with the adults in each having a greater understanding of the child's experiences in the other.

We have tried to develop ways of ensuring that busy parents who work or are students are also offered accessible ways to be involved. One method has been the use of home/centre books where parents and key workers enter into a dialogue by recording observations of the child's experience at home and at the centre. Another has been the use of regular newsletters and information sheets about the current work of the centre. Our website contains a wide range of information about the centre and offers opportunities for parents to get involved in current projects. The toy and book libraries also provide opportunities to bring centre and home life together.

There are also opportunities for parents to get involved in specific programmes. Peters and Kostelnik (1981) point out that practitioners often present irrelevant and ineffective materials in these situations, because they have neglected to find out more about the strengths and needs which parents are bringing to the programmes in the process. We have tried to ensure that we consider this when planning what to offer. In the groups, there is a strong focus on the children's learning and development, drawing on our in-house skills, reflecting the cultural and linguistic diversity of the community we serve, and again often using video. Workshops might be entitled 'What does a 2-year-old do all day?' or they focus particularly on interactions between adults and children. The discussion that has resulted has been rich and has offered parents and staff new insights to the children. Another group – again using video observations – has been used to consult with parents on what they would like to see for their children at the beginning and end of the 'extended day'. They fed back to staff that the priority for them was that their children should have as relaxed and calm a time as they might have had at home if they were there.

Parents, who first became interested in the question of how their children learn, have sometimes gone on to train as practitioners through the 'Introduction to Childcare' and then the accredited 'Level 2 Certificate in Childcare' courses, which we offer in partnership with the local college. For us, this also brings the opportunity to employ our practitioners from among parents in the local community, with all the benefits that brings. Other parents have trained with us as community interpreters or outreach workers, again building on the skills and knowledge of their communities.

Support for parents

All our work rests on an acknowledgment of the importance of parents and carers in their children's lives, and of the rewards – as well as the challenges and difficulties – involved in the parenting task. (In a 1998 survey of parents, 87 per cent of parents named joy as the emotion they felt most often – Barnardo's, 1998.) The staff are privileged to have come to know an enormous amount about families' lives; in the relatively informal setting of the drop-in, we have watched babies grow and develop, eat and sleep and – both literally and metaphorically – take their first steps. We have listened to their parents' worries and concerns, heard about their pregnancy and childbirth experiences, been part of workshops where they have shared a wide range of cultural expertise concerning children and child-care, and music sessions where songs and lullabies from many different languages are shared and learnt. Sometimes we have heard about difficulties with housing or money or immigration status and at times, hopefully, have been able to give useful advice in these areas. It is also not unusual for parents to share their worries about conflict with partners or other family members.

Two mornings a week, we are lucky enough to have a psychologist and psychotherapist, provided by the local Primary Care Trust, available in the centre to see parents who have particular concerns about their children. Parents who have worries about their children's behaviour often find it very hard to seek help, and may worry they will be blamed for these difficulties or 'reported' to Social Services. The service has worked very well and proved to be helpful to parents with a variety of concerns about their children's sleeping, eating or behaviour. It seems that because the service, though specialized, is based in a community setting, parents find it much easier and less threatening to use. An early evaluation showed that 93 per cent of parents attended their first appointments, compared with 68 per cent who are referred to psychologists in clinical settings. The psychology staff also co-run parents' group with centre practitioners, provide help for staff wanting to think about the needs of particular children or groups of children, and teach on courses for parents and practitioners.

There are very wide variations in beliefs (held by both practitioners and parents) about what is 'good for children'. Thomas Coram is situated in a cul-turally very diverse neighbourhood, and families attending the centre speak 48 different languages. Working in effective partnership with parents from differ-ent ethnic backgrounds requires both knowledge of and respect for these differ-ences, and a commitment to provide a service of equal quality to all their children. Parents who were not themselves educated in the UK may be unfa-miliar with the British education system and possibly are not confident it will serve their children well.

Having information and knowledge about parents' points of view is crucial. At a meeting of Bangladeshi parents brought together to discuss their perspectives on their children's education, they were for the first time given the information that as a group, Bangladeshi children – especially boys – were doing less well in school than most other ethnic groups. There was, understandably, a great deal of anxiety about their children's progress.

This anxiety had several causes: ignorance of the methods and expectations of English schools; embarrassment that as parents they lacked the education needed to support their children; and confusion about the English belief in learning through play. Parents were torn between trying to implement the kinds of learning they had experienced as schoolchildren, and trying to follow the advice of English practitioners. This confusion and contradiction was only slowly discussed and understood, through initial visits from outreach workers, visits to the toy library, recruitment to parents' classes in primary schools (part of the wider work of the Parents Centre) and continual discussion in groups at the Centre. Some parents remained uncertain of the benefits of the English school system, but all knew that they had to put their faith in it, and most became quite confident in dealing with schools and teachers, as well as in supporting children's learning at home. (Brooker, 2004)

At a series of 'International Parenting' workshops, groups of parents made presentations about their home cultures, particularly in relation to pregnancy, childbirth and child-rearing. Childcare practitioners who attended these workshops found them particularly valuable and the material was published in a booklet entitled 'Sharing our Stories'.

Research in the UK has shown that black and ethnic minority parents are less likely to attend family centres or 'parenting skills' classes than white parents, even though they have similar needs for support (Butt and Box, 1998). We looked for particular models of parenting support that would meet the needs of all parents and have for some years been running a programme called *Strengthening Families: Strengthening Communities* (Steele, 2000). This has many things in common with better known models, but two of its features are unique. One is that it emphasizes the strengths in a family's cultural history and looks at ways in which parents can pass these on to their children (rather than focusing on problems). The other is that it includes discussion of a 'spiritual' component in parenting, which can mean a variety of things from formal religious teaching to creating a moral framework for children's lives.

This has been eagerly welcomed by parents, who have taken from it not only new ideas about children's learning and behaviour, but also a determination to make the local neighbourhood a safer and happier place for their children to grow up.

The bombings in London in July 2005, some of which took place very close to Thomas Coram, not only made local families very fearful, but also presented a challenge to the community's capacity to tolerate the differences within it. Only a few days after the bombings, a large community festival – Bangladesh Mela – had been planned in a local park. Staff and parents from the centre had long been involved in the preparations for this event, and though there was talk of postponing it, it was agreed that it would make an important and positive statement if it went ahead. In the event, over 2,000 local families took part, including many from Thomas Coram.

Like the wider group of families, our Teenage Parent Project includes young parents from many different backgrounds, including some who are refugees from war-torn countries, as well as those who grew up in the UK. There are as many individual stories as there are individual young parents, including 16-year-old married couples, young care-leavers, and teenagers who arrived in this country pregnant having experienced severe trauma. The project has an educational focus and the young parents are given an opportunity to study, while keeping their children close by them (some in the same room, some in crèches and some given nursery places, according to their parents' wishes). Their successes have challenged the stereotype of feckless teen parents; their motivation to take part in various photographic and film projects about the lives of young parents have stemmed from their desire to put the record straight and to demonstrate their serious commitment to their children.

We have learned that it is important to provide specific services targeted at the particular needs of certain groups (such as young parents); after a while, though, they may welcome the opportunity to take part in more general activities. The same is true of fathers, whose particular needs and interests often get forgotten, even while we are talking about work with 'parents'. We have for some years employed a specially designated Fathers' Worker to co-ordinate particular activities for fathers and also to raise the general level of awareness among staff of 'the man's position' – important in such a generally female environment. To ensure that the Fathers' Worker does not become professionally isolated (in a mirroring of the father's role in the young family), he is part of a wider team of men employed by Coram Family's Boys2Men Project, who work with fathers in different children's centres across London.

Access to further training

The centre offers a number of ways in which parents can access further training. There is a well-resourced information technology room, in which we offer a range of courses as well as individual access to computers, and classes are also offered in sewing, first aid, ESOL and return to work. Ongoing support and encouragement from staff are important as a return to study can be daunting but, when parents are ready, we also offer accredited professional training in childcare, interpreting and outreach. Teenage parents, whose studies may have been interrupted by the birth of their babies, are able to continue to study, while keeping their children close to hand, and are also given support with their other concerns.

Since the recent publication of the new *National Occupational Standards for Work with Parents* (Lifelong Learning, 2005), we have offered a new training course for practitioners linked to these standards, drawing on the range of different kinds of work with parents at Thomas Coram. Parents – fathers and mothers – are regular contributors to this course, bringing the perspectives of different ages, backgrounds and needs.

Parental involvement in the management of the centre

Parents can also, if they wish, become involved in the management of the centre. The development of the local Sure Start programme has particularly supported them to gain the skills and confidence necessary to contribute to the planning and delivery of services. There are five parents on the governing body, one of whom is the deputy chair, and parents are represented on each of the sub-committees, chairing two of them. The parents' forum, which is organized and chaired by the parent governors, offers an opportunity for those parents who wish to get involved with the management of the centre. In order to get the views of as wide a range of parents as possible, the parents forum and others organize surveys of parents' views on key issues.

Conclusion

At Thomas Coram, we see one of our professional tasks as being to use our knowledge about what parents want and need – both individually and more generally – to work together with early years practitioners in the best interests of all. Parents' involvement with the centre will vary over time and from family to family, as will the nature of that involvement. We would argue that the opportunity to be involved, especially in their own child's learning and in the management and development of the centre, must be open to all, and that not only they, but also early years practitioners, will benefit from this partnership.

Points for discussion

❖ Are parents involved in all aspects of your setting?
❖ Are different kinds of parents equally involved, though not necessarily in the same ways?
❖ Does your setting have a policy on partnership with parents? Who has been involved in devising and developing it?

PART 3
RESEARCH

12

Effective Settings: Evidence from Research

Kathy Sylva and Helen Taylor

Chapter contents

- What is 'effectiveness' and why is it important?
- Identifying effective practice
- Observing pre-school practice associated with effectiveness
- Linking the centre characteristics in the EPPE sample settings to their children's learning
- Case studies on effective provision
- A brief summary of the effects of early childhood care and education
- Key findings at ages 5 and 7 – do the effects last?
- The impact of EPPE on policy and practice

What is 'effectiveness' and why is it important?

There are several ways to define effectiveness. One way is for practitioners to 'reflect' on their own experiences to try to come up with a set of practices they think will benefit their children. Another way is to ask experts such as inspectors or advisers what they record (often on pro formas or rating scales) about the settings which they judge, as professionals, to be particularly effective. Finally, we can think of effectiveness in terms of children's developmental outcomes; settings are effective if children thrive in them! This is the approach taken here. Settings are considered as 'effective' if their children make excellent developmental progress, much more than would be expected according to their family backgrounds or the neighbourhoods they live in. In the view taken here, the characteristics of those settings which formal assessments have shown led to successful child outcomes *are likely to be* indicators of high-quality practice. Thus, the characteristics of settings where children make great progress ('value-added gains') are those we can identify as 'quality characteristics'.

The three ways to define effectiveness – personal experience, expert judgement and measured child outcomes – are all valid, but they rest on different standards of evidence.

Effectiveness of early childhood settings, and what it is that makes them effective, is important for the development of local and national policy. Research on the effectiveness of pre-schools, using both quantitative and qualitative methods, gives a guide to the kind of practice that leads to developmental progress for children across a range of cognitive, social-behavioural and dispositional outcomes. In establishing educational effectiveness, account must be taken of children's background factors such as family socio-economic status (SES), mother's education and the ways that the parents stimulate their children at home, in order to study the effect of pre-school over and above social background. Clearly it is also necessary to take account of children's initial levels of development when establishing the 'value added' by educational experiences. This is sometimes called the baseline profile, against which progress can be measured over time.

Effectiveness research, therefore, can be pivotal in identifying effective practice, which in turn can be used to guide curriculum development, resource deployment, staff ratios, staff qualifications and ways to work with parents. An understanding of what makes an effective setting is also very important to help parents to make an informed choice about the type of pre-school setting they use. Research on the temporal patterning of pre-school attendance, how early it starts and how many days each week, will be important information for families when deciding when and where to find childcare for their child.

Identifying effective practice

The Effective Provision of Pre-school Education (EPPE) project is a major European longitudinal study which investigated the effectiveness of pre-school education and care in terms of children's development. The project has been led by the following investigators: Kathy Sylva, Edward Melhuish (Birkbeck College, University of London), Pam Sammons (University of Nottingham), Iram Siraj-Blatchford (Institute of Education, University of London) and Brenda Taggart (Institute of Education, University of London). It is an 'educational effectiveness' study of a national sample of randomly selected children aged 3–7 years old throughout England. The EPPE team collected a wide range of information on 3,000 children who were recruited at age 3+ and studied longitudinally until the end of Key Stage 1. Data were collected on children's developmental profiles (at ages 3, 4/5, 6 and 7 years), background characteristics related to their parents, the child's home learning environment and the pre-school settings the children attended. Settings (141) were drawn from a range of providers (local authority day nurseries, integrated centres, playgroups, private day nurseries, nursery schools and nursery classes). A sample of 'home' children (who had no or minimal pre-school experience) were recruited to the study at entry to school for comparison with the pre-school group. In addition to investigating the effects of pre-school provision, EPPE explored the characteristics of effective practice (and the pedagogy which underpins it) through 12 intensive case studies of settings where children had positive outcomes.

In the EPPE study, effective settings were initially found by identifying those classes in which children made the most cognitive and social-behavioural progress. After first controlling for the baseline and background factors such as parental characteristics and the home learning environment, the 'value added' to children's development by their pre-school setting could be calculated. In this way the EPPE researchers identified effective settings according to the impact they made on children's development over and above the influences of social background and developmental profile at the start of the pre-school provision.

The analyses of children's progress show that the individual pre-school centre attended by a child has an impact on cognitive progress as well as on social-behavioural development. In some centres children make significantly greater gains than in others. The effects of the unique setting a child attended, for example, the Market Road playgroup, are larger for 'emergent' literacy development than they are for early number concepts, showing that settings vary more in their provision for communication/language/literacy than they do in their work with numeracy. It may also reflect differences in the priority settings give to different types of learning goals such as those related to language and those related to mathematics. A number of settings were identified as 'outliers'– some very effective in terms of child outcomes and some less effective. Just over one in five centres (22 per cent) were found to be statistical outliers, that is, their children made more or less developmental progress than could be predicted by their attainment profiles at entry to the study and by children's social backgrounds. In a large and representative sample of children and settings in England, EPPE has shown that children's progress across a wide range of developmental outcomes can be traced to the individual pre-school centre each child attends. Moreover this has a lasting impact on children's cognitive gains as well as on their social/behavioural development (for example, the disposition to be an independent learner).

Typically centres vary in their effects on different developmental outcomes. The most common profile of a setting showed it had some strengths in one area but weaknesses in another. However, a number of centres could be distinguished with broadly positive or negative effects, demonstrating that profound and potentially transforming effects can be made on children's development in a sustained way. This gives cause for great optimism but also some grave worries. Why such different outcomes for children?

Observing pre-school practice associated with effectiveness

After identifying effective settings by looking at cognitive and social-behavioural progress made by their children, it was possible to study the practices and organization within these very effective settings. The goal was to distinguish the characteristics of the more effective settings that set them apart from the less effective ones. In other words, 'what makes them different?'

All the settings in the EPPE study were observed according to three quality 'profiles': The Early Childhood Environment Rating Scale – Revised (ECERS-R), the Early Childhood Environment Rating Scale – Extended (ECERS-E) and the Caregiver Interaction Scale (CIS). The first is a measure of quality that has been developed in the USA and is used widely in research and professional development. The ECERS-R was developed by early years practitioners and experts to create a numerical profile for rating the 'quality' of a setting across a set of sub-scales, each dedicated to a different aspect of practice. Munton et al. (1995) identified three basic dimensions that can be considered in describing the early years setting. These are the *structure* which includes both facilities and human resources; the educational and care *processes* which children experience every day; and the *outcomes* or the longer-term consequences of the education and care the child receives. The quality profiles used in EPPE attempted to capture the second in Munton's list – education and care processes that could be observed in everyday practice. The goal was to link measures of effectiveness of each setting (how much progress their children made) to its quality profiles. Did the highly effective settings appear different in terms of 'process' characteristics such as interactions, facilities, curricular balance, pedagogy or catering for diversity?

A widely used instrument for measuring ' process' characteristics of the environment is the ECERS-R (Harms et al., 1998). This measure describes the characteristics of the physical environment but, more importantly, it also rates the quality of the social and pedagogical environment which children experience. The revised ECERS-R has 43 items divided into seven sub-scales: space and furnishing, personal care routines, language and reasoning, activities, social interactions, organization and routines, adults working together. Each item is rated on a seven-point scale (1 = inadequate, 3 = minimal/adequate, 5 = good, 7 = excellent).

The word 'environment' is taken in its broadest sense to include the quality of social interactions, strategies to promote learning, and relationships between children as well as adults and children. The emphasis in the ECERS-R is very much on a balanced and 'whole child' programme. For example the sub-scale 'Organization and routine' has an item called 'Schedule' which gives high-quality ratings to a balance between adult-initiated and child-initiated activities. To score a 5 the centre must have 'a balance between structure and flexibility' but a score of 7 requires 'variations to be made in the schedule to meet individual needs, for example a child working intensively on a project should be allowed to continue past the scheduled time'.

The importance in the ECERS-R of high-quality interaction is illustrated by the many observational indicators which give high scores to the way staff engage with children, even when that is not the explicit focus of a particular item. For example, in 'Supervision of gross motor activities', a score of 7 requires that 'staff help children develop positive social interactions (for example – Help children to take turns on popular equipment; Provide equipment that encourages cooperation such as a two-person rocking boat, walkie-talkie communication devices)'. The 'Interaction' sub-scale places importance on the development of respect among the children, and supervision and discipline which are 'negotiated' rather than 'imposed'. Throughout many of the items there are criteria for scoring that take into account the role of the staff. For example, in 'Using language to develop reasoning skills' (in the 'Language-reasoning' sub-scale) a score of 5 requires that 'staff talk about logical relationships while children play with materials that stimulate reasoning' while for a 7, staff must 'encourage children to reason throughout the day, using actual events and experiences as a basis for concept development'. So, despite its title of 'Environment Rating Scale' the ECERS-R describes the processes of the educational and care environment even more than the physical space and materials on offer.

In the EPPE research the ECERS-R rating scale was supplemented by a new scale (ECERS-E or Extension; Sylva et al., 2003a). This new, supplementary scale was designed because the ECERS-R was thought to be insufficiently 'emergent' in its assessment of curricular provision for literacy and numeracy, and thus insensitive to important curricular activities conducive to children's intellectual and linguistic progress in the run-up to school. The ECERS-E was developed to extend the ECERS-R, especially in emergent literacy and numeracy, and also in science/environment and in 'diversity'. Some sample items from the ECERS-E appear as an appendix to this chapter.

The four sub-scales of the ECERS-E (literacy, maths, science/environment, diversity) are based on the *Curriculum Guidance for the Foundation Stage* (CGFS) (QCA, 2000), a document specifying national 'learning goals' (statutory curriculum objectives) and some 'stepping stones' (developmental steps children take before reaching each statutory goal). Thus, the ECERS-E is specifically designed to tap the dimensions of quality which should lead to the more 'academic' learning goals in the Guidance. For example, consider the ECERS-E literacy sub-scale item 'Sounds in words'. In it, high scores are obtained by settings where staff explicitly highlight rhyme, alliteration and syllabification in everyday activities such as nursery rhymes and clapping games. This relates closely to the early learning goals (in the CGFS curriculum) related to children's 'Linking sounds and letters'. Other examples include the ECERS-E mathematics sub-scale item 'Shape and space' which assesses the capacity of the setting to nurture children's development in the area of 'Shape, space and measures' which are part of the statutory learning goals.

Finally the diversity item 'Multicultural education' in the ECERS-E is closely linked to the early learning goals specified under 'Confidence and self-esteem' in the CGFS document.

Linking the centre characteristics in the EPPE sample settings to their children's learning

Higher quality in settings as assessed by the ECERS-E scale was positively related to children's cognitive progress in several areas: in settings that had high scores on the ECERS-E total, children made more progress in pre-reading (letters and sounds), early number concepts and non-verbal reasoning. Settings which scored high on the literacy sub-scale of the ECERS-E had children who made more progress in pre-reading and early number concepts, while the diversity sub-scale of the ECERS-E (which includes items on differentiation, observation, individual record-keeping and ability grouping) was significantly related to children making exceptional progress in pre-reading, early number concepts and non-verbal reasoning.

The pattern of results for the ECERS-R scales was somewhat different. Settings with high scores on the ECERS-R tended to have children who made good progress in social and behavioural outcomes such as co-operation and conformity rather than cognitive outcomes. For example, the social interaction sub-scale of the ECERS-R was positively related to children making good progress in their independence/concentration, co-operation/conformity and peer sociability. Overall, the ECERS-E rating scale was a much better predictor of children's intellectual and linguistic progress than was the ECERS-R. The American instrument predicted children's social development, but not their cognitive progress. To summarize, EPPE found that the ECERS-R was a sensitive assessment of those aspects of settings' quality which are associated with social progress. The ECERS-E, on the other hand, was more related to those aspects of quality which are associated with cognitive progress in young children. Clearly both are important!

A third observational measure of quality was applied to each setting. The CIS scale of adult–child interaction (Arnett, 1989) showed many effects upon children's development. In particular, the sub-scale 'Positive relationships' was related to children making greater progress in pre-reading but also on all the social outcomes except 'Anti-social/worried' behaviour. There are three sub-scales on the CIS that assess negative aspects of adult–child relationships and interaction: detachment, permissive and punitive style. All three were associated negatively with progress in pre-reading and early number concepts. (In other words, settings scoring low on detachment, permissiveness and punitiveness had children who made more cognitive progress.) Low quality scores on these negative sub-scales were related to social progress as well, for example, to children's developing co-operation and peer sociability. This is the first large-scale study in the UK to use the CIS and it has shown how adult interactions shape children's development; specifically too much permissiveness is associated with poor outcomes and positive relationships lead to cognitive as well as social progress.

Although the quality of pre-school shows a positive impact in reducing anti-social behaviour over the age of 3, there was also a weak association between very long duration of pre-school (with an early start aged under 2 years) and increases in scores on the anti-social measure in year 1. However high quality pre-school from age 3 upwards tended to reduce, but not eliminate, the raised anti-social scores associated with a very early start to day care.

Finally, children from all SES groups benefit equally from higher-quality provision, indicating that quality is vital in all SES groups; it is not something needed just by the poor. Taken together, the three observational measures (ECERS-R, ECERS-E and the CIS) demonstrate conclusively that the type and amount of developmental progress made by children in the pre-school period are positively related to quality.

When drawing together all the findings, the EPPE study showed that settings identified as 'effective' (that is, their children made more progress than expected) *also* had high-quality scores. The benefits that quality brought to children's development were similar in size for both socio-economically and educationally advantaged and disadvantaged groups alike. It is interesting, also, that boys and girls responded differently to low-quality centres, with boys' development more adversely affected than girls. For example, boys fared particularly poorly in early number concepts if they attended low-quality provision, which was not true for girls. Given that, as a group, girls made greater cognitive gains and had higher attainments at entry to pre-school in most areas, the positive impact of pre-school quality for boys' progress in early number concepts is of special interest. It suggests that raising the quality of pre-school provision may help promote boys' attainment levels and possibly reduce the gender gap.

Case studies on effective provision

The statistical analyses which identified 'effectiveness' of settings were used to single out settings that were most effective in furthering children's cognitive and social-behavioural development after taking account of background factors. Members of the EPPE team conducted qualitative case studies in 12 centres identified as being in the middle or upper range of effectiveness (Siraj-Blatchford et al., 2003). The aim of the case studies was to identify the characteristics of settings that gave children the biggest boost in their developmental outcomes, in an attempt to demonstrate in detail those aspects of pre-school practice that are most effective.

These intensive case studies provided insight into effective pre-school practice at a close-up level. The findings are reported in detail in EPPE *Technical Paper 10* (Siraj-Blatchford et al., 2003). Here, we will discuss one of the most striking findings from the case studies: the importance of 'sustained shared thinking'. Sustained shared thinking refers to an aspect of the quality of adult–child interactions, something which is tapped into by the ECERS-R and ECERS-E, although especially the latter.

The Researching Effective Pedagogy in the Early Years project (REPEY; Siraj-Blatchford et al., 2002) identified the practice most predictive of children's progress – sustained shared thinking. This is a process of cognitive construction which can only be achieved when the child is motivated and involved. In sustained shared thinking, the construction of ideas occurs through the co-operation of two or more individuals and uses the knowledge of each to extend an idea. In this way, learning is achieved through a process of co-construction, in which both parties are actively involved in working together to help clarify a concept, explain a statement, extend a narrative or solve a problem. Evidence from both REPEY and EPPE has suggested that involvement in sustained shared thinking, or what Bruner (1983; 1996) called 'joint involvement episodes' may be especially valuable in terms of child development in the early years. It is important to note, however, that this must be as part of a balance between adult- and child-initiated activity and free and directed play.

The qualitative (case studies) and quantitative (observational rating scales of quality) approaches come together in revealing the importance of joint involvement and 'sustained shared thinking' in everyday activities. Although the case studies allow deeper analysis of sustained shared thinking, discrete quality indicators in the ECERS-R and ECERS-E scales give higher scores to something resembling it. For example, in the ECERS-E item 'Talking and listening' the scoring of indicator 7.1 requires that 'adults provide scaffolding for children's conversations with them, that is, they accept and extend children's verbal contributions in conversation'. This is a good general definition of the principle of sustained shared thinking, as it requires the acceptance and extension of children's ideas.

Similarly, in the ECERS-R item on 'Supervision of gross motor activities', one of the indicators at level 7 requires that 'Staff talk with children about ideas related to their play (Ex. bring in concepts such as near-far, fast-slow for younger children; ask children to tell about building project or dramatic play)'. To satisfy this indicator, staff must engage in sustained shared thinking to help scaffold children's learning. Of course, sustained shared thinking was not the only aspect of provision that the case studies identified as being particularly effective; many others are discussed in detail in EPPE *Technical Paper 10* (Siraj-Blatchford et al., 2003).

A brief summary of the effects of early childhood care and education

This chapter has emphasized the contribution of quality to the effectiveness of early childhood settings. Other things contribute to effectiveness as well, and some of these will be summarized below so that the contribution of quality can be set in the context of other structures or processes that also matter.

Key findings at ages 5 and 7 – do the effects last?

The main effects of pre-school are present at school entry; these strong effects can be seen in the difference between school-entry profiles of the 'home' children and the pre-school group. The influence of pre-school is also demonstrated in the 'dose effect' by which the more pre-school experience a child has, the more progress they make in the period 3–5 years. However, once children enter school at reception, the pre-school children do not make more gains than the 'home' children. This suggests that the impact of pre-school operates through a stronger start to school and *not* through increased capacity to learn more in subsequent years.

Irrespective of level of disadvantage, the 'home' children (with no pre-school experience) show poorer cognitive and social-behavioural outcomes at entry to school and at the end of Key Stage 1 when compared with those who attended pre-school. They are more likely to be identified by teachers as having some form of SEN. By the end of Key Stage 1 the attainment gap was still evident for reading and mathematics, but was no longer significant for social behaviour.

Figure 12.1 shows graphically the size and continuation of pre-school effects. Other findings can be found in 'Effective Pre-school Education' (Sylva et al., 2004; see also www.dfes.gov.uk/research/data/uploadfiles/SSU_FR_2004_01.pdf).

Figure 12.1 shows the effects of pre-school versus no pre-school on children's tests of literacy and numeracy at ages 4, 6 and 7. They are expressed as effect sizes, which give a measure of the strength (or measured benefit) of attending a pre-school versus not attending a pre-school on attainment. The effects are calculated after controlling for the contribution of child, family and home learning environment factors. It can be seen that the pre-school influence is strongest for early number concepts when children start primary school (at age 4 years plus, mean age 4 years 9 months) but reduces for mathematics attainment over years 1 and 2. For pre-reading the effects are more modest, but the impact shows less decline across Key Stage 1. For social-behavioural outcomes such as peer sociability and self-regulation, the effect sizes are strong at entry to primary school but no longer significant by the end of year 2. It appears that the pre-school impact is more long-lasting for attainment in reading and mathematics than it is for social behaviour.

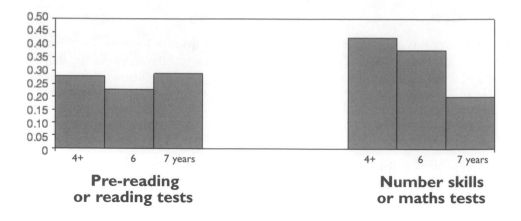

Figure 12.1 *Bar chart of the effect of home v pre-school attendance on cognitive attainment (contextualized models)*

Summary of the effects of pre-school at age 5 and 7

- *Impact of attending a pre-school – lasting effects* (Sammons et al., 2004)
  - Pre-school experience, compared to none, enhances all-round development in children.
  - The duration of attendance is important, with an earlier start being related to better intellectual development.
  - Full-time attendance led to no better gains for children than part-time provision.
  - Disadvantaged children in particular can benefit significantly from quality pre-school experiences, especially where they are with a mixture of children from different social backgrounds.
  - The beneficial effects of pre-school remained evident throughout Key Stage 1, although some outcomes were not as strong as they had been at school entry.

- *Effects of quality*
  - Pre-school quality was significantly related to children's scores on standardised tests of reading and mathematics at age 6. At age 7 the relationship between quality and academic attainment was somewhat weaker and the effect of quality on social-behavioural development was no longer significant.

- Settings that have staff with higher qualifications have higher quality scores and their children make more progress.
- Effective pedagogy includes interaction traditionally associated with the term 'teaching', the provision of instructive learning environments and 'sustained shared thinking' to extend children's learning (Siraj-Blatchford et al., 2002).

- *Does type of pre-school matter?*
  - There are significant differences between individual pre-school settings and their impact on children; some settings are more effective than others in promoting positive child outcomes.
  - Good quality can be found across all types of early years settings; however even after taking account of a child's background and prior intellectual skills, the type of pre-school a child attends has an important effect on developmental progress. The EPPE project found that integrated centres (these are centres that fully combine education with care and have a high proportion of trained teachers) and nursery schools tend to promote the strongest intellectual outcomes for children. Similarly, fully integrated settings and nursery classes tend to promote better social development even after taking account of children's backgrounds and prior social behaviour.

- *Effects of duration*
  - The number of months a child attended pre-school continued to have an effect on their progress throughout Key Stage 1, although this effect was stronger for academic skills than for social behavioural development.

- *The importance of home learning*
  - For all children, the quality of the home learning environment promotes more intellectual and social development than parental occupation or qualification. The EPPE project has shown that girls experience a richer home learning environment than boys. Do parents 'favour' their daughters or are girls just more interested than boys in learning activities at home?

The impact of EPPE on policy and practice

The EPPE project was designed as a 'policy relevant' study and it has been influential in shaping government policy (see Sylva and Pugh, 2005, for details). In less than seven years EPPE had recruited a sample of 3,000 families, constructed developmental trajectories for children between the years of 3+ and 7, and described the early years practices associated with children making a flying start to school. This large-scale longitudinal study required the contribution of six local authorities, five full-time regional officers responsible for keeping track of and assessing hundreds of children in their region, and many part-time data analysts and research assistants. The research was guided by a steering committee, selected by the DfES, which included a range of experts encompassing research, policy and practice. The EPPE project also benefited from an equally helpful consultative committee composed mainly of practitioners who ensured that the research questions/methods were related to current concerns 'on the ground'.

The case studies (Siraj-Blatchford et al., 2003) have always been a vital part in the design; they show in detail how staff teams can function effectively, how children's play can be extended and lifted to new heights of intellectual challenge, and how parents and staff can work together so that the 'learning environments' of home and pre-school are harmonized and stretched.

The impact of EPPE has been seen at four levels:

- National policy – through evidence at Parliamentary Select Committees, ministerial briefings, contributions to the Treasury Spending Reviews and evidence to teams preparing government reports and policy documents. The ten-year childcare strategy (HMT, 2004) quoted EPPE evidence in its rationale for increasing spending on early education and care and the 2005 Childcare Bill (House of Commons, 2005) used EPPE evidence that the new policies outlined in the bill will benefit families and children.
- Local authority policy – through disseminations to local officers and elected members of local authorities seeking to reconfigure their early years services. Also locally through workshops and training usually organized by the Early Years Development and Childcare Partnerships.
- Practitioners and parents – through lectures, seminars and workshops focused on practical pedagogies. The EPPE project has been reported widely in practitioner publications, for example, *Nursery World*, *Primary Practice*, and so on. One of the unanticipated impacts of EPPE has been the way it has raised awareness of rigorous methods in carrying out 'policy-sensitive research'. There is anecdotal evidence showing that people at every level of expertise are now asking 'How do you know it works?'
- Academic/research community – the EPPE project has published 12 technical papers, explicitly showing the workings out of the analyses and descriptions of the research instruments. Papers have also appeared in research journals. The EPPE project has contributed to the debate about methods for establishing the effects of education.

The EPPE project is now well known for its contribution to 'evidence-based policy' in early years education and care. Its findings are based on sound and innovative research methods. The implications for policy of the EPPE project have been spelled out clearly and are being discussed – and acted upon – at national and local level. The research is now extended in the continuation study EPPE 3–11, also funded by the DfES, to find out if the effects of early education that were so evident at ages 5 and 7 continue through to age 11. Moreover, the team will investigate the way in which educational experiences in Key Stage 2 interact with the earlier pre-school experiences in the shaping of cognitive and social-behavioural outcomes for children.

The chapter began with some definitions of effectiveness, then continued by showing how the EPPE research used an 'educational effectiveness' research design to pinpoint effective early childhood settings in a large, randomly selected sample. One of its most striking findings is that the quality of the individual settings attended by children has a measurable impact on their tested progress up to age 7. Quality was described through observational rating scales *and* through case studies. It was one of the vital ingredients that distinguished effective from ineffective settings. And it matters for all children.

Appendix 1: Example ECERS-E item 'Adult reading with the children', taken from the 'Literacy' sub-scale

Item	Inadequate 1	2	Minimal 3	4	Good 5	6	Excellent 7

Item 3. Adult reading with the children

Item	Inadequate 1	2	Minimal 3	4	Good 5	6	Excellent 7
1.1 Adults rarely read to the children. *			3.1 An adult reads with the children most days. **		5.1 Children take an active role in group reading during which the words and/or story are usually discussed.		7.1 There is discussion about print and letters as well as content.
			3.2 Children are encouraged to join in with repetitive words and phrases in the text (where appropriate).		5.2 Children are encouraged to conjecture about and comment on the text.		7.2 There is support material for the children to engage with stories by themselves, e.g. tapes, flannel board, displays, etc.
							7.3 There is evidence of one to one reading with some children.

Notes:
* Score yes if no reading with the children is seen during the observation (formal or informal, include reading with small groups or individuals).
** Score yes if you observe an adult reading with groups or individual children during the observation.

Source: Sylva et al., 2003a

Appendix 2: Example ECERS-E item 'Food preparation' taken from the 'Science/environment' sub-scale

Item	Inadequate		Minimal		Good		Excellent
	1	2	3	4	5	6	7

Item 5 Science Activities: Science processes: Food preparation

Note + In order to assess this you must have observed staff interacting with children. For higher levels, look for evidence for engagement with children in scientific processes, i.e. close observation, raising questions/making guesses (hypothesising), experimenting (see what happens) and communicating and interpreting results (why has this happened?).

Item	Inadequate (1)	Minimal (3)	Good (5)	Excellent (7)
	1.1 No preparation of food or drink is undertaken in front of the children.	3.1 Food preparation is undertaken by adults in front of the children.	5.1 Food preparation/cooking activities are provided regularly.	7.1 A variety of cooking activities in which all children may take part are provided reglarly.
		3.2 Some children can choose to participate in food preparation. But this is random, not planned in advance.	5.2 Most of the children have the opportunity to participate in food preparation.	7.2 The ingredients are attractive and the end result is edible and appreciated, e.g. eaten by children, or taken home.
		3.3 Staff discuss with the children food that has been prepared by adults, where appropriate, e.g. burnt toast or new biscuits or food brought in by children.	5.3 The staff lead discussion about the food involved and use appropriate terminology, e.g. melt, dissolve.	7.3 The staff lead and encourage discussion on the process of food preparation, such as what needs to be done to cause ingredients to set or melt.
			5.4 Children are encouraged to use more than one sense (feel, smell, taste) to explore raw ingredients.	7.4 Staff draw attention to changes in food and question children about it, e.g. what did it look like before, what does it look like now, what has happened to it?

Source: Sylva et al., 2003a

PART 4
TRAINING

13

Training and Workforce Issues in the Early Years

Sue Owen

Chapter contents

- The current context
- New reforms under Every Child Matters
- New professionals and leaders
- Conclusion: a better future?

> The next few years could turn out to see radical changes in the nature and availability of Early Years training and the professionalisation of the roles of early years workers. (Abbott and Hevey, 2001: 192–3)

When Lesley Abbott and Denise Hevey wrote this in the last edition of this book, the early years world had experienced four years of an unprecedented political interest in the provision of care and education for young children. There had been many initiatives to improve the planning of services, the number of places available for children and the quality of those places. In terms of training, Abbott and Hevey singled out the creation of a National Qualifications Framework as central to change: raising the standard of training, making qualifications clearer and making it easier for workers to progress. All these elements need to be present if early years work is to become a career which is recognized, valued by the public and attractive to high-quality applicants.

Now, four years on, we are facing even more, and more radical, changes in the field of training and qualifications. These have built on developments such as the National Qualifications Framework and the creation of Early Childhood Studies degrees and, it is to be hoped, are now being located within a nationally planned framework for services which meet the needs of children, families and the practitioners who work with them. Many of the issues which are driving change in training, qualifications and workforce organization have been covered in other chapters. They include a growing understanding, through research, of the needs of young children and their families, the continuing low status of the work and pay differentials within the sector, low levels of qualifications, high rates of turnover, the persistence of low standards in some provision, and the need to work to the government's new Every Child Matters agenda, including its vision of an integrated children's workforce. These all present challenges that need to be addressed as part of the government's current, ambitious strategy to increase both the amount and quality of provision.

In this chapter I will chart some of the developments which have led to the current situation, describe the main initiatives which are being proposed and consider how they might affect early years practice as a career.

The current context

Table 13.1 *Characteristics of the childcare workforce*

	Women %	Under 25 %	NVQ3 equivalent or above %	Hourly pay £
Childcare workers	98	41	52	5.50
Childminders	99	6*	15	N/A
Childminders in 'Children Come First' networks	98	2	51	N/A
Nursery workers	99	16	76	7.10
Playgroup workers	99	7	44	5.40
Teachers (for comparison)	72	5	97	11.07

Note: * 20–29 years.
Sources: adapted from Day Care Trust, 2004; Moss, 2004; Owen, 2005

As can be seen from Table 13.1, despite the huge changes in early years policy and the big expansion of places since 1997, some characteristics of the workforce have hardly changed at all. It is still a workforce which is overwhelmingly female and low paid, and the levels of qualifications vary considerably across the sector. Qualified teachers stand out as different in this company, a stark contrast which accounts for some of the arguments (outlined below) for moving the sector towards teacher training rather than creating a new specifically early years focused professional role. The qualifications structure for the sector is still complex, with the Qualifications and Curriculum Authority's website listing 77 qualifications on child development alone as part of the National Framework of Qualifications (QCA 2005b). No one has planned this situation, it has just evolved over the years to meet needs as they have arisen. For people who want to work with young children this has resulted in confusion over the best career path to take or, indeed, whether to see this work as a career at all.

Some of the initiatives, such as the National Framework, which were coming on stream in 2001 have developed very differently from expectations. The Framework did not lead to a smaller number of qualifications, nor to clear routes into other areas of work with children and, because training courses are not mapped, workers are still doing a lot of training which does not count towards formal qualifications. It also coexists with a long 'acceptable list' of qualifications which are not on the Framework but which are acceptable for regulatory purposes.

A more long-standing initiative, National Vocational Qualifications, has also suffered some new problems over the past five years. NVQs were brought in for all industries in 1992 as a radically different approach to qualifications, based on the existing competence of the candidate and his or her ability to demonstrate that competence in real-life situations, rather than on a course of training leading to an examination. They were designed to be rigorous qualifications in which practical competence is underpinned by knowledge and understanding, and in which candidates are mentored and assessed individually, working through the qualification at their own pace and in relation to their practice, the training courses which they take, and the support of their assessor. They are based on a set of National Occupational Standards (NOS) to ensure that all workers cover the same range and standard of knowledge and practice, and these are reviewed regularly to keep pace with changes in the sector. The NVQs are particularly well suited to workers with experience but no formal qualifications, and so they found a ready market among childcare workers, many of whom had entered the profession when their own children were young and might have done extensive training which was not related to formal qualifications.

The nature of this qualification means that qualifying can take varying lengths of time depending on the experience and knowledge of each candidate. National Vocational Qualifications were initially developed for the childcare workforce at levels 2[1] and 3 and they replaced the course-based qualifications such as the National Nursery Examination Board (NNEB). The early years sector became one of the most successful at recruiting and qualifying candidates, partly because the workforce was so ideally suited to this type of qualification (Owen and Thorpe, 1998). However critics have always argued that the model rarely happens in practice, as funding constraints have forced training providers and assessment centres to cut corners and move candidates through the qualifications too fast to ensure high-quality practice. These problems have surfaced even more frequently in the last few years as there have been cut backs in further education funding and serious problems in recruiting and retaining tutors and assessors.

In addition, although NVQs seem so ideal for the early years workforce, the funding arrangements developed nationally have discriminated against the kind of candidates who need the qualifications most. Targets set for the Learning and Skills Council (which has controlled vocational qualification funding since 2000) concentrated on young people obtaining basic skill and job qualifications at level

2 and some local authorities have found it very difficult to negotiate funding for the older, level 3, students who were needed within the expanding early years sector. During consultation exercises which the National Children's Bureau carried out for the DfES in 2004 on integrated working in children's centres, local authorities reported real concerns over the quality of NVQ candidates. Some had taken matters into their own hands and would work only with trusted training providers who were prepared to work to the local authority's own quality standards.

The level 4 NVQ, which was developed in 2000, has also suffered from setbacks and it has had little impact on the sector. This is mainly because of the creation, in 2001, of foundation degrees. These were designed to provide an accessible route into higher education for non-traditional students who, on completion, could apply to move into the later stages of a related honours degree. A sector-endorsed foundation degree was developed for early years practitioners and was launched with a generous package of support including the loan of laptop computers to students. The qualification could be studied part-time, while people continued to work, and it has been extremely popular. The direct and clear link into the traditional higher educational sector, and then, for those who want it, into teaching, makes it far more attractive than an NVQ level 4 which requires the same depth and range of study but without such an obvious payback for the effort.

Another major development in the field of higher education came with changes to early childhood studies degrees. These were first developed as a response to strong lobbying from the sector that work with young children is complex and it is vitally important, and that those who work with them should have the highest level of skills and knowledge. Most followed the pattern of other degrees in being three-year courses of study. However, many offered practice placements or allowed part-time study for workplace-based students, and all were interdisciplinary, attempting to create a body of knowledge which integrated childcare and education at degree level. As with NVQs, these degrees found a ready market both with students straight from school and more experienced practitioners, and they have grown rapidly. In 1997 there were 15 (Fawcett and Calder, 1998) and now there around 40 such degree courses in UK universities (*Nursery World* 2005). However, there was criticism that they could produce graduates with no practical experience and competence and, indeed, some job applicants with degrees found that they were losing out to candidates with level 2 or 3 NVQs which, on the face of it, are lower-level qualifications. As a result, the Early Childhood Studies Degrees Network (set up to support university staff offering these degrees) began a process of developing a nationally recognized 'practice option' which could be inserted into the degree and taken by students with no current experience of an early years setting.

A disappointment for early years qualification candidates has been the difficulty of moving into teaching. The NVQ route, early childhood studies degrees and foundation degrees have all, at one time or another, held out the promise that they would ease the path into teaching qualifications for non-graduates or those without a subject specialism, but this has not proved to be the case. The graduate teacher route is one way in which people with early years degrees can gain qualified teacher status but it is not an easy route, as they need to complete the course in nine months while employed in a school which will provide support for their work, including a day off each week. It is only recently, following the involvement of the Teacher Training Agency (now the Training and Development Agency for Schools, TDA) in the wider children's workforce debates, that there is some possibility of change.

A more positive development over the past few years has been in the effectiveness of training related to the roll out of the *Curriculum Guidance for the Foundation Stage* (QCA, 2000) to early years providers. A nationally led team of Foundation Stage advisers from the Primary National Strategy has produced exemplification materials which have been very popular and has also supported practitioners on a regional basis through nominated qualified teachers in each local authority area. These staff have supported practitioners in voluntary and private settings who draw down the nursery education grant for children aged 3 and 4, for instance, these childminders who work as part of organized networks studied in 2004–05:

> I know I work completely differently now than I did last year, more balanced across all six areas of learning.

> it makes you think about why you are doing things, about progression and planning (Networked childminders, quoted in Owen, 2005)

This type of support has encouraged many practitioners to seek out further training and qualifications

Training and qualifications for childminders has, in fact, been another area of vast improvement over the past five years. In the 2002–03 Childcare and Early Years Workforce Survey (quoted in DfES, 2005f) only 16 per cent of childminders had a level 3 qualification, the lowest rate of qualification in the childcare workforce, but the development of organized childminding networks with a requirement to work towards level 3 qualifications has changed this dramatically. In the study quoted above, over 70 per cent of networked childminders either already had a level 3 or equivalent qualification, or were working towards one. The ability to access training and qualifications was the most frequently mentioned positive aspect of networks, and childminders highlighted the following factors which had impacted on their ability to take this training:

- funding so that it was free or cheap
- accessibility in terms of the days and hours on which it was offered
- appropriateness, that is, having it run by people who understood childminding practice

- planning – customizing training packages for individual needs
- peer support – providing training as part of a network means that childminders can take it as part of a supportive group within a culture of learning and change.

Undoubtedly, all these factors will also be true for other groups of early years workers and these active strategies have a transformative effect; just making training courses available is not enough, they need to be accessible, affordable and required. In other words, training needs to be delivered in the same way as it has traditionally been provided for the maintained sector.

New reforms under Every Child Matters

So the latest developments in training and qualifications have had a mixed effect on the sector, but overall it has been the uncertainty of the last few years which has been the main problem for employers and service managers in voluntary organizations and local authorities. Reforms have been piecemeal and the structures set up to deliver them have sometimes been short-lived. The government created the Every Child Matters agenda in 2003 (DfES, 2004c) as a new approach which would integrate all work done with children and families on a continuum from universal services for all children to targeted work with the most vulnerable.

The Treasury led on the introduction of a ten-year childcare strategy (HMT, 2004), underpinned by new legislation and, most importantly for this discussion, a workforce strategy to address the problems of the children's workforce as a whole. This included commitments that, in the long term, all managers of full day-care settings will be graduates, bringing business and management as well as professional competence[2] and that there will be support for more early years workers, including childminders, to gain level 3 qualifications. However, this was all within a context of uncertainty. The national training organizations were being disbanded in favour of sector skills councils (but one had not been identified for the children's sector), the National Occupational Standards for early years and childcare had been reviewed (but their status was unclear in light of the creation of a more integrated workforce crossing age groups), and the problems with the National Qualifications Framework have been mentioned above. This was an untenable situation for a low-wage sector in which staff often invest their own time and money in professional development.

However, there was no confusion over the important role of training and qualifications:

> The single biggest fact that determines the quality of childcare is the workforce. The current childcare workforce includes many capable and dedicated people. However … qualification levels are generally low … if the system is to develop into one that is among the best quality in the world, a step-change is needed in

the quality and stability of the workforce. Working with pre-school children should have as much status as a profession as teaching children in schools. (HMT, 2004: 44–5)

We have now entered a period in which the government is attempting to rationalize the situation rather than simply adding extra layers of reforms. In essence, the ten-year childcare strategy is designed to rationalize, redesign and re-badge the existing early years initiatives so that they fit within the Every Child Matters framework and become a coherent strategy for improving the quality of services. There are seen to be three components to this quality initiative: a better qualified workforce, a single quality framework from birth to 5 (the Early Years Foundation Stage Framework) and a new registration and inspection framework under Ofsted.

A missing element is that of continuous quality improvement within individual settings, the type of process typically undertaken through quality assurance (QA) schemes. As part of the consultation process for the ten-year strategy and the 2005 Childcare Bill (its underpinning legislation) the DfES suggested abandoning its own kitemark for QA schemes, Investors in Children (IiC), on the grounds that the three elements mentioned above would suffice to improve quality in settings (DfES, 2005a). The response to the Childcare Bill Consultation (Sure Start, Extended Schools and Families Group, 2005) showed great concern over this on the part of the early years sector and the national network for QA scheme managers offered to take over the operation of this benchmarking system from the DfES and also to run a much higher profile publicity campaign on continuous quality improvement. It was argued that QA has been a big driver for improved training and qualifications and for a general improvement in the morale and status of the workforce, but that there has been disappointment at the low level of publicity about it to parents. It was also felt that QA should be knitted into the other workforce initiatives so that practitioners do not see it as an additional responsibility but as something which is a building block in their own and their setting's development. For instance, the standards set as part of the IiC endorsement process should be clearly signposted within the Early Years Foundation Stage Framework, should be mapped against elements in the Ofsted framework and should count towards units of qualifications on the Integrated Qualifications Framework.

This type of rationalization is consistent with the approach of the Every Child Matters agenda. *Every Child Matters: Next Steps* (DfES, 2004c) announced a consultation document on a pay and workforce strategy which would begin to rationalize the situation for the children's workforce as a whole. The document did, however, place a great deal of emphasis on the early years workforce as being key to the Every Child Matters reforms and as being particularly in need of change. A federated sector Skills Council for Social Care, Children and Young People (SSC) was announced, to cover the whole of the UK and all staff working in social care and with children. A Children, Young People and Families Work-force Development Council (CWDC) would represent England on both this UK SSC and on a UK Children's Workforce Network which would bring together the SSCs for other sectors such as playwork, health and the school-based workforce. The CWDC has a strong representation from the early years sector which comprises over half its workforce (see Figure 13.1).

This appears to be a complicated structure, but it is designed to deal with a complicated situation. There are numerous agencies representing different work-force and employer interests in different ways in different countries of the UK and in the short term a structure was needed which would allow all these inter-ests to meet together on a basis of equality and to move, in the long term, towards a more rational and planned approach to the new integrated children's workforce without alienating existing representative organizations.

The consultation on the workforce strategy took place over the spring and summer of 2005 and included a number of face to face consultation events with the early years sector as well as written responses. Before the consultation docu-ment was published the word 'pay' was quietly dropped from the title of the strategy and Jane Haywood, the Chief Executive of the CWDC, stressed that improvements in this would have to evolve over time: 'the CWDC will have no control over this. So Haywood's strategy is to work instead on training and qualifications to produce a highly trained and skilled workforce so they will have "a much stronger argument for better pay"' (Miller, 2005: 15).

At the time of writing the final shape of the workforce reform has not been decided but it is expected that an 'early years professional' role will be created for the sector, at graduate level, and that local authorities and individual settings will be supported to move staff as quickly as possible into these qualifications via a Transformation Fund of £125 million per year.

The Early Years National Occupational Standards have just been reviewed but the CWDC now has a brief to review all the NOSs for the children's workforce in order to integrate them in readiness for the development of new qualifica-tions and a new national qualifications framework, which will be called the Integrated Qualifications Framework because it will cover the whole of the chil-dren's workforce and will offer clearer progression routes which link specific qualifications to job roles. The Framework will probably be built up from common units related to the *Common Core of Skills and Knowledge for the Chil-dren's Workforce* which was published in 2005. These are designed to provide a basic minimum of skills and knowledge for anyone working with children and young people around six areas of expertise:

- effective communication and engagement
- child and young person development
- safeguarding and promoting the welfare of the child
- supporting transitions

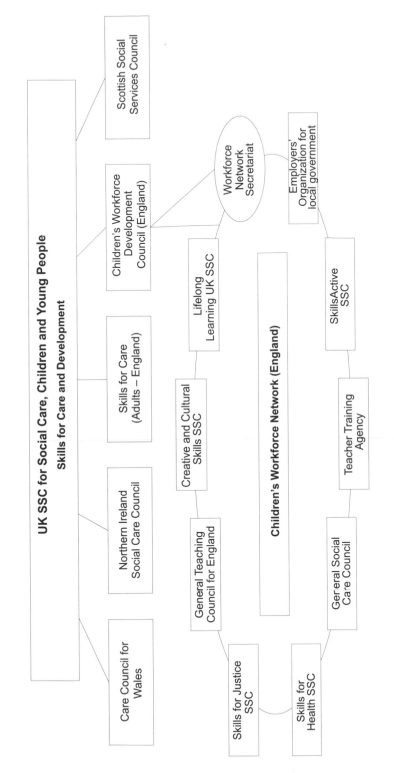

Figure 13.1 *Proposed structure for the new Sector Skills Council which covers the children's workforce (DfES, 2005g: 14)*

- multi-agency working
- sharing information (DfES, 2005f: 4).

Qualified early years workers would have no difficulty in covering such a core as these areas are already included within early years training and qualifications. However, the *Common Core* does provide one more tool for integrating the sector and facilitating smoother transitions for workers between various job roles.

In November 2005 the CWDC announced its priorities for the coming year which included the above reviews alongside the development of the early years professional role, supporting local authorities to develop local workforce strategies, and working to increase the recruitment of children's social workers and foster carers. They also have the brief to develop a clear action plan arising from the responses to the Children's Workforce Strategy. These are all reforms which are long overdue and have been welcomed by the early years sector, even if the detail has been slow to emerge.

New professionals and leaders

One of the aspects which has occasioned great debate has been the title and job role for the new early years 'professional'. In a paper for the Day Care Trust in 2004 Claire Cameron described the role taken by 'social pedagogues' in Scandinavian countries and used this as a model for what is needed in an integrated workforce in the UK: 'The essential point is to lift working with children out of a series of task-based occupations and towards the idea of a critical thinking, creative, team working professional' (Cameron, 2004: 19).

Social pedagogues have a graduate level training which enables them to work across all age groups, including adults, but also to specialize. This, or a similar training focused only on children, is a model which has been proposed for the UK and was one of the options put forward by the government in the Children's Workforce Strategy consultation paper. The other was an 'early years qualified teacher', a practitioner with a basis of traditional teacher training but with additional elements of child development and integrated work practices with children from birth onwards. There were strong lobbies around both these options. The government-funded longitudinal study on Effective Practice in Pre-school Education (EPPE) showed that the intervention of a trained teacher made a significant difference to children's later school attainment across a range of measures (Sylva et al., 2004). However, EPPE researchers were only in a position to look at the work of traditionally trained teachers because they comprised 95 per cent of the graduate-level practitioners in the study and they did not have data for people who had obtained level 5 qualifications through other routes such as Early Childhood Studies degrees. It has been argued that further work is needed if we are to have real evidence for the effectiveness of different types of graduate level training within a delivery model centred on integrated care and education. However, the impact on child outcomes was not the only argument put forward in favour of the teacher model, others felt strongly that a new early years profession should be based on the status and pay levels accruing to teachers rather than on the widely criticized pay and conditions of other workers in the sector. This is a strategy which is being adopted in New Zealand with the aim of improving the status and pay of early childhood staff as well as the quality of provision for children.

Critics of this approach argue that it devalues the contribution of other graduates, could lower the morale and, therefore, the confidence and effectiveness of other workers, and that it is both financially unrealistic and socially undesirable to move towards a wholly graduate profession. In seminars which the National Children's Bureau organized as part of the Children's Workforce Strategy consultation, the term 'professional' was generally more popular than pedagogue, and felt to be less contentious and easier to understand. It also has the advantage of being able to be used at all levels from school leaver to graduate as long as the profession as a whole is coherent with clear standards and principles and with recognized qualificatory routes.

Finally, among these reforms is the important issue of leadership within this new workforce. The ten-year childcare strategy committed to graduate-level leadership for all full day-care settings as a first step in a better qualified workforce, and it is undoubtedly true that the leadership of multi-agency teams, together with an understanding of how young children's learning can be supported through all the activities of a childcare setting, is a skilled and demanding job. In 2004 a new National Professional Qualification in Integrated Centre Leadership (NPQICL) was piloted by the National College for School Leadership in partnership with the Pen Green Research, Training and Development Centre. Forty students graduated from this course in October 2005 and it was then opened up for delivery by other universities and colleges around the country. Four hundred other senior staff were then able to take up places, thus offering the potential to create a cadre of highly and specifically qualified leaders, drawn from education, social care, early years and health backgrounds, to take forward the vision of the new integrated children's workforce. However, there will need to be effective links between this and the National Professional Qualification for Headship if the early years strand of this workforce is to flourish on a basis of equality with other specialisms. Only with raised status, pay and esteem will we be able to recruit and retain workers who can provide the highest standards for young children and their families.

Conclusion: a better future?

The new initiatives outlined above, twinned with the developments which have already taken place, promise a better future for the early years workforce and, consequently, a better future for children. Because early years work relies on the development of strong and respectful relationships, this is a profession in which the quality of the outcomes can be directly tied to the quality of the people working within them. The importance of relationships also means that only so much can be effected through changes in structures, it is also vital that we decide what we want for young children in any setting and any community. It is then possible to support practitioners to reflect on their work and develop relationships based on deep knowledge of the children and families they work with. This is why the inclusion of quality improvement processes within the government's new structures and links between them and qualifications is so vital. Getting better at your job should be a way of life, not just the result of a training course.

Points for discussion

❖ Should early years continue to be a specialism in its own right within an integrated children's workforce and, if so, how would this work?
❖ Consider some of the ways in which quality assurance schemes or other quality improvement processes could be linked directly into the qualifications structure.
❖ List the advantages and disadvantages of developing a 'new teacher' as opposed to a 'pedagogue' model as the new early years professional role.

Notes

1 The most basic NVQ level (level 1) was considered inappropriate for anyone working with young children and so the basic qualification is at level 2, at which level practitioners are expected to be working under supervision.
2 'Competence' is defined as knowledge plus skills.

References

Abbott, L. and Hevey, D. (2001) 'Training to work in the early years: developing the climbing frame', in G. Pugh (ed.), *Contemporary Issues in the Early Years: Working Collaboratively for Children.* 3rd edition. London: Sage. pp. 179–93.

Abbott, L. and Langston, A. (2005) *Birth to Three Matters: Supporting the Framework of Effective Practice.* Maidenhead and New York: Open University Press.

Abbott, L. and Moylett, H. (eds) (1997) *Working with the Under-Threes: Training and Professional Development.* Buckingham: Open University Press.

Abbott, L. and Nutbrown, C. (eds) (2001) *Experiencing Reggio Emilia: Implications for Preschool Provision.* Milton Keynes: Open University Press.

Adams, S., Alexander, E., Drummond, M.J. and Moyles, J. (2004) *Inside the Foundation Stage: Recreating the Reception Year.* London: ATL.

Alderson, P. (2000) *Young Children's Rights: Exploring Beliefs, Principles and Practice.* London: Jessica Kingsley/Save the Children.

Anning, A. (2005) 'Investigating the impact of working in multi-agency service delivery settings in the UK on early years practitioners' beliefs and practices', *Journal of Early Childhood* Research, 3(1): 19–50.

Arnett, J. (1989), 'Caregivers in day-care centres: does training matter?', *Journal of Applied Developmental Psychology*, 10: 541–52.

Athey, C. (1990) *Extending Thought in Young Children: A Parent–Teacher Partnership.* London: Paul Chapman Publishing.

Audit Commission (1996) *Counting to Five.* London: Audit Commission.

Aynsley-Green, A. (2004) 'Change for children: how can current government policy be implemented to improve the lives and health of children and young people?', paper presented at Coram Family's Annual Lecture, London.

Bailey, D. and Hall, S. (1992) *Critical Decade: Black British Photography in the 80s.* Ten-8 2,3

Ball, C. (1994) *Start Right: The Importance of Early Learning.* London: Royal Society of Arts.

Ball, S.J. and Vincent, C. (2005) 'The "childcare champion"? New Labour, social justice and the childcare market', *British Journal of Educational* Research, 31(5): 557–70.

Barnardo's (1998) *Attitudes towards Parenting.* London: National Opinion Polls.

Bennett, J. (2003) 'The persistent division between care and education', *Journal of Early Childhood Research*, 1(1): 21–48.

Bennett, J. (2004) 'Curriculum issues in national policy making', keynote address at the EECERA Conference, Malta, 2 September.

BERA Early Years Special Interest Group (EYSIG) (2003) *Early Years Research: Pedagogy, Curriculum and Adult Roles, Training and Professionalism*. Southwell: BERA.

Bergman, M. (1993) 'Early childhood care and education in Sweden', in T. David (ed.), *Educational Provision for our Youngest Children*. London: Paul Chapman Publishing. pp.112–32.

Bertram, T., Pascal, C., Bokari, S., Casper, M. and Holterman, S. (2002) *Early Excellence Centre Pilot Programme: Second Evaluation Report 2000–2001*. DfES Research Report RR361. London: HMSO.

Beveridge, S. (2005) *Children, Families and Schools, Developing Partnerships for Inclusive Education*. London: Routledge/Falmer.

Bion, W. (1962) *Learning from Experience*. London: Heinemann.

Blakemore, C. (2001) 'Early learning and the brain', Royal Society of Arts lecture, 4 February.

Bowlby, J. (1988) *A Secure Base*. London: Routledge.

Bronfenbrenner, U. (1979) *The Ecology of Human Development*. Cambridge, MA: Harvard University Press.

Brooker, E. (2004) Summary of lessons learned from evaluations of work with parents in Coram Parents Centre (unpublished).

Brown, J.S. and Duguid, P. (2000) *The Social Life of Information*. Boston, MA: Harvard Business School Press.

Bruner, J. (1983) *Child's Talk: Learning to Use Language*. New York: W.W. Norton.

Bruner, J. (1996) *The Culture of Education*. Cambridge, MA: Harvard University Press.

Butt, J. and Box, L. (1998) *Family Centred – a Study of the Use of Family Centres by Black Families*. London: Race Equality Unit.

Caldwell, B.M. (1989) 'All day kindergarten – assumptions, precautions, ... and over-generalisations', *Early Childhood Research* Quarterly, 4: 261–6.

Cameron, C. (2004) *Building an Integrated Workforce for a Long-Term Vision of Universal Early Education and Care*. London: Day Care Trust.

Campell-Barr, V. (2005) 'The economy of childcare', unpublished thesis submitted to CCCU/UKC, Canterbury.

Carpenter, B. and Egerton, J. (eds) (2005) *Early Childhood Intervention: International Perspectives, National Initiatives and Regional Practices*. West Midlands: SEN Regional Partnership Publication.

Claxton, G. (2005) 'Learning to learn: a key goal in the 21st century curriculum', in *Futures; Meeting the Challenge – a Curriculum for the Future*. London: QCA.

Cohen, B., Moss, P., Petrie, P. and Wallace, J. (2004) *A New Deal for Children?* Bristol: Policy Press.

Critchley, D. (2002) 'Children's assessment of their own learning', in C. Nutbrown (ed.), *Research Studies in Early Childhood Education*. Stoke-on-Trent: Trentham Books.

Dahlberg, G., Moss, P. and Pence, A. (1999) *Beyond Quality in Early Childhood Education and Care: Postmodern Perspectives*. London: Falmer Press.

David, T. (1990) *Under Five – Under-educated?* Milton Keynes: Open University Press.

David, T. and Powell, S. (2005) 'Play in the early years: the influence of cultural difference', in J. Moyles (ed.), *The Excellence of Play*. Maidenhead: Open University Press and McGraw-Hill. pp. 242–54.

David, T., Raban, B., Ure, C., Goouch, K., Barrière, I. and Lambirth, A. (2000) *Making Sense of Early Literacy: A Practitioner's Perspective*. Stoke-on-Trent: Trentham Books.

Day Care Trust (2004) 'A new era for universal childcare?', www.daycare.trust.org.uk.

Delfos, M.F. (2001) *Are You Listening to Me? Communicating with Children from Four to Twelve Years Old*. Amsterdam: SWP.

Department for Education and Employment (DfEE) (1994) *Special Educational Needs Code of Practice*. London: HMSO.

Department for Education and Employment (DfEE) (1998a) *Meeting the Childcare Challenge*. London: HMSO.

Department for Education and Employment (DfEE) (1998b) *Meeting Special Educational Needs: a Programme of Action*. London: HMSO.

Department for Education and Skills (DfES) (2000) *National Standards for Under Eights Day Care and Childminding*. London: DfES.

Department for Education and Skills (DfES) (2001) *Special Educational Needs Code of Practice*. London: DfES.

Department for Education and Skills (DfES) (2002) *Birth to Three Matters – a Framework to Support Children in their Earliest Years*. London: DfES.

Department for Education and Skills (DfES) (2003a) *Birth to Three Matters*. London: HMSO.

Department for Education and Skills (DfES) (2003b) *Every Child Matters*. Green Paper. London: The Stationery Office.

Department for Education and Skills (DfES) (2003c) *National Standards for Under Eights Day Care and Childminding*. London: DfES.

Department for Education and Skills (DfES) (2003d) *Sure Start Children's Centre Start up Guidance*. London: Sure Start Unit.

Department for Education and Skills (DfES) (2004) *The Key Aspects of Development and Learning*. London: DfES.

Department for Education and Skills (DfES) (2004a) *Removing Barriers to Achievement: The Government's Strategy for SEN*. Nottingham: DfES Publications.

Department for Education and Skills (DfES) (2004b) *Every Child Matters: Change for Children*. Nottingham: DfES Publications

Department for Education and Skills (DfES) (2004c) *Every Child Matters: Next Steps*. London: DfES, www.everychildmatters.gov.uk, accessed 10 October 2005.

Department for Education and Skills (DfES) (2004d) *Sure Start Guidance 2004–2006* (SS Guidance 0406). London: DfES.

Department for Education and Skills (DfES) (2005a) *Childcare Bill Consultation. Consultation on Legislative Proposals for the Future of Childcare and Early Years Provision in England: Implementing the Ten Year Strategy for Childcare*. London: DfES.

Department for Education and Skills (DfES) (2005b) *Extended Schools: Access to Opportunities and Services for All, Prospectus*. London: DfES.

Department for Education and Skills (DfES) (2005c) 'Multi agency toolkit' www.everychildmatters.gov.uk/deliveringservices/multiagencyworking/teamtoolkit

Department for Education and Skills (DfES) (2005d) *Children Act 2004: Guidance on the Duty to Cooperate*. London: DfES.

Department for Education and Skills (DfES) (2005e) *Common Core of Skills and Knowledge for the Children's Workforce*. London: DfES.

Department for Education and Skills (DfES) (2005f) *Children's Workforce Strategy, Consultation Paper*. London: DfES.

Department for Education and Skills (DfES) (2005g) *Youth Matters*. Green Paper. London: The Stationery Office.

Department for Education and Skills (DfES) (2005h) *A Sure Start Children's Centre for Every Community, Phase 2 Planning Guidance (2006–9)*. London: DfES.

Department for Education and Skills (DfES) (2005i) *Consultation on the Draft Code of Practice on Funding Early Education*. London: DfES.

Department for Education and Skills (DfES) (2005j) *Sure Start Children's Centres Start Up Guidance*. London: DfES.

Department for Education and Skills/Qualifications and Curriculum Authority (DfES/QCA) (2003) *Foundation Stage Profile Handbook*. London: QCA.

Department of Education and Science (DES) (1990) *Starting with Quality: Report of the Committee of Enquiry into the Quality of Education Experience Offered to Three and Four Year Olds* (Rumbold Report). London: HMSO.

Department of Education and Science (DES) (1998) *Education for Citizenship and the Teaching of Democracy in Schools* (Crick Report). London: QCA.

Department of Health and Department for Education and Skills (DH and DfES) (2004) *National Service Framework for Children, Young People and Maternity Services*. London: DH Publications.

Desforges, C. and Abouchaar, A. (2003) *The Impact of Parent Involvement, Parent Support and Family Education on Pupil Achievement and Adjustment: A Literature Review*. Research Report 433. London: DfES Publications.

Diamond, M. and Hopson, J. (1998) *Magic Trees of the Mind*. New York: Datton.

Donaldson, M. (1983) *Children's Minds*. Glasgow: Fontana/Collins.

Drummond, M.J., Rouse, D. and Pugh, G. (eds) (1992) *Making Assessment Work*. London: NES Arnold and National Children's Bureau. Maidenhead and New York: Open University Press.

Duffy, B. (2006) *Supporting Creativity and Imagination in the Early Years*. Buckinghamshire: Open University Press.

Dunn, J. (1987) 'Understanding feelings: the early stages', in J. Bruner and H. Haste (eds), *Making Sense: The Child's Construction of the World*. London: Routledge. pp. 26–40.

Dweck, C.S. and Leggett, E. (1988) 'A social-cognitive approach to motivation and personality', *Psychological Review*, 95(2): 256–73.

Easen, P., Kendall, P. and Shaw, J. (1992) 'Parents and educators: dialogue and development through partnership', *Children & Society* 6(4): 282–96.

Edwards, R. (2002) *Children, Home and School*. London: Routledge.

Eisner, E. (1992) 'Objectivity in educational research', *Curriculum Inquiry*, 22(1): 9–15.

Elfer, P., Goldschmied, E. and Selleck, D. (2003) *Key Persons in Nurseries: Building Relationships for Quality Provision*. London: Early Years Network.

Emmerling, L. (2003) *Pollock*. London: Taschen.

Evangelou, M. and Sylva, K. (2003) *The Effects of the Peers Early Education Partnership (PEEP) on Children's Developmental Progress*. London: DfES.

Fawcett, M. and Calder, P. (1998) 'Early Childhood Studies degrees', in L. Abbott and

G. Pugh (eds), *Training to Work in the Early Years: Developing the Climbing Frame*. Buckingham: Open University Press.

Filippini, T. and Cecchi, V. (1996) (eds) *The Hundred Languages of Children: The Exhibit*. Reggio Emilia: Reggio Children.

Flouri, E. and Buchanan, A. (2004) 'Early father's and mother's involvement and child's later educational outcomes', *British Journal of Educational Psychology*, 74: 141–53.

Folque, M., and Siraj-Blatchford, I. (2003) 'Children and pedagogues learning together in the early years: the collaborative process of the Portuguese MEM pedagogy', European Early Childhood Educational Research Association Conference, 3–6 September, University of Strathclyde.

Formosinho, J. (2003) 'Transformational leadership in early childhood centres', conference paper, Pen Green Centre, Corby.

Freire, A. and Macedo, D. (eds) (1998) *The Paolo Freire Reader*. New York: Continuum.

Freire, P. (1970) *Pedagogy of the Oppressed*. Harmondsworth: Penguin.

Fullan, M. (2001) *Leading in a Culture of Change*. San Francisco, CA: Jossey-Bass.

Gerhardt, S. (2004) *Why Love Matters: How Affection Shapes a Baby's Brain*. London: Brunner-Routledge

Ghate, D. and Hazel, N. (2001) *Parenting in Poor Environments: Stress, Support and Coping*. London: Policy Research Bureau.

Gillborn, D. and Gipps, C. (1997) *Recent Research on the Achievements of Minority Ethnic Pupils*. London: HMSO.

Glass, N. (1999) 'Sure Start: the development of an early intervention programme for young children in the UK', *Children* & Society, 13(4): 257–65.

Goldschmied, E. (1989) *Infants at Work: The Treasure Basket Explained*. National Children's Bureau, 8 Wakley Street, London EC1V 7QE.

Goldschmied, E. and Jackson, S. (2004) *People Under Three: Young Children in Day Care*. 2nd edition. London: Routledge.

Gopnik, A., Metfzoff, A. and Kuhl, P. (2001) *How Babies Think*. London: Phoenix.

Goutard, M. (1993) 'Preschool education in France', in T. David (ed.), *Educational Provision for our Youngest Children*. London: Paul Chapman Publishing. pp. 35–55.

Grossberg, L. (1994) 'Introduction: Bringing it all Back Home – Pedagogy and Cultural Studies' in Giroux and McLaren (eds), *Between Borders: Pedagogy and the Politics of Cultural Studies*. London: Routledge.

Guba, E. and Lincoln, Y. (1989) *Fourth Generation Evaluation*. London: Sage.

Hall, S. (1992) 'Race, culture and communications: looking backward and forward in cultural studies', *Rethinking Marxism*, 5: 10–18.

Hallgarten, J. (2000) *Parents Exist OK – Issues and Visions for Parent-School Relations*. London: Institute for Public Policy Research.

Handy, C. (1994) *The Empty Raincoat: New Thinking for a New World*. Reading: Arrow Books.

Hardy, T. (1891, republished 1983) *Tess of the D'Urbervilles*. Harmondsworth: Penguin.

Harms, T., Clifford, M. and Cryer, D. (1998) *Early Childhood Environment Rating Scale, Revised Edition (ECERS-R)*. New York: Teachers College Press.

Hartley, D. (1993) *Understanding the Nursery School: A Sociological Analysis*. London: Cassell.

Pg 154

Henry, M. (1996) *Young Children, Parents and Professionals*. London: Routledge.

Her Majesty's Inspectorate (HMI) (2002) Inspection Report, Randolph Beresford Early Years Centre, Ofsted.

Her Majesty's Inspectorate (HMI) (2004) Inspection Report, Everton Early Childhood Centre, Ofsted.

Her Majesty's Inspectorate (HMI) (2004) *Children at the Centre: an Evaluation of Early Excellence Centres*. London: Ofsted.

HM Treasury (HMT) (2004) *Choice for Parents, the Best Start for Children: A Ten Year Strategy for Childcare*. London: The Stationery Office.

Home Office (1998) *Supporting Families*. Green Paper. London: HMSO.

House of Commons (2005) *Childcare Bill*. London: The Stationery Office.

House of Commons Education Select Committee (2005) *Every Child Matters: 9th Report of Session 2004–5*.

Isaacs, S. (1929) *The Nursery Years*. London: Routledge and Kegan Paul.

James, A. and Prout, A. (1990) 'Contemporary issues in the sociological study of childhood', in A. James and A. Prout (eds), *Constructing and Reconstructing Childhood*. London: Falmer Press.

Johnson, M.C. (2000) 'The view from the Wuro', in J. DeLoache and A. Gottleib (eds), *A World of Babies*. Cambridge: Cambridge University Press. pp. 171–98.

Kagan, S.L. (2004) 'Key elements of quality oriented policy for the Early Years', keynote address, International Convention of the Free University of Bolzano, Bressanone, Italy, 14–16 June.

Keating, D.P. and Mustard, F.J. (1993) 'Social economic factors and human development', in D. Ross (ed.), *Family Security in Insecure Times*. Ottawa: National Forum on Family Security. pp. 87–105.

Kelly, A.V. (2004) *The Curriculum Theory and Practice*. London, Thousand Oaks, CA, and New Delhi: Sage.

Konner, M. (1991) *Childhood*. London: Little Brown.

Ladson-Billings, G. and Gillborn, D. (2004) *The Routledge Falmer Reader in Multicultural Education*. London: RoutledgeFalmer.

Laming, Lord (2003) Presentation at Coram Family's Annual Lecture, London.

Lancaster Y.P. (2003) 'Promoting Listening to Young Children: the reader', in Y.P. Lancaster and V. Broadbent (eds), *Listening to Young Children*. Maidenhead: Open University Press.

Lancaster Y.P. (2004) 'Listening to Young Children: promoting the "voices" of children under the age of eight', in the Rt Hon. Lord Justice Thorpe and Justine Cadbury (eds), *Hearing the Children*. Bristol: Jordan.

Lancaster Y.P. and Broadbent V. (2003) *Listening to Young Children*. Maidenhead: Open University Press.

Lansdown, G. (2001) *Promoting Children's Participation in Democratic Decision-making*. Florence: UNICEF.

Lansdown, G. (2005a) 'Can you hear me? The right of young children to participate in decisions affecting them', working paper in Early Childhood Development, Bernard Van Leer Foundation, The Hague.

Lansdown, G. (2005b) *The Evolving Capacities of the Child*. Florence: UNICEF and Save the Children.

Lansdown, G. and Lancaster Y.P. (2001) 'Promoting children's welfare by respecting their rights', in G. Pugh (ed.) *Contemporary Issues in the Early Years: Working Collaboratively for Children*. 3rd edition. London: Paul Chapman Publishing.

Learner, S. (2005) 'Sure Start for all of us', *Children Now*, 16–22 March, 22–3.

Leseman, P. (2003) *Early Childhood Education and Care for Children from Low Income or Minority Backgrounds*. Paris: OECD.

Lifelong Learning UK (2005) *National Occupational Standards for Work with Parents*. London: Lifelong Learning UK.

Lloyd, B. (1987) 'Social representations of gender', in J. Bruner and H. Haste (eds), *Making Sense: The Child's Construction of the World*. London: Routledge. pp. 147–62.

London Borough of Camden (2004) *The Shortage of Under Fives Childcare in Camden*. London: LBC.

Lubeck, S. (1986) *Sandbox Society*. Lewes: Falmer Press.

Macdonald, G. and Roberts, H. (1995) *What Works in The Early Years? Effective Intervention for Children and their Families in Health, Social Welfare, Education and Child Protection*. Barkingside: Barnardo's.

MacPherson, W. (1999) *Report of the Stephen Lawrence Enquiry*. London: HMSO.

Makins, V (1997) *Not Just a Nursery: Multi-Agency Early Years Centres in Action*. London: National Children's Bureau.

Malaguzzi, L. (1993) 'History, ideas and basic philosophy', in E. Edwards, L. Gandini and G. Forman (eds), *The Hundred Languages of Children* – the *Reggio Emilia Approach to Early Childhood Education*. Greenwich, CT: Ablex.

Matthews, P. and Sammons, P. (2004), *Improvement through Inspection*. London: Ofsted and the Institute of Education, University of London.

McNeish, D., Newman, T. and Roberts, H. (eds)(2002) *What Works for Children? Effective Services for Children and Families*. Buckingham: Open University Press.

Melhuish, E., Sylva, K., Sammons, P., Siraj-Blatchford, I. and Taggart, B. (2001) *The Effective Provision of Pre-school Education (EPPE) Project: Technical Paper 7 – Social/Behavioural and Cognitive Development at 3–4 Years in Relation to Family Background*. London: DfEE and Institute of Education, University of London.

Miller, A. (2005) 'Feeling the force' (interview with Jane Haywood), *0–19*, November.

Moran, P., Ghate, D. and van der Merwe, A. (2004) *What Works in Parenting Support? A Review of the International Evidence*. Research Report 574. London: DfES Publications.

Moriarty, V. and Siraj-Blatchford, I. (1998) *An Introduction to Curriculum for 3 to 5 Year-olds*. Nottingham: Education Now Books.

Moss, P. (1997) 'Transforming nursery education – or more of the same', conference paper, Pen Green Centre, Corby.

Moss, P. (2004) 'Why we need a well qualified early childhood workforce', Power-Point presentation.

Munton, A., Mooney, A. and Rowland, L. (1995) 'Deconstructing quality: a conceptual framework for the new paradigm in day care provision for the under eights', *Early Child Development and Care*, 144: 11–23.

Mustard, F.J. (2002) *Early Childhood Development: Investing in the Future*. Washington, DC: World Bank.

National Audit Office (NAO) (2004) *Early Years: Progress in Developing High Quality Childcare and Early Education Accessible to All*. London: HMSO.

National Children's Bureau (2004) Spotlight briefing, March.

National Commission on Education (1993) *Learning to Succeed*. London: Heinemann.

National Institute of Child Health and Human Development (NICHD) (1997) *Mother–Child Interaction and Cognitive Outcomes Associated with Early Childhood Care: Results of the NICHD Study*. Society for Research in Child Development Meeting Symposium, Washington.

NESS (2005) *Early Impacts of Sure Start Local Programmes on Children and Families*. National Evaluation Report 013, Nottingham: DfES Publications.

Neuman, M. (2005) 'Governance of early childhood education and care: recent developments in OECD countries', *Early Years*, 25(2): 129–42.

Nursery World (2005) 'Honours degrees', training supplement, Summer.

Nutbrown, C. (1997) *Recognising Early Literacy Development: Assessing Children's Achievements*. London: Paul Chapman Publishing.

Nutbrown, C. (1998) *The Lore and Language of Early Education*. Sheffield: USDE.

Nutbrown, C. (1999) *Threads of Thinking: Young Children Learning and the Role of Early Education* (2nd edition). London: Sage.

Nutbrown, C. (2005) *Key Concepts in Early Childhood Education and Care*. London: Sage.

Nutbrown, C. (2006) *Threads of Thinking: Young Children Learning and the Role of Early Education*. London: Paul Chapman Publishing.

Nutbrown, C. (ed.) (1996) *Respectful Educators, Capable Learners: Children's Rights and Early Education*. London: Paul Chapman Publishing.

O'Brien, L. (2002) 'A response to "Dewey and Vygotsky: Society, Experience, and Inquiry in Educational Practice"', *Educational Researcher*, 31(5): 21–3.

O'Neill, J. (1994) *The Missing Child in Liberal Theory*. Toronto: University of Toronto Press.

Oberhuemer, P. (2004) 'Controversies, chances and challenges: reflections on the quality debate in Germany', *Early Years*, 24(1): 9–21.

Office for Standards in Education (Ofsted) (2004) *Transition from the Reception Year to Year 1: An Evaluation by Her Majesty's Inspectors*. London: HMSO.

Office for Standards in Education (Ofsted) (2005a) *Early Years: Firm Foundations*. London: Ofsted.

Office for Standards in Education (Ofsted) (2005b) *Are You Ready for your Inspection? A Guide to Inspections of Childcare and Nursery Education Conducted by OFSTED*. London: Ofsted Publications.

Office for Standards in Education (Ofsted) (2005c) *Inspecting Outcomes for Children: Guidance for Inspectors*. London: Ofsted.

Office for Standards in Education (Ofsted) (2005d) *Every Child Matters: Framework for the Inspection of Children's Services*. London: Ofsted Publications.

Office for Standards in Education (Ofsted) (2005e) *Every Child Matters: Framework for the Inspection of Schools in England from September 2005*. London: Ofsted.

Office for Standards in Education (Ofsted) (2005g) *Every Child Matters: Joint Area Reviews of Children's Services*. London: Ofsted.

Organisation for Economic Co-operation and Development (OECD) (2001) *Starting Strong: Early Childhood Education and Care*. Paris: OECD.

Organisation for Economic Co-operation and Development (OECD) (2004) *OECD Country Note: Early Childhood Education and Care Policy in the Federal Republic of Germany*. Paris: OECD.

Osler, A. and Starkey, H. (2005) 'Learning for cosmopolitan citizenship', Ad-Lib, University of Cambridge Institute of Continuing Education, issue 28, www.Cont-Ed.Cam.Ac.Uk/BOCE/Adlib28/Article1.Html.

Owen, S. (2005) *Children Come First: The Future of Childminding Networks*. Bromley: National Childminding Association, and at www.ncma.org.uk.

Owen, S. and Thorpe, G. (1998) 'Praxis Early Years Assessment Centre – a case study: putting the candidate at the heart of the process', in L. Abbott and G. Pugh (eds), *Training to Work in the Early Years: Developing the Climbing Frame*. Buckingham: Open University Press.

Peacock, J.J. (2005) Inspection Report, New Hartley First School, Ofsted.

Penn, H. (2005) *Understanding Early Childhood: Issues and Controversies*. Buckingham: Open University Press.

Peters, D. and Kostelnik, M. (1981) 'Current research in day care personnel preparation', *Advance in Early Education and Day* Care, 2: 29–66.

Primary National Strategy (2004) *Learning and Teaching in the Primary Years – Professional Development Resources*. London: DfES.

Prout, A. (2001) 'Representing children: reflections on the Children 5–16 programme', *Children & Society*, 15: 193–201.

Pugh, G. (1988) *Services for Under Fives: Developing a Coordinated Approach*. London: National Children's Bureau.

Pugh, G. (1994) 'Born to learn', *Times Educational Supplement*, 11 November, 15.

Pugh, G. (1999) 'Young children and their families: a community response', in L. Abbot and H. Moylett (eds), *Early Education Transformed*. London: Falmer Press.

Pugh, G. (2003) 'Children's centres and social exclusion', *Education Review*, 17(1): 23–9.

Pugh, G. (ed.) (1996) *Contemporary Issues in the Early* Years. 2nd edition. London: Paul Chapman Publishing.

Pugh, G., De'Ath, E. and Smith, C. (1994) *Confident Parents, Confident Children*. London: National Children's Bureau.

Qualification and Curriculum Authority (QCA) (1999) *The National Curriculum Handbook for Primary Teachers in England*. London: QCA.

Qualification and Curriculum Authority (QCA) (2000) *Curriculum Guidance for the Foundation Stage*. London: QCA.

Qualification and Curriculum Authority (QCA) (2004) *Foundation Stage Monitoring Report 2003/04*. London: QCA.

Qualification and Curriculum Authority (QCA) (2005a) *Futures: Meeting the Challenge – a Curriculum for the Future*. London: QCA.

Qualifications and Curriculum Authority (QCA) (2005b) 'QCA's database of accredited qualifications', www.openquals.org.uk, accessed 2 November 2005.

Qualification and Curriculum Authority (QCA)/Department for Education and Skills (DfES) (2003) *Foundation Stage Profile Handbook*. London: QCA.

Quinton, D. (2004) *Supporting Parents: Messages from Research*. London: Jessica Kingsley.

Quortrup, J., Bardy, M., Sgritta, S. and Wintersberger, H. (1987) *Childhood Matters: Social Theory, Practice and Politics*. Aldershot: Avebury.

Raban, B. (forthcoming) 'The early years', article prepared for publication – personal communication.

Roberts, R. (1995) *Self-esteem and Successful Early Learning*. London: Hodder and Stoughton.

Roberts, R. (1998) 'Thinking about me and them: personal and social development', in I. Siraj-Blatchford (ed.), *A Curriculum Development Handbook for Early Childhood Educators*. Stoke-on-Trent: Trentham Books. pp. 155–74.

Rogoff, B. (1990) *Apprenticeship in Thinking: Cognitive Development in a Social Context*. Oxford: Oxford University Press.

Rosenthal, M. (2003) 'Quality in early childhood education and care: a cultural context', *European Early Childhood Research Journal*, 11(2): 101–16.

Sammons, P., Smees, R., Taggart, B., Sylva, K., Melhuish, E.C., Siraj-Blatchford, I. and Elliott, K. (2002) *SEN across the Preschool Period*. EYTSEN Technical Paper 1, University of London Institute of Education, 20 Bedford Way, London, WC1H OAL.

Sammons, P., Sylva, K., Melhuish, E., Siraj-Blatchford, I., Taggart, B., Elliot, K. and Marsh, A. (2004) *The Continuing Effects of Pre-school Education at Age 7 Years: Technical Paper 11*. London: DfES and London Institute of Education.

School Curriculum and Assessment Authority (SCAA) (1997) *National Framework for Baseline Assessment: Criteria and Procedures for the Accreditation of Baseline Assessment Schemes*. London: DfEE and SCAA.

Schweinhart, L.J. and Weikart, D.P. (1993) *A Summary of Significant Benefits: The High Scope Perry Pre-School Study Through Age 27*. Ypsilanti, MI: High Scope Press.

Shore, R. (1997) *Rethinking the Brain*. New York: Families and Work Institute.

Siraj-Blatchford, I. (1994) *The Early Years: Laying the Foundations for Racial Equality*. Stoke on Trent: Trentham Books.

Siraj-Blatchford, I. (1996) 'Language, culture and difference', in C. Nutbrown (ed.), *Children's Rights and Early Education*. London: Paul Chapman Publishing. pp. 23–33.

Siraj-Blatchford, I. (ed.) (1998) *A Curriculum Development Handbook for Early Childhood Educators*. Stoke-on-Trent: Trentham Books.

Siraj-Blatchford, I. and Clarke, P. (2000) *Supporting Identity, Diversity and Language in the Early Years*. Buckingham: Open University Press.

Siraj-Blatchford, I. and Siraj-Blatchford, J. (1999) 'Race, research and reform: the impact of the three Rs on anti-racist pre-school and primary education in the UK', *Race, Ethnicity and Education*, 2(1): 127–48.

Siraj-Blatchford, I., Sylva, K., Muttock, S., Gilden, R. and Bell, D. (2002) *Researching Effective Pedagogy in the Early Years (REPEY)*. DfES Research Report 356. London: DfES.

Siraj-Blatchford, I., Sylva, K., Taggart, B., Sammons, P., Melhuish, E. and Elliot, K. (2003) *The Effective Provision of Pre-School Education (EPPE) Project: Technical Paper 10 – Intensive Case Studies of Practice across the Foundation Stage*. London: DfES and Institute of Education, University of London.

Sloper, P. (2004) 'Facilitators and barriers for co-ordinated multi agency services', *Child: Care, Health and Development*, 30(6): 571–80.

Smith, A.B., Grima, G., Gaffney, M., Powell, K., Masse, L. and Barnett, S. (2000) *Strategic Research Initiative Literature Review: Early Childhood Education Report to the Ministry*. Dunedin: University of Otago.

Sparkes, A. (1992) 'Validity and the research process: an exploration of meanings, University of Exeter', *Physical Education Review*, 15(1): 29–45.

Special Educational Needs and Disability Act (SENDA) (2001) London: The Stationery Office.

Starkey, H. (1997) 'Freinet and citizenship education, pleasure of learning et travail coopératif: les méthodes éducatives et la philosophie pratique de Célestin Freinet', Séminaire International a L'alliance Francaise de Londres, June.

Steele, M. (2000) *Strengthening Families: Strengthening Communities: An Inclusive Parent Programme*. London: Racial Equality Unit.

Street, A. (2005) *Caring for Children and Yourself Project*. Corby: Pen Green Centre.

Sure Start Unit (2003) *Children's Centres – Developing Integrated Services for Young Children and their Families*. Start up guidance, February. London: DfES, Sure Start Unit.

Sure Start, Extended Schools and Families Group (2005) *Report on Responses to Consultation on Legislative Proposals for the Future of Childcare and Early Years Provision in England*. Sure Start, 1 November.

Sylva, K. and Pugh, G. (2005) 'Transforming the early years in England', *Oxford Review of Education*, 31(1): 11–27.

Sylva, K., Siraj-Blatchford, I. and Taggart, B. (2003a) *Assessing Quality in the Early Years: Early Childhood Environment Rating Scale-Extension (ECERS-E): Four Curricular Subscales*. Stoke-on-Trent: Trentham Books.

Sylva, K., Melhuish, E.C., Sammons, P., Siraj-Blatchford, I. and Taggart, B. (2004) *The Effective Provision of Pre-School Education (EPPE) Project: Technical Paper 12 – The Final Report: Effective Pre-School Education*. London: DfES and Institute of Education, University of London.

Sylva, K. and Siraj-Blatchford, I. (1996) *Bridging the Gap Between Home and School: Improving Achievement in Primary Schools*. Paris: UNESCO.

Sylva, K., Melhuish, E., Sammons, P., Siraj-Blatchford, I., Taggart, B. and Elliot, K. (2003b) *The Effective Provision of Pre-School Education (EPPE) Project: Findings from the Pre-School Period, Summary of Findings*. DfES research brief, Institute of Education, University of London.

Sylva. K., Siraj-Blatchford, I., Melhuish, E., Sammons. P. and Taggart, B. (1999) *Effective Provision for Pre-school Education Project: Technical Paper 6*. London: DfEE and Institute of Education, University of London.

Taggart, B. et al. (2004) *SEN in the Early Years: The Parents' Perspective*. EYTSEN Technical Paper 3, University of London Institute of Education, 20 Bedford Way, London, WC1H OAL.

Taggart, B., Sylva, K., Siraj-Blatchford, I., Melhuish, E. and Sammons, P. (2000) *Technical Paper 5*. London: DfEE and Institute of Education, University of London.

Tait, C. (2004) *Growing Together Training Resources*. Corby: Pen Green Centre.

Tawney, R.H. (1966) *The Radical Tradition: Twelve Essays on Politics, Education and Literature*. Harmondsworth: Penguin.

Thomas, G. and Pring, R. (eds) (2004) *Evidence-based Practice in Education*. Maidenhead: Open University Press and McGraw-Hill.

Thompson, F. (1939) *Larkrise to Candleford*. Oxford: Oxford University Press.

Thorpe, S. and Gasper, M. (2003) *Who Cares for the Carers? An Exploration of Support Provided for Leaders of Integrated early Years Centres*. DfES Research Bursary on Leadership and Management. Corby: Pen Green Centre.

Tofler, A. and Tofler, H. (1993) *War and Anti-war*. London: Little, Brown.

Tomlinson, K. (2003) *Effective Inter-agency Working: A Review of the Literature and Examples from Practice*. Report no. 40. Windsor: National Foundation for Educational Research.

Vincett, K., Cremin, H. and Thomas, G. (2005) *Teachers and Assistants Working Together*. Maidenhead: Open University Press.

Vong, K.I. (2005) 'Towards a creative early childhood programme in Zhuhai-SER and Macau-SER of the People's Republic of China', unpublished doctoral thesis, University of London.

Vygotsky, L.S. (1978) *Mind in Society*. Cambridge, MA: Harvard University Press.

Warnock, M. (Chair) (1978) *Special Educational Needs* (Warnock Report). London: The Stationery Office.

Whalley, M. (1994) *Learning to Be Strong: Setting Up a Neighbourhood Service for Under-fives and their Families*. London: Hodder and Stoughton.

Whalley, M. (1999) 'Women leaders in early childhood settings', PhD thesis, University of Wolverhampton.

Whalley, M. (2005) *National Professional Qualification in Integrated Centre Leadership, Rollout Training Guidance*. Nottingham: National College for School Leadership.

Whalley, M. and the Pen Green Centre team (1997) *Working with Parents*. Sevenoaks: Hodder and Stoughton. (2nd edition, 2000.)

Whitaker, P. (2002) 'Designing and developing integrated services for children and families', conference paper, Pen Green Centre, Corby.

White, M. (1997) 'A review of the influence and effects of portage', in S. Wolfendale (ed.), *Working with Parents after the SEN Code of Practice*. London: David Fulton.

Wilson, R. (2003) *Special Educational Needs in the Early Years*. 2nd edition. London: Routledge.

Winnicott, D.W. (1965) *The Theory of the Parent–Infant Relationship (1960) in the Maturational Processes and Facilitating Environment*. London: Hogarth Press.

Wolfendale, S. (2000) 'Special needs in the early years: prospects for policy and practice', *Support for Learning*, 15(4): 147–51.

Wolfendale, S. (ed.) (1997) *Working with Parents after the SEN Code of Practice*. London: David Fulton.

Wolfendale, S. (ed.) (2002) *Parent Partnership Services for SEN: Celebrations and Challenges*. London: David Fulton.

Wolfendale, S. and Bastiani, J. (eds) (2000) *The Contribution of Parents to School Effectiveness*. London: David Fulton.

Wolfendale, S. and Einzig, H. (eds) (1999) *Parenting Education and Support: New Opportunities*. London: David Fulton.

Wolfendale, S. and Robinson, M. (2004) The developing role and influence of the educational psychologist working within early years, *Educational and Child Psychology*, themed issue on early childhood education and care, 21(2): 16–25.

Wood, E. and Attfield, J. (2005) *Play ,learning and the early childhood curriculum*. London, Thousand Oaks, CA, and Delhi: Paul Chapman Publishing.

Woodhead, J. (2001) 'Using attachment theory and the concepts of holding and containment in groupwork with parents and infants from birth to three years', unpublished paper, Pen Green Centre, Corby.

Woodhead, M. (1996) *In Search of the Rainbow*. The Hague: Bernard van Leer Foundation.

Index